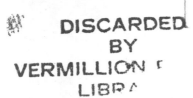

POLICE PROCEDURAL:

A Writer's Guide
to the Police
and How They Work

POLICE PROCEDURAL:
A Writer's Guide
to the Police
and How They Work

by
Russell L. Bintliff

WRITER'S DIGEST BOOKS
CINCINNATI, OHIO

Police Procedural: A Writer's Guide to the Police and How They Work. Copyright © 1993 by Russell L. Bintliff. Printed and bound in the United States of America. All rights reserved. No part of this book may be reproduced in any form or by any electronic or mechanical means including information storage and retrieval systems without permission in writing from the publisher, except by a reviewer, who may quote brief passages in a review. Published by Writer's Digest Books, an imprint of F&W Publications, Inc., 1507 Dana Avenue, Cincinnati, Ohio 45207. 1-800-289-0963. First edition.

97   96   95   94   93   5   4   3   2   1

Library of Congress Cataloging in Publication Data

Bintliff, Russell L.
    Police procedural: a writer's guide to the police and how they work / by Russell L. Bintliff.
       p. cm. — (The Howdunit series)
    Includes index.
    ISBN 0-89879-596-6 (pbk.)
    1. Criminal investigation. 2. Police I. Title. II. Series
HV8073.B53   1993
363.2'5 — dc20
                                                            93-8576
                                                                CIP

Edited by Jack Heffron
Designed by Brian Roeth

Dedication

To my Family

Acknowledgments

A special thanks to the G.A. Thompson Company

About the Author

Russell Bintliff has worked in investigations for more than twenty years as part of the Arkansas State Police, the Criminal Investigation Division of the Army, and the CIA. He has written a number of books on corporate security as well as several police training manuals. William Heffernan's *The Corsican*, published by Simon & Schuster, was based on parts of Bintliff's life, and he was technical advisor for the film *Nighthawks*.

Table of Contents

Introduction

The law enforcement profession continues to improve, moving into a high-tech world, increasing training requirement levels, tightening officer selection and standards criteria. Criminals who would have escaped arrest and prosecution just a few years ago are regularly tracked down today with amazing skill. Much of the credit goes to computer systems, collating vast amounts of information in a fraction of the time required by previous methods and linking departments nationally and internationally with instantaneous communications. Some credit must also go to the law enforcement profession itself, which abounds in professional officers desiring improvement; through their efforts, law enforcement is earning the professional career status it deserves. Most states now have minimum standards for candidate selection and performance certification programs that go a long way toward insuring that men and women carrying badges and guns are competent. Certification programs administered by the International Association of Chiefs of Police also set rigid standards for administration, operations and performance.

American police officers play a unique role in our society because they're entrusted with considerable power, such as the powers of arrest and use of force, while remaining locally controlled. Conversely, police in other Western countries are formally coordinated or directed by their national government. England, for example, has about forty-three police departments, all controlled or receiving direction and most of their funding from that country's Home Office. In the United States, nearly forty thousand local, county and state police departments operate independently from the national government. Officers also must have a thorough understanding of law and procedures. The era of pinning on a badge and "winging it" has faded into history.

Police procedures vary by jurisdiction, but all law enforcement departments follow basic principles. Although each detective may have a distinctive style, all proceed in a similar manner. Each case is unique, but all contain discernible common features. What works best for one person may not work effectively for another, but knowing the successful techniques of others with extensive investigative experience helps. In this book, I supply you with the "standards" of police organization, procedure and investigation, leaving to you their applications for your book or screenplay characters.

In this book you will find authentic information stemming from my thirty years of personal experience in law enforcement. Your work will be much more accurate if you rely on the information in this book rather than on the myths and misrepresentations we commonly find in otherwise excellent books, motion pictures or television shows. For example, in popular television police shows such as *Kojak*, *Columbo* and others, we see a small army of technicians swarming over a crime scene searching for fragments of evidence. We have seen this so often that victims of crimes, and the general public, believe their complaint will receive that kind of attention.

In reality, the police officer or detective rarely has the luxury of laboratory technicians and scores of other officers available to help process a crime scene and continue the investigation. In most departments, small to large, one or two detectives have to make or break the case alone. Across the country, small law enforcement departments have few full-time police officers to serve their community twenty-four hours a day, 365 days a year. The only technicians available to them include those in the state crime laboratory who analyze the evidence sent to them. The officer directing traffic might be investigating a homicide an hour later. The average police officer or detective wears many hats. He or she needs to know how to search a crime scene properly, as well as take photographs and collect, preserve and secure the evidence. Ironically, I have found over the years that police officers and detectives who must out of necessity do all or most of the investigative work themselves have the best skills and also solve the most cases. One important reason for their success is continuity. When an officer starts at the beginning and continues with a follow-up investigation, he or she becomes intimately familiar with the case. Information that might elude a detached detective operating among an army of technicians can be the catalyst that brings a major case to a successful conclusion.

Although the real world of law enforcement differs considerably from the one we regularly read about or view, I believe writers can use that reality and authenticity to their advantage when crafting a story involving the police. In my view, the genuine portrayal makes the character interesting and often larger than life. Whatever your choices as you create a story involving the police, I will supply you with reality throughout the book and leave the decision of "literary license" to your writer's judgment.

O N E

POLICE ADMINISTRATION AND PATROL OPERATIONS

One of the common myths we find in books and films is that of the tired, disillusioned cop who gets beaten down by the system. I suppose if one looked hard among the one million plus law enforcement officers across the country, some percentage would have a disgruntled attitude. However, I want to emphasize from my personal experiences over thirty years in law enforcement that, despite all the problems, most police officers keep their affection for the profession close to the vest. Law enforcement is a profession that "gets in the blood." Even retired or former law enforcement officers like me feel an occasional "twinge" or yearning to get back into the harness. That's also true of professionals such as fire fighters, race car drivers and others I've talked with over the years. Becoming a police officer brings many aggravations and frustrations. However, it also brings many advantages, benefits and fond memories. Police officers learn early in their career how vulnerable they are to civil liability and intradepartment rivalry. For example, an error in handling a situation can land an officer and, normally, his department in civil court to defend their actions or handling of persons taken into custody or shot during or after the commission of a crime. Interpersonal rivalry among officers often creates tension and can lead to considerable difficulty. Just as do their counterparts in other organizations, police officers seek promotion; some exhibit lower standards of ethics than others. An ambitious officer might become the "fair-haired" favorite of a supervisor and create tension in a squad. He or she may be distrusted by other officers who believe the favored officer will report anything viewed or overheard to the supervisor. In spite of these difficulties, an overwhelming majority of police officers would have it no other way than to become and remain a law enforcement officer.

This chapter provides an overview of the uniformed police, their departments, training and other important aspects that can help you portray them as they are by understanding where they came from, how they got here, and who they really are today.

Modern Spectrum of Police Services

Metropolitan police agencies make up most of the law enforcement community's numbers. For example, New York City employs about twenty-five thousand officers, while a rural or small-town department might have a single full-time police officer with part-time personnel or volunteers called when needed.

Local Police

Most larger urban departments operate independently under the control of elected boards or commissioners without significant political or operational control from higher governmental authority. However, many small- to medium-sized police departments remain indirectly controlled by the executive level of a local government, by the city's mayor, manager or council (or equivalent), who control the hiring and monitoring of the police chief.

Many police departments now have unions for all officers not considered part of management. The influence of police unions varies, but they try to set standards for salaries, benefits and working conditions much like in a small to large business operation.

Illustration 1-1 (page 11) shows the basic organizational structure of a typical metropolitan police department. Police agencies have a diverse role depending largely on locale and jurisdiction.

Some of their daily activities might include identifying criminal suspects; investigating crimes; apprehending offenders and participating in their trials; deterring crime through patrol; aiding persons in danger or in need of help; supplying emergency services; resolving conflict and keeping the peace; maintaining a sense of community security; keeping automobile traffic and pedestrian movement efficient; promoting civil order; and operating and administering the police department.

County Police

The county police department takes one of two forms in different parts of the country. The first form is a conventional police department, in which the county sheriff limits his or her duties to supporting the court, transporting prisoners and performing other judicial duties. The second is an independent police department whose senior officer, the sheriff, is an elected official. The county sheriff's role descends from the early English shire reeve, whose main duties included assisting the royal judges when trying prisoners plus enforcing the law outside cities in the countryside. From the time of westward expansion in the United States until municipal police departments developed, the county sheriff often acted as the sole legal authority for large territories.

The duties of a conventional county sheriff's department vary according to the size and degree of development of the county. Officials within the department may serve as coroners, tax assessors, tax collectors, overseers of highways and bridges, custodians of the county treasury, keepers of the county jail, court attendants and executors of criminal and civil processes; in years past, sheriff's departments also conducted executions. Today many sheriff's department functions remain limited to unincorporated areas within a county, although officers can respond to city departments' requests for aid in such matters as patrol or investigation. Some sheriff's departments have only one or two deputies, others have several hundred, and a few exceed a thousand.

Because the county sheriff and town or municipal constable are traditionally chosen by election, sheriffs often receive more political than professional recognition. For example, most states now require minimum standards for becoming a police officer and demand minimum initial training (at a state academy or equivalent) plus annual qualification with firearms and other elements such as use of force.

Although sheriff's deputies must conform to standards leading to and maintaining "certification" to work as a law enforcement officer in a state, the sheriff, being elected, does not have to meet any of the standards. Other factors affecting the elected sheriff stem from early state constitutions that specifically provided for the offices and made their abolition or even the sheriff's dismissal impossible. These constitutional deficiencies remain in some states. Although many sheriffs today come from within the trained, experienced and certified officer ranks, others do not. For example, a used car salesman with no previous law enforcement experience might become the elected county sheriff and begin work without meeting a single qualification.

State Police

State police agencies were created to address two problems: the public's low regard for the crime-fighting ability of local police agencies and the increased mobility of law violators. Using automobiles, thieves could strike at will and be out of a local or county jurisdiction before an effective response or investigation could be mounted. The state police concept also gave governors a powerful enforcement arm under their personal control.

The major roles of state police are: controlling traffic on the highway system, helping trace stolen automobiles, and aiding in disturbances and crowd control. In states with large and powerful county sheriff's departments, the state police normally focus on highway patrol activities. In others, where the county sheriff's law enforcement role is limited or the department has few deputies, the state police normally take a more active investigative and enforcement role.

The Texas Rangers, established in 1835, were the first state law enforcement officers in the United States. However, the Rangers were more a quasi-military force that supported the Texas state militia than a true law enforcement body. Today, they continue in a criminal investigation role while the Texas Highway Patrol focuses primarily on patrolling for traffic violations. Massachusetts organized a variety of state law enforcement in 1865, and Connecticut followed at the turn of the century.

By 1930 twenty-two states had state police agencies, and by 1939 another twenty-four had joined the trend. Today, all states have a variety of state law enforcement departments under various names and titles.

Federal Police

The United States Marshal was the first law enforcement officer in the federal government, created by the Judiciary Act of September 14, 1789. The Revenue Cutter Service (later the Coast Guard) came into being in 1790 to deal with smuggling and collection of maritime revenues. That inroad led to creation of the Customs Service in 1799. The establishment of regular land patrols at the borders followed, culminating in the creation of the Border Patrol during 1920.

Congress passed legislation during 1865 creating the Secret Service as part of the United States Treasury Department to combat increasing reports of counterfeit currency, which had reduced public confidence in the country's money. The Secret Service restored this confidence by enforcing the counterfeiting laws. After the assassination of President McKinley in 1901, the Secret Service informally received the task of protecting the president and, in 1903, formally added these duties.

In time, other federal law enforcement agencies evolved. In 1908, the Justice Department created the Bureau of Investigation, which became the Federal Bureau of Investigation in 1935. The FBI itself was a product of a reorganization in 1924 under the directorship of J. Edgar Hoover. Still other federal enforcement bodies, including the Drug Enforcement Administration and the Internal Revenue Service, provide services to the American public today.

The Police at Work

Before looking at how the police work, we should make a number of observations. First, not all police agencies are alike. They differ in the scope of their routine enforcement responsibilities; in the territorial and population size of their jurisdictions; in the composition of the populations they serve; in their size, training and salaries; and in their internal organization. Second, not all police officers are alike. They differ in background, personality, experience, attitudes, behavior on the job, qualifications and interests. Third, though collectively referred to as the police, the occupational demands placed on any one officer differ from those placed on another. There is no

one type of police work. A division of labor or occupational specialization exists in police work just as it does in most other work organizations. For at least these three reasons, then, we should remember
that when speaking of the police we are not dealing with a collection
of homogeneous organizations, people or activities. We are dealing
with a group of people and agencies that share a common occupational responsibility: the enforcement of laws and the preservation
of domestic order.

Joining the Force

Much of what police officers do could be called "dirty work," work
that most people might shun, prefer not to think about, or leave for
others to perform. It is work that is demanded and rejected, disgust-
ing and indispensable. It garners little prestige and recognition for
its practitioners but is touted as essential for maintaining the
"proper" moral and social standards of the community. It is work
that protects the in-group from the out-group, but those who consider themselves as insiders hire outsiders to perform it.

The dirty aspects of police work—handling drunks, dead bodies and accident victims; dealing with family squabbles, prostitutes,
muggers and other "deviants"; sometimes using violence to achieve
control—merely strengthen the view that such work is not for everyone. To most citizens, it is precisely this facet of police work that
identifies the real job of the police. How often do police officers
hear, "Instead of bothering me, why don't you go and arrest real
criminals like we're paying you to do?" or "Why don't you clean up
the streets so that respectable people like me can walk safely at
night?"

It is reasonable to wonder whether there is any striking com-
monality among persons who enter this occupation. Studies indicate, however, that police recruits share the same background with
those who enter myriad other occupations. The evidence on personality traits also offers no sound basis for distinguishing recruits from
their peers.

When asked about their reasons for joining a police force, officers regularly voice the same reasons that move people to seek nonpolice jobs. Among the most often cited reasons are security and
retirement benefits. Few officers speak of excitement, action, or the
dirty facets of police work as reasons for joining, and few recruits

come to police work for idealistic reasons, such as helping to rid society of criminals or contributing to law and order. These findings reinforce the view that those who enter police work are in no way a special category of people and are no different from others with similar backgrounds.

Contemporary Police Departments

Since the business of law enforcement has many aspects and complexities, this chapter focuses on the "front line," often referred to as "the blue line," and on daily operations. Two categories, *line* (direct public contact such as patrol) or *nonline* (supporting elements such as administrative and technical), characterize all police functions. Line functions include tasks that directly enable the police to serve and protect the community. The nonline functions supplement and support the line operations. Although nonline police categories receive less acknowledgment, these services have equal importance.

Primary Patrol (Line) Functions

Patrol activities of the police department remain the primary line function, considered first priority. The police patrol division has initial responsibility on the streets for crime prevention, and detection and apprehension of offenders. Theoretically, the police patrol force that's 100 percent effective in its assigned tasks would eliminate the need for specialized units such as traffic and detective divisions. The uniformed patrol function serves as the backbone of the police service.

Secondary Line Functions

Historically, police departments limited themselves to police patrols (uniformed). Many small departments continue to do that today, largely because they have few officers, limited budgets, low crime rates and limited jurisdiction. However, in many municipalities, population and geographical growth have greatly increased the burden on uniformed police patrols, as have more complex laws and procedures, increasing crime rates, higher standards, transportation improvements and the technology boom. These departments have added uniformed personnel and a variety of supplemental divisions, including traffic control and detectives, juvenile and vice officers.

Nonline Functions

Nonline functions of police departments include those services that support the line. Traditionally, nonline or support activities consist of two major categories: staff and auxiliary services.

Police Staff Services. Staff services include department command and administration, patrol supervision, personnel recruiting and development, and a variety of training programs. Budget, planning and research, inspection, and similar activities also fall under the heading of administration and supervisory activities.

Auxiliary Police Services. All nonline activities not regarded as staff services fall under "auxiliary" services. Typically, nonline police department members provide technical and nontechnical support services to both line and other nonline activities. For example, polygraph examiners, photographers, fingerprint and crime-scene technicians and the police laboratory fall under the "technical" auxiliary services that support the line activities. Nontechnical auxiliary services that support both line and nonline activities include jails and communications systems. Other activities become difficult to classify as either staff or auxiliary. Often, they perform a dual service. For example, a police department's community relations unit, although performing secondary line services, might also have an auxiliary or a staff function depending on the department's structure. Illustration 1-1 (page 11) presents the various functions within a model of a contemporary municipal police department. All the functions play a role in any sized police department. However, in small departments officers may perform several functions instead of having specialized officers assigned to each function.

Principles of Police Organization

To better understand the organization and operation of police departments, you'll need to grasp certain general principles of police organization. These principles of organization generally originated and evolved from the military services. Members of police departments, including sheriff's and state police, wear uniforms and observe rigid standards and regulations. Police hold formations and inspections, march in ceremonial gatherings, and use rank to designate authority. Chiefs of police often wear general's stars, just as state police colonels wear the military colonel's eagle. Other ranks

A Contemporary Municipal Police Department

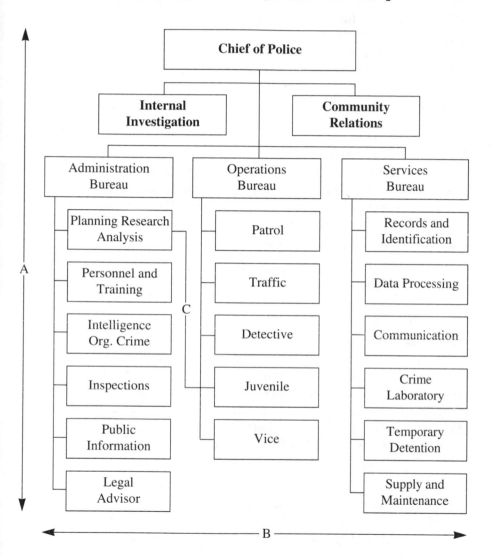

include lieutenant colonel, major, captain, first and second lieutenants, sergeants of various levels, corporal, private first class and private. The departments operate by orders, regulations and manuals and are administered by commanders who maintain internal discipline and order much like that of military organizations.

In the following sections I've summarized central aspects of average operations for a contemporary police department. These assume greater or lesser importance depending on the size of a department, the geographical area, and other elements that are tailored to circumstances.

Division of Resources

An effective police department must have a clear design to accomplish its tasks, functions and activities with the human, financial and equipment resources available. Normally, a police department like the one shown in Illustration 1-1, for example, divides its resources in the following segments.

Department. The common short designation for "Police Department." This term encompasses the entire law enforcement operation of a village, town, city or county and is often used by state and federal agencies.

Headquarters. Where the chief and his or her command and administrative officers and civilian employees manage the department. This designation might also include the only police station in small departments. This term will also include most state police organizations. Normally the headquarters for the sheriff's department has the traditional title "Sheriff's Office," primarily because a sheriff holds a political office. "Headquarters" may also describe some federal law enforcement centers.

Police Station. "Police station" might remain a more common term than headquarters in smaller cities, because the designation "headquarters" implies a metropolitan jurisdiction. It can also describe one of multiple operations centers, often called "precinct police stations," under a central headquarters in some cities.

Bureau. Usually the largest enforcement unit within a municipal, state or federal department.

Division. Part of a bureau while having a department-wide function (e.g., Detective Division, Traffic Division).

Section or Squad. One of several functional elements of a division (e.g., Robbery Section).

Watch or Shift. The day-to-day group of officers, detectives and others working, which changes every eight hours.

Team. A special group of officers such as a Special Weapons and Tactics (S.W.A.T.) team, or a pair of detectives or other officers.

Command Concepts

Unity of command requires that a department officer stay directly accountable to only one superior at a time, just as in the military. No one officer can effectively serve two superiors. This often becomes a problem when police departments and local politics clash and police commissioners, chiefs and others in the hierarchy of law enforcement get personally involved in local situations. Ideally, the chain of command remains clear and each officer need obey only one superior. When officers receive conflicting orders from commanders and authorities other than their direct supervisor, it hinders their performance and may create a serious morale problem. Line A in Illustration 1-1 represents the vertical chain of command: the relationship of the chief to the bureaus, and the areas controlled by each bureau.

Coordination Factors

The police department organizational structure must foster close cooperation between line and staff activities. Effective coordination depends entirely on adequate communication among all elements of a police department, coupled with a clear and uninterrupted chain of command. Line B in Illustration 1-1 represents the horizontal dimensions of the department. Often, elements within the department must function horizontally and diagonally (Line C, Illustration 1-1) to achieve their objectives. Line C illustrates a relationship of units within a department. They work separately on specific tasks but jointly on others.

Time Factors

The police service is among the few public services that maintain a twenty-four-hour schedule. Some law enforcement departments that serve small towns or villages may have only one or two full-time officers and maybe one or two part-time officers; these departments might operate part of the twenty-four-hour period on-call. An average department must assign enough officers to meet the law enforcement and protection demands of the community at any given time.

Allocation of personnel is often a complex problem. On the surface, it appears logical to divide the total police complement into three equal parts or shifts. However, for any given city, experience shows that, during certain hours of the day, activities that call for police service increase and decrease. All department functions are subject to this type of scheduling.

Territory Factors

Territorial distribution is necessary to ensure the availability and general suitability of the patrol service throughout an area of jurisdiction. The following are some common descriptions involving geographical or territorial divisions within a police department:

1. **Post:** A fixed or stationary point of location (for example, a specific street intersection, a surveillance site, or an assigned desk or office).

2. **Route or Line Beat:** A length of street normally assigned to a traffic or patrol officer (whether on foot or mobile).

3. **Beat:** A geographical area, assigned to a foot or mobile patrol and traffic officer. To visualize a beat, think of one square city block. The officer assigned to this beat is responsible for patrol activities within it, including all the buildings, streets, side streets and alleys, and any specific calls needing a response. Assume that a major street is within this beat and requires a major part of the patrol officer's time and energies. Under these conditions, the major street would be assigned to another officer, who would devote full attention to this single length of street (a route beat) while the beat officer would be better able to patrol the now reduced beat. The beat is a basic unit of police organization and among the terms commonly associated with police work.

4. **Sector:** Two or more beats, route beats, motorized patrols, stationary posts, or any combination of them.

5. **District or Precinct:** A geographical subdivision of a city for police patrol purposes. A district for a state police department usually has several counties. Typically a district contains a sta-

tion and maybe some other physical facilities.

6. **Area:** Two or more districts.

Police Operations

Another word in the large collection of police service terminology is "operations," synonymous with line functions. This all-encompassing phrase includes protecting lives and property and providing all other services expected of the police department by a community. Illustration 1-2 (page 16) shows the organizational structure of a police operations bureau.

Police Patrol Operations

The uniformed patrol officer of a local police or sheriff's department is the personification of law enforcement in the United States. Most people who encounter patrol officers on a day-to-day basis respect them as their protectors. Others, however, see uniformed officers as a nuisance; still others look upon them as the enemy. It is the officer's responsibility to serve all members of a community with equal dedication and respect and to demonstrate a clear sense of justice.

Activities of the Patrol Division

The following information describes the general activities of an average patrol division of a police department. Keep in mind that more than 80 percent of this nation's police departments employ fewer than twenty officers. Those smaller departments probably assign all of their officers, or all but one or two to field responsibilities, with additional special duties on an as-needed basis. Consider a village or small town with only one office; the chief is also the juvenile officer, records clerk, traffic investigator, patrol officer and writer of parking tickets during slack hours. In a one-officer department, the chief will spend the greatest percentage of time with field police activities. As a police department grows to stay abreast with increasing population, expanding geographical boundaries, and growing diversity of the jurisdiction, a chief must add to the force of uniformed officers. As the department continues to grow, officers move from the field to specialize in traffic investigation and control, juvenile victims and perpetrators, plainclothes de-

Organizational Structure of a Police Operations Bureau (Representative Model)

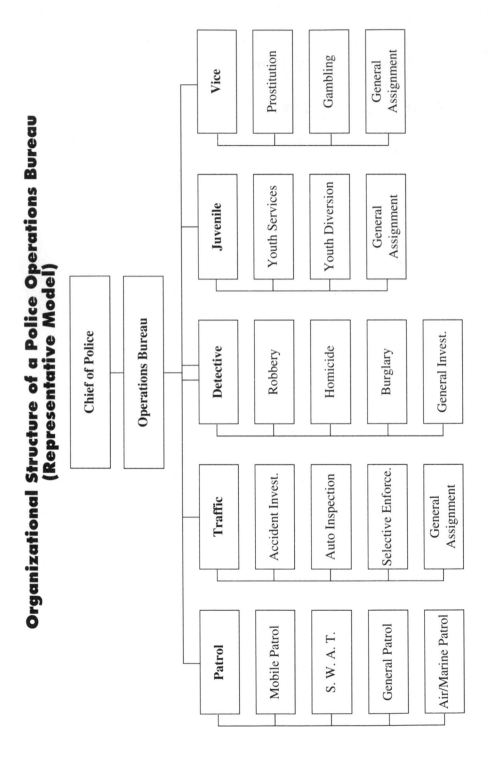

tective activities and other specialized functions. No matter what the size of the department, patrol continues to be the department's principal function.

Routine Patrol and Observation

A uniformed patrol officer performs many basic, often mundane functions. Much of the officer's attention goes to benevolent and community services such as refereeing neighborhood or family quarrels, helping people get into their homes or automobiles when locked out, getting cars started, or changing tires for an elderly person stranded on a street. Patrol officers also routinely perform watchman or security services, advising a concerned business owner about locks, burglary and robbery prevention, and "rattling" doors throughout the night. Patrol officers regularly inspect and report problem areas on sidewalks and streets as well as other safety-related hazards to the public. They might become involved in inspections for building code violations or for health threats in unsanitary restaurants, grocery stores and butcher shops. Officers remain alert for obscured traffic signs and signals, professional and business license violations and flouters of leash laws. Lastly, the patrol officer issues tickets for overtime parking and cites offenders for motor vehicle infractions involving licensing, safety inspections, speeding or other moving violations.

Most calls for police service, however, do not concern matters that lead to an on-the-spot arrest or other action beyond investigating a vandalized fence in a residential area, looking for lost children, responding to a minor traffic accident, or handling a shoplifter held by a store manager. The patrol officer routinely monitors legal repossessions and property rights, landlord-tenant arguments, employer and employee relations, and a long list of daily "gripes" emerging from community residents. When an elderly, bedridden person falls out of bed and needs help, an explosion occurs at an industrial site, a burglar alarm is set off by the wind, or a person threatens to jump off a bridge, patrol officers respond, and the community paying their salary expects them to supply solutions. These examples and many others fall within the patrol officer's purview and, depending on the location, involve two primary ways of conducting "routine patrol."

Types of Police Patrols

Walking the Beat — Foot Patrols. Dating from the first organized police force, foot patrols or "beat cops" have historically played an important part in law enforcement and crime prevention. The numbers of traditional walking beat or foot patrols have declined as departments have moved to more mobile patrols. In many cities, however, the need for a more focused enforcement effort has caused a gradual return of the walking patrol, especially in high-crime urban areas.

Police officers who work on a foot patrol in a limited area know their beat intimately. They know the people living or working in a neighborhood, including each small business owner. The size of the walking patrol depends on the crime rate in an area, density of population and, often, the stamina of officers. An officer will be more effective on a comfortable, cool day or evening than when it's raining, snowing and freezing cold or during a heat wave. Many cities have rotating foot patrols, such as four hours on a beat, four hours in a car, or limit the beat to times of the day or night when the area has the most crime or other types of problems.

Although portable communications enable foot patrol officers to stay in close contact with their headquarters, officers remain vulnerable to attack. When a walking beat cop calls for help, he or she must wait until a mobile patrol becomes available. Often, the location of the walking beat cop forces the mobile officer to park and search for the other officer on foot. Mobile patrol officers, on the other hand, can stay within the protection of their car, using it for psychological advantage and to draw attention to police presence in an area.

Automobile Patrols. The motor vehicle allows law enforcement officers to stay mobile while carrying a variety of emergency equipment. The automobile also supplies protection against inclement weather and enables officers to maintain constant contact with the police communications center. It allows officers to pursue and apprehend criminals and enforce traffic violations.

Motorized patrols are normally assigned to areas that don't require public contact. In communities that do not have walking beats, mobile patrolling must try to supply the best possible protection. However, according to several studies, much of the crime such as robberies, mugging, rapes and murders increase and decrease depending on the mix between walking and mobile patrols.

Motorized patrols originally assigned two officers to each car, but recently most police departments have used only one officer because of limited budgets.

Horse Patrols. Once a common sight in metropolitan or rural areas, horse patrols have faded significantly in recent years. However, New York City, Chicago, Atlanta and other cities use horses in parks and for crowd control. Horse-mounted officers supply mobility and psychological advantages under certain conditions that vehicles cannot offer. Motorized officers cannot race across lawns, or through wooded areas or pedestrian malls with automobiles. Horse patrols also satisfy a need in remote rural areas when supplied by volunteers as part of a county sheriff's mounted posse.

Specialized Motor Vehicles. Motorcycles, dune buggies, and four-wheel drive, safari-type vehicles share a wide-ranging advantage over automobiles. In some jurisdictions such as coastal areas that also have hills and woods, as well as in metropolitan and residential areas, all types of patrol vehicles are used. Motorcycles, for example — another disappearing vehicle once considered standard in most departments — serve well for traffic control and enforcement, escorts, and other situations in which maneuverability is important. Other types of specialized motor vehicles found in law enforcement use include snowmobiles, dog sleds, gliders and boats.

Aircraft. Helicopters and fixed-wing aircraft play an important role in police patrol, although they are very costly to operate. The first airborne unit was created in New York City in 1930. The New York police unit had responsibility for controlling reckless flying over the city when daredevil pilots were commonplace. The unit included one amphibian plane and three biplanes that operated well into the 1950s, when they were replaced by a fleet of helicopters.

Fixed-wing aircraft prove excellent for traffic control on open stretches of highway, for search and surveillance, and for transportation of people and supplies. The helicopter has increased the air capabilities of the police, especially patrol operations, because it can fly slowly, hover, fly at a variety of altitudes, provide officers with good visibility, and take off and land vertically.

Common police applications of the helicopter and some fixed-wing aircraft include rescue, medical evacuation, traffic control, general patrol, criminal apprehension, crime prevention and repression, emergency transportation, surveillance, searches, and other activities supporting ground police patrols.

Preliminary Investigation Role

Patrol officers have a high profile and remain constantly available to take immediate action in response to a traffic collision or criminal law violations. In small towns and rural areas, the patrol officer might conduct the preliminary and follow-up investigations. In many departments patrol officers make most arrests for narcotics and vice activities.

As the first officer on the scene, the patrol officer looks after the safety of the victim and witnesses and arrests suspects when they remain at the location. The officer must also protect the crime scene from contamination by weather or onlookers and communicate to the department immediate information about the status of the scene, seriousness of the situation and action he or she has taken. The importance of the patrol officer during preliminary investigations stems from his or her presence while the scene is still fresh and victims and witnesses still have a candid view. The success of a follow-up investigation often depends entirely on how well the patrol officer performed upon arrival.

When there's a threat to evidence at a collision or crime scene, the patrol officer must collect it, handle and secure it properly, take notes, make sketches and perform other tasks. Common threats to the crime scene include inclement weather and onlookers who might appear as witnesses or victims who instead wander in and contaminate the scene by obscuring evidence underfoot, handling or moving items critical to evidence and generally creating confusion.

Arrest and Booking Role

Second only to caring for the injured at a crime scene, the patrol officer's primary responsibility is locating and arresting the offender. In an armed robbery, rape or shooting, that arrest might be made with the help of other patrol officers. The offender might have fled, but victims or witnesses may supply a license number or some other information. The responding officer communicates this information to the department, which in turn relays it to all police units, including walking patrols.

After an arrest, the police officer normally follows up with one or two "booking" actions. In some misdemeanor cases, the officer might issue a citation and allow the violator to sign a promise to appear in court on or before a specified date. The citation method is used for traffic offenses and other minor crimes that pose no threat to life or property. Other misdemeanors and all felony arrests call for the patrol officer to "book" the offender and place him or her in jail. Within a specified number of hours, the arresting officer must take the jailed offender to appear before a judge to justify the arrest and custody and to set or deny bail. In some misdemeanor cases (not life or property threatening), the offender is released without a court hearing after posting a prescribed bail. Other circumstances will dictate placing offenders in a station detention cell until bail or other arrangements are made for their release.

Writing Reports

Patrol officers spend much of their time writing routine reports that record what they observed, details about the incident and action they took, and other pertinent information. Nearly everything a patrol officer does requires a written report of some type. When an officer collects evidence at a crime scene, he or she must check it in to a department evidence repository, completing the necessary forms and other requirements.

The forms police officers most frequently fill out are offense, complaint and arrest reports.

Traffic Operations Role

Typically, the traffic function involves three tasks: traffic control, accident investigation and law enforcement. In smaller departments, the patrol division is responsible for all police operations including traffic. Larger cities normally establish specialized functional traffic units, usually at the bureau level. Traffic control and accident investigation become the responsibility of the traffic bureau. Traffic officers, however, continue to perform a patrol function as needed. When, for example, a traffic officer observes a serious crime, he or she has a sworn duty to take action and, when possible, to apprehend the offender. A patrol officer not assigned to traffic duties also must render assistance when observing a traffic accident but normally would secure the situation until the arrival of the specialist.

Training, Certification and Police Perspectives

Many departments offer extensive training courses for their new recruits. Often, after basic police academy training, departments send recruits to universities and colleges with special law enforcement curricula. These training programs introduce the newcomer to the legal, ethical, organizational and operational facets of police work. While enrolled in the programs, recruits get a taste of what it means to be a police officer. It is also during this period of formal training that an intensive socialization process begins and the cord binding the rookie to the civilian world is cut.

In their training by police instructors, rookies are exposed to the ambiguities and conflicts inherent in police work. The new recruits learn that the public expects them to enforce all criminal laws, but in practice they must be selective and keep the spirit of the law. For example, a police officer who arrests everyone breaking any law would fill the jails to overflowing, like Barney Fife on the *Andy Griffith Show*. Recruits learn the public can be something akin to an enemy. They learn to be cautious about walking into a setup and never to rely on help from citizens. They learn that, while the public demands they combat crime and arrest criminals, police officers must follow procedures, even when following procedures sometimes allows a criminal to escape. They learn that police work is also public relations work, and that honesty and zeal in job performance may get them into trouble with superiors who prefer not to rock the boat. They also learn that the content of lectures at the police academy often differs markedly from what they know from experience as private citizens. Whatever idealism a police recruit brings to the academy will soon be forgotten.

Defensiveness, Professionalism, Depersonalization Concepts

The police academy suggests that one of its primary training goals is to develop uniform behavior among officers so there is less room for personal judgment and individualized behavior. Recruits must be stripped of their identity and taught to assume a police identity—to think like, act like, and be a police officer. Three themes emerge during recruit training that help generate in candidates a proper police perspective. The first theme, perhaps essential, is defensiveness. Recruits are told to be alert to the many dangers of police work and to build defenses against them. These dangers are not merely physical. They include the dangers of procedural violations that can lead to criminal charges, civil suits, reprimands, lost cases and dismissal. They also include the dangers of corruption, inefficiency, emotional involvement in police-citizen encounters, and provocation of hostile and punitive reactions among members of the public who can make trouble for the department.

The second theme is professionalism — the development of a professional image, techniques, esprit de corps, service ideals, and a sense of "us" as opposed to "them." The third theme, depersonalization, has two sides. On one hand, persons with which recruits interact, including the public and their own supervisors, often treat them as faceless. Recruits also learn that some occupational demands require them to deny their own personal qualities such as compassion. One of the easiest ways for a police officer to get into trouble is to give an attractive woman a break. Doing so might stimulate speculation and questions about the officer's motives. Police officers learn quickly that personalizing their official relationships with the public, even when it seems the right thing to do, can be twisted and used to get them in trouble. The other side of depersonalizing involves the officer's own adoption of stereotypes, black-and-white distinctions, and intolerance of out-groups, whose members, in turn, become faceless. Police officers must walk a thin line between prudence, common sense and impartiality regardless of how their social upbringing and tradition pull them toward doing something else.

There are seven levels of police training: basic, field, advanced, specialized, in-service, seminars and video training. Most departments help officers pay for college courses of various types. Many colleges and universities offer courses in criminal justice subjects; a few even offer degrees in criminal justice. States across the country have adopted minimum standards for the professional training and certification of law enforcement officers. An officer who fails to complete the mandatory training courses cannot receive state certification and without it can't make arrests or perform law enforcement duties. Although used for decades by federal agencies, standards and certification requirements did not become a reality in local, county and many state departments until the 1970s. Problems continue, however, because each state has its own standards and certification program. There is no nationwide model program for standardized training and certification. A veteran officer from one state might not qualify for certification as a law enforcement officer in another state. The same problem exists for federal officers who decide to join a state, county or local department: Although federal officers normally receive far more professional training and have a broad base of experience, they probably would not qualify for town marshal in a village of five hundred people because that job calls for certification from the state, and the state rarely recognizes federal training. States that do recognize the training and requirements of other states or the federal government normally also require that applicants attend state-controlled training before certifying them. Standardization of training is important, and states are slowly moving toward that goal.

Basic Police Training. Except for officers in a few large cities that operate their own police academies, most recruits receive training at a state-sponsored and operated police academy. The course normally supplies about 650 hours of formal training that cover the basic knowledge an officer needs to begin performing police duties. The following summary lists the courses taught to each officer in the basic training, although it varies state to state between federal agencies, who normally conduct their own academy focused on the jurisdiction and mission.

POLICE BASIC TRAINING CURRICULUM

Arrest of Persons	Authority and Jurisdiction
Basic Law Application	Choke Defenses
Club Technique and Defense	Communications
Conduct of Search & Seizure	Court Testimony
Crime Scenes	Directing Traffic
Driver's Defensive Training	Drug Abuse
Elements of Proof	Ethics
Examinations	Fingerprinting
Interviews and Interrogations	Investigative Procedures
Legal Rights, Warnings and Waivers	Notetaking
Patrol Operations	Police Information
Practical Exercises (Day)	Practical Exercises (Night)
Records and Forms	Report Writing
Restraints and Use of Force	Search and Seizure
Traffic Accident Investigation	Traffic Accident Reports
Traffic Control Operations	Unarmed Defense
Unarmed Self-Defense	Weapons and Firing Ranges

Field Training. The field training program helps new patrol officers quickly build proper job attitudes and behaviors. An FTO (Field Training Officer) program provides close coaching and monitoring of a new officer's demeanor by a senior officer (the FTO) who has received special training. A supervisor, normally a corporal or sergeant, depending on the department's rank configuration, will often have the FTO assignment. The FTO works for several weeks with a new officer after he or she graduates from a police academy. For two or three weeks the new officer observes more than she participates, and listens to instructional guidance from the FTO. When the FTO believes the officer has a clear understanding and sufficient self-confidence, the new officer can begin handling minor problems with the FTO observing and ready when necessary to salvage the situation. When the FTO feels the officer can function competently on her own, a recommendation will normally place the new officer on patrol alone. Most new officers serve probationary periods of about twelve months; during that time, an FTO or supervisor can judge an officer to be unfit for police duties.

Advanced Training. Advanced training varies from department to department. The amount and levels of training depend largely on budget limits and crime rates in the area. Training courses range from those showing supervisors how to be better leaders to advanced training that includes courses on administration, handling specific problems such as civil unrest, handling crimes as a patrol officer, and becoming a police in-service trainer.

Specialized Training. Specialized training for patrol officers normally includes Special Weapons And Tactics (S.W.A.T.), Riot Control, Counter Terrorism, Intelligence Operations, and other types of special tasks that patrol officers perform either full-time or on-call. Such courses are offered at the state level, at federal schools, and at a variety of seminars and courses throughout the country. Some departments hire professional trainers. These trainers supply more economical and often higher quality training that is tailored to a department's needs and working environment.

In-Service Training. In-service training within a department helps patrol officers review prior training and learn new skills. This training often satisfies requirements set by the state minimum standards boards or commissions, especially in use of force and firearms qualification, as well as treating other subjects relevant to the needs of individual communities, departments and officers.

Seminars and Workshops. Throughout the country, colleges and universities, law enforcement departments and academies offer seminars and workshops on a variety of law enforcement subjects. These courses offer basic or advanced instruction and deal mostly with investigative subjects. Many seminars address patrol officer topics; others help officers work toward qualifying as detectives.

Video Training. Training videotapes have largely replaced the old training films and have improved the quality and quantity of training within departments. Several companies rent or sell a large inventory of police training videotapes. A service called LETN (Law Enforcement Television Network), which began broadcasting to about three thousand subscriber departments across the country, supplies short training sessions that can be used during roll calls, in-service training sessions, or department-sponsored seminars.

The Station House

Police departments or stations provide a location from which to direct and control police operations. The police station is the center of activity for all police services. Its location often determines how effectively these services are delivered. In a village or small town, the police station might have only one room. In large cities, the central headquarters can occupy a large, multistoried building with several substations or precinct stations. While no one station design will fit all needs and budgets, certain features consistent with the departments' responsibilities should be found in all stations. The following features must be considered in the design and construction of a police station (not all stations will have every feature, but most will have some combination of them):

- Outside lighting completely encircling the station and a fifty-foot "stand off" area free from private vehicle parking.
- Controlled or monitored access to the station at every door. Special entrances for police officers arriving at and leaving the station.
- Interior and exterior doors with Plexiglas windows for maximum visibility except for doors leading from the public waiting

areas to detention areas, which should block observation. Electrically controlled doors leading into and out of a detention area to maximize control.

- Minimum number of exterior windows. Where they are required, Plexiglas instead of plate glass.
- Emergency lighting and power.
- Separate restroom facilities for the public, prisoners and police officers.
- Separate office for Shift or Watch commander.
- Separate office for Patrol Supervisor.
- Property and Evidence storage area.
- Communications Center situated internally for security.
- Storage area for equipment and emergency items.
- Booking and Processing Room.
- Detention Cells.

Station Security

Efficient design and organization of the police station can do much to minimize personnel requirements, enhance security, and ensure effective use of station facilities.

Controls normally prevent visitors and unauthorized people from wandering through the station. Such controls should not interfere with personnel conducting business. Control measures may include a visitor sign-in book, information desk, or electrically operated doors.

Station Desk

The station desk handles incoming offenders and generally manages the station house facilities. Normally, the station desk is managed by a desk sergeant (a senior sergeant). Other police officers assist the desk sergeant in administrative functions, including answering the telephone, filing, managing records checks and helping arresting officers in booking and detention. In some jurisdictions, a minor offender may stay in detention only long enough for a bondsman or lawyer to arrange bail and have the client released. In these situations, the offender will stay in station detention rather than be transferred to a city or county jail.

The station desk area should be separate from the area where the public might come to seek information or complain. Although some police departments, police stations or precincts allow the public to enter a police operations area to talk with the desk sergeant or another supervisor, it's not a desirable setting.

The desk location should enable desk personnel (desk sergeant and administrative officers) to have an unobstructed view of the station entrance and the area around the desk. Desk construction should place desk personnel, when seated, at eye level with a person standing in front of the desk. The height of the desk may vary, but it should be high enough to present an obstacle or barrier to persons trying to harm desk personnel and should minimize the physical and psychological disadvantages for seated personnel.

A restraining bar is sometimes used to keep people at a certain distance. A sharp incline outward from floor level to the desk top makes it difficult for anyone to climb over the desk. The front of the desk in some stations is reinforced to provide protection from small arms fire and shrapnel from bombs or grenades.

Complaint and Information Desk

This desk is freely accessible to the public. Desk personnel supply information to walk-ins, receive complaints by telephone, and issue statements to the media. This desk is normally located in a separate area of the station and is manned by one senior patrol officer and several less experienced officers or cadets.

Report Writing Room

The report writing room must be near the operations area, but far enough from the mainstream of station activity to allow officers to complete their paperwork undisturbed.

Police Communications Center

The police communications center houses radio, telephone, facsimile (fax) and computer equipment, including 911 service. Dispatchers must be intimately familiar with the geographical areas of the jurisdiction, must stay calm under pressure, and must be well organized, since they often do several tasks simultaneously.

Other Station Facilities

Other facilities include a roll-call or briefing room. Locker rooms, showers, lounges, training rooms and similar areas are normally in the basement of the station. Detectives and juvenile, vice, traffic and other officers are usually found on the second and third floors, while the chief and department command and management are located on the top floor of the station.

Illustration 1-3 (page 30) shows the main floor layout of a typical police station that carries on twenty-four-hour, day-to-day operations. A station can have more facilities or remain a one-room facility, depending on the size of the department, budget limits, number of officers and other considerations.

An Average Police Department Layout

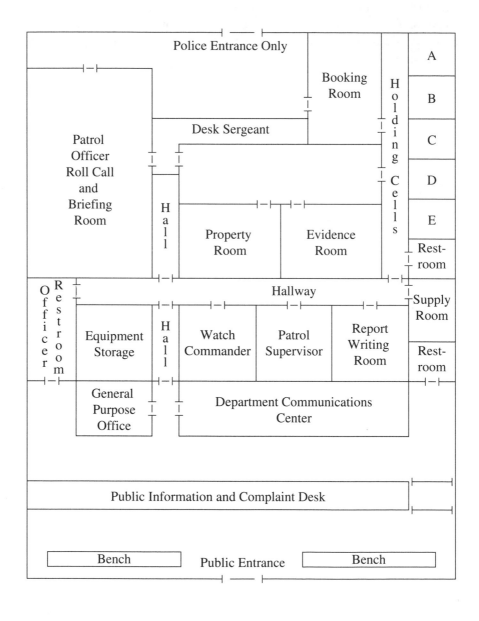

THE DETECTIVE

The second important police role is investigation and crime detection. The detective has been a figure of great romantic appeal since the first independent bureau was established by the London Metropolitan Police in 1841. Portrayal of the detective as the elite or the idiots of police departments comes to us in countless books, films and television productions. Most young police officers aspire to join the detective division. To them, an investigator's job is 99 percent adventure and 1 percent paperwork. Having worked over half of my thirty-year law enforcement career as a criminal investigator for federal, state and county agencies across the country, I can attest that the opposite ratio is more accurate.

The main function of a detective division is to support the patrol division by conducting the special crime investigations that lead to the arrest and conviction of offenders not apprehended at the scene by patrol officers. Because of time limits and personnel restrictions, the patrol division cannot complete all criminal investigations. The detective division conducts follow-up investigations.

Structure of a Police Detective Division

Detective divisions can be structured in two ways: generalized or specialized. A general investigative approach is most affordable for smaller departments with limited personnel and no predominant crime category, while groups of specialized detectives prove the most effective and efficient for larger departments.

In a generalized structure, detectives perform all or most of the investigative tasks themselves. These tasks include the preliminary investigation, evidence gathering, interviewing and interrogating, eliminating suspects, apprehending offenders, and court case preparation and presentation. A detective's responsibility begins with the receipt of the crime report and continues until the investigation concludes in court. In some instances, especially in small departments, a uniformed officer may perform the dual functions of patrol and investigation. These departments normally rely on specialized help from outside agencies such as the sheriff's department and state police.

In larger departments, specialization becomes more viable and often a necessity because of the heavy case load. Using specialized techniques enables detectives to focus on specific categories of crimes, such as homicide, robbery, rape, burglary and arson.

Illustration 2-1 (page 33) shows a typical detective division structure in a large department.

How Detective Divisions Work

Normally, a police department detective division is responsibile for continuing the investigation of a crime beyond the preliminary stage. Composition of the various assigned elements will depend on the extent of the department's generalization or specialization; it will also be affected by population, geography of jurisdiction, officer strength of the division, budget, crime rates, types of crime experienced and department objectives. The detective division will often include the following:

Office of the Chief of Detectives

The chief of detectives administers and supervises the detective division. The office is staffed by the chief, the chief's deputies, and supervisory officers detailed as commanding officers of the various principal subdivisions.

Typical Police Department Detective Division

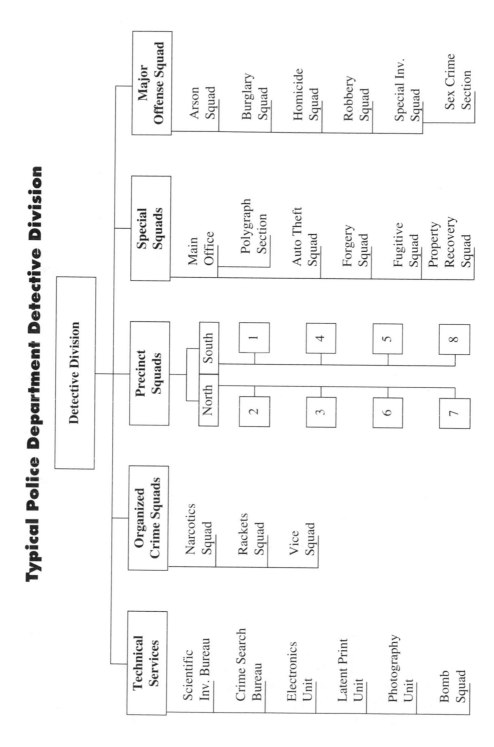

Precinct, District or Station Detective Squads

The size of precinct detective squads will depend on the size of the department and precincts (zones) into which it is subdivided. These squads are organized in independent divisions, such as North, South, East, West or whatever geographical, numerical or alphabetical designation works best for the department.

Precinct detectives become the "front-line troops" of the detective division. Usually one squad operates from each of the precinct station houses. Precinct detectives conduct the initial investigation of most crimes referred to the detective division. Cases of a specialized, complex or technical nature are referred to detectives of organized crime squads, special squads, major offense squads or the technical service bureau. The precinct squad detective originally responsible for an investigation can be temporarily assigned to a concerned special unit, according to the priorities and continuity needed for the case.

Detectives assigned to organized crime squads, special squads, major offense squads and technical service bureaus generally investigate one crime or groups of related crimes or occurrences. However, as the need arises, officers assigned to these units can be assigned anywhere in the detective division. Sizes of precinct or special detective squads in metropolitan police departments will be proportionate to the crime levels and degree of generalization or specialization. A large city department may have a hundred or more detectives working out of a precinct. The personnel staffing level must compensate for days off, vacations, sick leave, court appearances, training and other administrative duties. Actual time spent investigating a case is often only a fraction of the time reported for payroll.

Property Recovery Squad

This squad conducts investigations at pawnshops, secondhand dealers, jewelers and elsewhere in an attempt to recover stolen or lost property. It sends reports to precinct detective squads, the burglary squad and the bureau of special operations regarding property sold to pawnshops and secondhand dealers, with the names and addresses of the persons who sold these goods. If these persons have prior criminal records, it's noted on the reports. The squad maintains a daily liaison with other police departments regarding property recovery. It also keeps a central file on all property lost, stolen or found within the municipal jurisdiction, indexed by type of property, serial numbers or other identifying data, and an alphabetical file of all persons doing business with pawnshops or second-hand dealers within the squad's jurisdiction.

Bomb Squad

The bomb squad enforces all laws involving explosives, dangerous substances, dangerous articles, gases and radioactive materials. It is also responsible for defusing bombs and explosive devices and for rendering harmless dangerous substances, articles, gases and materials, as well as safeguarding and storing volatile evidence and giving court testimony associated with that evidence.

The bomb squad primarily investigates possible offenses in the eight areas listed below:

1. Technical aspects of explosions, bombs, explosives or related items.
2. All injuries resulting from explosions of bombs, devices, substances, articles, gases or from radiation.
3. Pyrotechnic and rocket displays.
4. Ammunition and powder sales.
5. Firearms problems with dealers and gunsmiths.
6. Federal violations involving firearms.
7. Pistol and rifle ranges and their safety and construction.
8. Firearms turned in at police headquarters or shipped to local terminals of Railway Express, United Parcel Service or other common carriers.

The bomb squad also maintains a liaison with the following agencies:

1. Bureau of Alcohol, Tobacco and Firearms (firearms and explosive devices).
2. Federal Bureau of Investigation (explosions and intelligence about bomb threats).
3. FBI Bomb Data Program (bombs, explosions, and technical data about explosives).
4. International Association of Bomb Technicians and Investigators (information exchange).

This squad maintains and operates special equipment associated with its responsibilities, including:

1. Portable X ray machines capable of fluoroscopy and Polaroid X ray pictures through objects of up to one-inch-thick steel.
2. Cryogenic (supercold) equipment that freezes bombs and their internal components.
3. A bomb equipment truck that carries special equipment for explosives.
4. A tractor-trailer truck that carries a special bomb transport vessel.

Central or Main Office

This office operates twenty-four hours a day, seven days a week to supply support services to detective units. An information and coordination center, the central office also acts as custodian of investigative supplies and equipment issued as needed to detectives. Equipment reserves might include items such as:

- Cameras and film
- Binoculars
- Gasoline credit cards
- Auto rental cards
- Leg irons and waist restraining chains
- Handcuffs for mass-arrest situations
- Shotguns, machine guns and ammunition
- Tear gas guns and shells
- Gas and smoke grenades
- Gas masks and bulletproof vests
- Computer warrant terminal
- Motor-vehicle computer terminals
- Detective division portable radios
- Refrigerator for storing perishable evidence
- Night-vision devices for night surveillance
- Evidence lockers
- Disaster and mass-arrest kits
- Microfilm readers
- Other items tailored to the needs of the division

The main office also houses technically oriented units such as the polygraph section and others as needed by the division.

Major Offense Squads

The major offense squads investigate major crimes and are grouped according to the following descriptions:

Arson Squad. This police detective squad works closely with a state fire marshal's office to investigate incendiary fires, fires of undetermined origin and false alarms. The squad maintains a variety of files, such as: (1) location file — all reported fires by fire district; (2) date and time file — all reported fires in order of occurrence; (3) owner-occupant file — owners or occupants of premises reporting a fire loss; (4) suspects file — all persons causing or suspected of causing a fire.

Burglary Squad. The burglary squad helps precinct detective squads investigate major burglaries or a concentration of burglaries in a specific area. It also maintains a liaison with and coordinates burglary investigations between precinct detective squads and other law enforcement agencies. It is responsible for the follow-up investigation of all burglaries involving safes and maintains surveillance of known or suspected burglars, often conducting day and night patrol in high-frequency locations. The squad conducts security surveys of public buildings and shows owners and managers of businesses optional preventive techniques that safeguard against burglaries. It also gives lectures for citizen groups as part of a burglary prevention program.

The burglary squad normally maintains the following files and equipment: (1) suspect file — known or suspected burglars with photos when available; (2) suspect file by last known place of residence; (3) burglary file — all burglaries committed in specific areas.

Homicide Squad. This detective squad investigates deaths, or serious injuries ostensibly resulting in death, in the following categories:

1. Criminal violence or assault.
2. Accidents including criminal negligence.
3. Vehicle, railroad, airplane and boat accidents.
4. Suicides.
5. Drownings.
6. Sudden death, or death happening under any suspicious or unusual circumstance.

7. All deaths during confinement in jail or in detention cells.

The homicide squad also maintains a liaison with the medical examiner's or coroner's office and the homicide bureau of the prosecutor's office and keeps files on all deaths in its jurisdiction investigated by the police.

Robbery Squad. The robbery squad helps precinct detective squads in robbery investigations. It also maintains a liaison with and coordinates investigations between precinct squads and other law enforcement agencies. The squad keeps surveillance on known or suspected robbers and conducts patrols and stakeouts in high-frequency locations.

The robbery squad normally creates and maintains files that would include:

1. Suspect file — an alphabetical listing (cross-indexed with photographs when available) of known perpetrators of robberies in the squad's jurisdiction, or perpetrators of robberies anywhere if their residence is in the department's jurisdiction.

2. Robbery location files — listing all robberies committed in its jurisdiction, categorized by type (for example, bank or gas station), where they happened, time of day or night, race and number of perpetrators, weapons displayed or used, and oddities of the case.

3. Bank file — containing photographs of exteriors of banks in the squad's jurisdiction, with integral security details and names and addresses of managers or security officers.

Special Investigations Squad. This unit is responsible for special or extraordinary investigations such as cases involving government officials or other officers or departments, cases with high media interest and coverage, or cases that have the general public deeply concerned. The squad normally conducts previsit investigations and helps plan for security and protection in local appearances of governmental and other dignitaries. It also polices planned large-scale public gatherings to ensure safety of life and property.

The special investigations squad will often maintain the following files and records:

1. Known subversives or extremists file — cross-referenced and indexed alphabetically by last names with their membership in various groups noted.

2. Motorcycle gangs.

3. Aerial photograph file — including photographs depicting various locations throughout the squad's jurisdiction where past large-scale public gatherings have occurred or are likely to occur, to aid in arranging for security.

This squad also regularly includes a sex-crimes unit or section. This section helps investigate all sex crimes and is responsible for interviewing female victims. All sex crimes are reported daily from the various precincts or substations. Information taken from these reports provides this squad with a picture of sex-crime activity in areas under its jurisdiction. Often, the sex-crime unit will conduct lectures for women and other groups about defensive and crime preventive measures.

The special investigations squad normally creates and maintains files as follows:

1. Known sex offender file — with photographs of the offenders.

2. Information file — listing sex offenders and their particular modus operandi.

3. Confidence game file — listing confidence-games offenders and their particular modus operandi.

Technical Service Bureau

The elements or units of this bureau have responsibility for many technical and scientific aspects of crime investigation. This bureau will often have the following internal specialized units and officers:

Crime Scene Search Unit. This unit processes crime scenes for physical evidence. The officers assigned to this unit may not be experts in any one field, but they have considerable knowledge in many. Due to the time they spend on each crime scene and to their limited numbers, these specialists normally become involved only in serious crime cases, especially those suggesting homicides, some bank robberies and violent sex offenses. The crime scene team might also have other responsibilities such as:

1. Conducting all crime scene, as well as aerial crime scene, photography.

2. Searching for, photographing and lifting latent fingerprints.

3. Recovering bullets, fragments and casings.

4. Casting footprints, tire marks and toolmarks.

5. Recovering paint scrapings.

6. Swabbing for gunpowder residue.

7. Testing for and recovering blood evidence.

8. Recovering flammables.

9. Measuring and sketching the crime scene.

10. Marking evidence and transporting it to the latent fingerprint unit and scientific investigation bureau.

11. Using metal detectors to recover hidden metallic articles.

12. Sweeping scenes with an evidence vacuum cleaner.

13. Gathering hair and fiber samples.

14. Taking fingernail scrapings of suspects and victims.

15. Photographing and sketching scenes of fatal auto accidents.

16. Fingerprinting and photographing arrested persons confined to hospitals.

17. Fingerprinting and photographing deceased persons at a medical examiner or coroner morgue.

18. Collecting evidence from post-bombing situations.

Latent Fingerprint Unit. Latent fingerprint evidence found at the scene of a crime by either the investigating officer or the crime scene search officers will eventually come to this unit for further developing and evaluation through several conventional or chemical methods. This unit normally supplies the following support services:

1. Manages the facility for photographing evidence and latent prints of all types.

2. Identifies the latent prints found at a crime scene. This might happen through a process of eliminating the prints of the complainant, members of the complainant's family, and authorized visitors who had legitimate access to the location where the crime happened. Where department budgets allow, this unit might use computerized equipment and programs to do much of the elimination and matching work.

3. Obtains classifiable fingerprints of unidentified deceased persons or ensures a positive identification when necessary.

4. Identifies palm prints and footprints.

5. Processes motor vehicles for latent prints.

6. Often supplies fingerprint powders and lifts to all precincts and other investigative squads.

7. Develops latent prints on human skin.

Photography Unit. The photography unit maintains and operates the photography laboratory. To support the detective division this unit processes all departmental negatives and makes copies and enlargements as needed. The unit often takes aerial photographs and photographs evidence (for example, jewelry or weapons) and often creates photographic training and investigative aids. This unit normally has primary responsibility for:

1. Inspecting, maintaining and repairing departmental photo equipment.

2. Ordering all photographic supplies for the police department.

3. Operating the identification camera for the departmental identification photo file.

4. Photocopying sketches, documents and photographs.

5. Creating and maintaining a negative file of crime scene and prisoner photos indexed by identification number.

6. Preparing composite drawings of suspects or perpetrators who are at large.

Scientific Investigation Bureau (Police Crime Laboratory)

The scientific investigation bureau typically has five sections.

Biology. This section's responsibilities include:

1. Blood identification by major group typing.

2. Identification of minor blood groups.

3. Isoenzyme identification using electrophoretic methods for further analysis of blood types.

4. Bloodstain pattern examination to determine origin and direction of blood spatters.

5. Spermatozoa identification.

6. Differentiation of seminal and vaginal fluids.

7. Major blood grouping of seminal and vaginal fluids.

8. Salivary amylase examination for saliva identification.

9. Major grouping of body fluids.

10. Differentiation of hair by particular species (human, animal or synthetics).
11. Race identification by hair samples.
12. Comparison of hair that has been collected as evidence with known standards.
13. Examination of crime scenes and preservation of fragile evidence in certain cases.

Criminalistics. The criminalistics section provides chemical analysis in the following areas:

1. Examination of flammables in arson cases for identification and flash-point determination.
2. Urine analysis for drug content in vehicular homicides.
3. Blood alcohol analysis for DWI.
4. Examination of alcoholic beverages.
5. Examination and identification of poisons.
6. Examination of gunpowder and gunshot residues.
7. Examination of paint scrapings.
8. Examination of metals.
9. Examination of sneak-thief detection powders and other substances.
10. Identification of glass fragments and determination of direction of fracture.
11. Identification of fibers.
12. Identification and comparison of foot, heel and vehicle tire impressions.

Document Examination. The document examination section examines documents to:

1. Determine age.
2. Restore charred or water-damaged papers.
3. Identify paper.
4. Identify writing material.
5. Restore erasures, obliterations or alterations.
6. Make handwriting and handprinting comparisons.

Firearms. The firearms section has responsibility for:

1. Identifying firearms and their working condition.
2. Determining possible source of cartridge casing or identifying type of firearm it came from.
3. Chemical testing for gunshot residue — uses neutron activation analyses.
4. Restoring obliterated serial numbers.
5. Comparing toolmark impressions with recovered tools.
6. Identifying pick marks on lock cylinders.
7. Determining distance between victim and firearm when fired by examining test patterns.
8. Assisting in recovery of firearms evidence at crime scenes.
9. Acting as liaison with firearms manufacturers and dealers regarding the sale and history of particular weapons.
10. Acting as liaison with other law enforcement agencies in major crimes involving firearms.

Controlled Substances Analysis. The controlled substances analysis section does quantitative and qualitative analyses of controlled substances. Examples include narcotics and drugs including synthetic or designer drugs. Prevalent drugs include marijuana, hashish, THC, cocaine, amphetamines, barbiturates, narcotic alkaloids, opium alkaloids, hallucinogens, heroin, morphine and LSD.

Detective Division Case Management

Once an initial investigation is completed, usually on the first day, and it appears that continued investigation is necessary, proper case management becomes a necessity. The supervising detective who made the original case assignment now continues to monitor the investigator's work.

When a case requires an intensive, concerted effort, more than one investigator may need to be assigned. When necessary, specialized units might take part. As the case progresses, the supervisor will need to manage and coordinate the various units and detectives involved. The investigation of each case must be done in an orderly and structured fashion.

Reviews of supplemental progress reports, statements, neighborhood canvas results, areas of concentration, index-file results of lead sheets and laboratory analysis reports help the supervising detective evaluate the potential for successful case conclusion.

The relationship between the crime investigator and the prosecutor becomes enhanced with close case scrutiny at the supervisory level. Many investigations require considerable time to dovetail all the connected facts into a proper case presentation. When daily activity reports come to the supervisor, he or she should be able to present a well-rounded picture of the case structure. The case manager can identify a case's strengths and weaknesses to the prosecutor, and working together they can often determine the next investigatory step. Certain evidentiary areas may need to be firmed up for proper trial presentation. As the person who will be presenting the case before the courts, the prosecutor proves invaluable at this stage of the investigation. When enough incriminating evidence exists for the issuance of an arrest warrant or a presentation before a grand jury, the prosecutor's assistance again is critical.

Managing the Case Load

Detectives cannot succeed when their case load fragments their efforts. A good case manager will ensure that incoming cases are distributed so that no one detective will have more work than can be completed effectively. The manager must also develop a system of case priority assignment that ensures maximum results.

Case Priority Assignment

Generally, the selection of cases for investigative priority should be guided by clues uncovered in the preliminary investigation. Cases of major concern, such as homicide, violent sex offenses, robbery and kidnapping, are usually exempt from priority ranking because they routinely require priority police effort from the first notification of occurrence. Burglary, larceny, auto theft, vandalism, and other categories of crimes unlikely to be witnessed by a complainant will receive less concentrated effort, unless significant reason for further investigation develops from a preliminary investigation. Effort and time should be concentrated on solving offenses offering the best evidence, including witnesses, and the best chance of a solution. Detective assignment made according to individual areas of expertise also helps ensure the most professional follow-up. This approach is not selective enforcement; instead, it focuses a detective's efforts in the direction of greatest probable achievement and uses police resources most efficiently.

For greatest effectiveness and efficiency, many police detective divisions manage their case load using three key elements:

1. Intrajurisdiction. The detectives and case load are assigned to sections of the department by area of jurisdiction. For example, a city might be divided geographically into four parts, six parts, eight parts or more according to available detectives.

2. By Watch or Shift. Each detective shift works the cases received on that shift; however, each shift receives a briefing about the crimes committed earlier to ensure that detectives will recognize important information or suspects.

3. By Types of Cases. In larger police departments, detective division case loads are also divided into three types:

   • Crimes against persons
   • Crimes against property
   • General and special crime assignments

   The *crimes against persons* category comprises all crimes involving the health and safety of any person. Crimes in this classification include:

   1. Murder
   2. Sex offenses:
      Sexual battery
      Sodomy
      Other sexual assaults
   3. Robbery
   4. Kidnapping
   5. Extortion
   6. Suicide
   7. Natural deaths
   8. Assault and battery
   9. Theft from person's body (for example, purse or wallet snatching)
   10. Other crimes in the department's jurisdiction according to state statute

   The *crimes against property* category involves all crimes that endanger or deprive a person of property. Some of the crimes in this category include:

1. Burglary
2. Larceny (theft)
3. Receiving and concealing stolen property
4. Lost and found property
5. Worthless documents:

   Bad checks

   Invalid or stolen credit cards
6. Explosions
7. Bomb threats
8. Breaking and entering:

   Coin-operated machines

   Motor vehicle
9. Auto theft
10. Vandalism

The *general and special crime assignment* category includes crimes that do not fall into the categories of crimes against persons or property, such as:

1. Swindles or con games
2. Embezzlements (all types)
3. Malicious mischief
4. Animal bites
5. Disorderly conduct
6. Arson
7. Trespassing
8. Obscene phone calls
9. Accidental injury
10. Traffic fatalities and assaults with automobiles

The case load might also be divided by division, zone or section. Detectives investigate all crimes committed in their assigned zone. This method is inefficient because detectives must become investigative generalists instead of specialists, and they may find it difficult to maintain continuity in homicide, sexual battery, burglary, worthless documents, juvenile crime and auto theft cases where specialization and continuity are essential.

Many departments now use a unique concept called team policing. In team policing, there is no patrol division or detective division in a traditional sense. The city is divided into large districts, and a team of police officers, supervised by a sergeant and lieutenant, is assigned to patrol and investigate criminal matters within each district. The sergeant and lieutenant in charge of each team have a great deal of discretion in managing the district and the assigned officers. For example, one particular area of the district might have a high crime rate; the sergeant or lieutenant in charge might assign five or six officers on the team to work only that area instead of dividing the officers equally into the different areas as is traditionally done. In team policing, an officer dispatched to a complaint call investigates that case to its conclusion. The first police officer dispatched will write the initial report, search the crime scene, collect evidence, interview the victim and witnesses, and complete all follow-up work normally done by a detective. Later, he or she will organize all information about the crime into a case, arrest the suspect when possible, and present the completed case to a prosecutor for trial. One of the key advantages of team policing is continuity— one officer understands all facets of the crime from beginning to end. The success or failure of this type of program depends on whether officers receive the necessary training to do these specialized tasks, and whether the budget can accommodate the required equipment and personnel. When an officer stays tied up with a case, he may not resume patrol for hours or even days. This concept is not workable for every department or jurisdiction.

Finding Police Detective Candidates

Law enforcement officers assigned to a detective division emerge from the ranks of the patrol officers. Detective candidates must be perceptive, have a strong sense of confidence, and possess a vivid imagination. These qualities help the investigator develop hypotheses relevant to the circumstances surrounding an offense and the offender's deviant thinking. Awareness of the who, what, when, where, why and how questions regarding a particular crime enhances the detective's ability to establish a plan of action. The detective must also be able to mentally take the role of the offender and try to re-create the offender's thoughts, motives and movements.

Guidelines Used in a Police Detective Selection Process

With rare exception, police detectives are selected from within the ranks of the police department. The following guidelines are used in selecting patrol officers to become detectives:

Experience. Most police agencies call for three to five years experience before considering a patrol officer for transfer to a detective division. When an officer meets the experience qualifier, other factors such as patrol performance, administrative proficiency, education, self-discipline, motivation, the ability to work unsupervised, personal demeanor and organizational skills come into play.

Testing. Some police departments have a rigid candidate testing process for transfer to the detective division, although this selection method is most common in large city departments where competition and numbers of personnel demand a fair elimination process. Testing normally includes a lengthy written test that encompasses laws, procedures and investigative processes. A review board of senior officers and detectives rates the candidates with a uniform numerical system. The board rating also includes their perception of the candidates' demeanor, ability to express themselves succinctly (important in court testimony about complex cases and under extreme stress, especially during cross-examination), general knowledge, and motives for becoming a detective.

Administrative Process. Ideally, the request for a particular officer should come from the commander of the detective division. In a small- to medium-sized police department, administrators can have personal knowledge of officer qualifications. In large departments, administrators cannot personally know or regularly observe officers. They must discuss possible candidates with working detectives whose feedback, when used correctly, can be valuable in determining which candidates will do the best job as investigators. Although feedback from veteran investigative officers and recommendations offered by the investigation commander are important, the chief of police must often make the final choice.

Probationary Period. Despite the rigorous selection process and training regime, some candidates who become police officers and receive promotions to detective status don't perform well. Some people excel on written tests but cannot apply their knowledge on the job. Others do well in their interviews before a board but do poorly on the job. Some officers who have dreamed about becoming detectives may become disillusioned or disappointed because the reality turns out to be different from their expectations. Because these problem areas cannot be completely eliminated through a selection process, a beginning police officer usually has a six-month to one-year probationary period during which he or she can be dismissed without cause from the department, from a promotion to higher grade, or from a detective position. This means the officer has no appeal rights and must accept the decision without recourse. Except in cases involving a recruit, promotions and detective assignments that don't work out satisfactorily normally result in an officer returning to his previous grade and status. If the officer or detective performs to acceptable standards, he receives a permanent status after completing his probationary period. New officers assigned to a detective division are evaluated throughout their probationary period. Although the new detective may have proved herself to be a valuable patrol officer, she may not have the attributes necessary to be a good criminal investigator. When officers are not effective as police detectives, they return to the patrol division.

Desirable Attributes in the Selection Process. The police detective (criminal investigator) must have all the competencies required of a regular patrol officer, plus some advance abilities and specialized skills. The detective's abilities must surpass those of a patrol officer. The following list describes fifteen attributes of a good police detective.

1. A detective's observation powers should be highly developed and specialized.
2. Report writing must be of high quality because a detective's finished report will determine whether the case will go to court.
3. A detective must be able to make an arrest in plain clothes without the advantage in authority a uniform provides.
4. A detective must feel he is doing a good job and is performing an important and useful function.
5. A detective must be able to talk with strangers and gain their confidence within a short time.
6. A detective must have confidence in her professional abilities.
7. A detective must have a keen interest in criminal investiga-

tions, and a natural curiosity or inquisitiveness.

8. A detective must be able to work without close supervision, to complete a task on his own initiative.
9. A detective must be open-minded and resist jumping to any conclusions.
10. A detective must be patient enough to handle details, stake-outs, long, drawn-out court proceedings and relentless cross-examinations.
11. A detective should be able to logically and imaginatively reconstruct the sequence of a crime's events.
12. A detective must have above-average intelligence and learning ability, excellent memory and recall, and the ability to identify a method of operation, the similarities among cases, and the value of evidence and information.
13. A detective must be able to investigate crime impartially, collecting information without bias or prejudice. She must also have the integrity to reject bribes.
14. A detective must be knowledgeable about the legalities involved in charging a suspect with a crime and prosecuting the crime in court.
15. A detective must appear physically average and inconspicuous.

Training Police Detectives

Although the recruit receives basic police training at a police academy, he or she will need specialized training to perform competently as a detective. In larger police departments, formalized training does not present a problem. However, in small- to medium-sized departments, new detectives are simply assigned to senior partners who have demonstrated skill and knowledge in criminal investigations. Smaller departments can normally secure investigative training assistance from larger municipal or county sheriff's departments. Often, the county district attorney or prosecutor's office has ample staff to help train new detectives. The prosecutor also benefits from participating in the training program by ensuring that investigative officers will later supply solid cases that can be prosecuted successfully in court.

Another excellent source of general and specialized training for investigative officers comes from over 1,100 colleges that offer criminal justice, law enforcement and assorted police courses. Seminars and specialized training courses for law enforcement investigators held at various colleges and federal agencies offer another training alternative.

Supervision and Administration

Police detectives must be dedicated to their job and willing to endure the obstacles often confronting them. Because detectives perform their duty in plain clothes and use an unmarked police vehicle, they enjoy considerable freedom. Unlike the supervisor of a patrol division whose patrol officers are in uniform, confined to a particular area, beat or zone or in a highly visible marked police car, the supervisor in the detective division must rely on personal integrity to guarantee a full day's or night's work.

Four types of records are used to help supervisors control the detective division: the daily call sheet, the case assignment record, the monthly summary report, and the investigator's case disposition report.

Daily Call Sheet. Although most detectives work during the day shift, when the greatest amount of information is available, there will also be off-hour investigation time. By maintaining a daily call sheet, the supervisor will be able to record the hours worked and the availability of each detective. A detective must expect to work an eight-hour shift; overtime is usually compensated with time off or added salary computed at one and one-half times an officer's regular hourly wage.

Case Assignment Record. Controlled by the Chief of Detectives or an equivalent position, this record supplies accountability and means of monitoring an investigation. Each case is assigned a control number—the year, month and day the case was opened—a letter or series of letters designating the type of case, and a sequential control number for the number of cases opened. Each department will design their own particular style of numbering since there is no universal type. A case assignment number might appear as 93-02-09-B-00050, which translates as a case opened February 9, 1993, Burglary, and the fiftieth burglary case opened in 1993.

Monthly Summary Report. This is a computation of the cases handled and cleared through the month. It is a brief summary of the detective's performance. Obviously, different types of cases call for different amounts of investigation time. Some investigations, because of their difficulty or lack of leads, may never be successfully completed. The supervisor can use this report to determine case assignments, performance of the officer and other statistical requirements.

Investigator's Case Disposition. Some police departments require that detectives write a separate monthly report on each case assigned to them. This report provides an update on the case and shows whether the detective has worked on it during the month. If the detective has a heavy case load, he often will not have time to work on each case during the month. This method is time-consuming and forces the detective to spend valuable time away from the cases.

Standard Equipment for Police Detectives

Effective police criminal investigations require proper tools for collecting and managing information, including physical evidence. The following kits supply detectives with minimum effective collection and recording capabilities. In most smaller departments, the detectives carry most or all of these kits in the trunk of their vehicle. In large cities, where supplying each detective is too costly, the precinct usually issues complete kits as needed or stores them in one or more vans that respond when needed by detectives.

General Evidence Collection Kit. This kit is used in a great number of evidence-collection situations. It contains scissors, wire cutters, tweezers, pliers, knives, syringes, and a variety of other tools, as well as everyday implements such as pens, pencils, envelopes, plastic bags, flashlights and measuring tape.

Drug and Narcotic Field-Testing Kit. Detectives often need to make on-the-spot tests of substances they believe are illegal. This kit contains a wide variety of reagent systems that identify amphetamines, barbiturates, LSD, PCP, cocaine, heroin, marijuana and other illegal drugs.

Photographic Kit. In many situations, the detectives need two cameras—a 35mm camera (with day and date imprint on the negative), and a Polaroid instant photograph camera. This kit contains both types along with the usual accessories, such as a flash and tripod. Some departments now use video cameras extensively, but the cost and skill required for operation continue to limit their use, especially in large detective divisions.

Latent Fingerprint Collection Kit. This kit contains a variety of latent and magnetic powders for lifting fingerprints. It also includes hinged and rubber lifters, lift tape, a toothbrush, a fingerprint pad, and a magnifying glass and other helpful tools.

Casts and Molds—Impressions and Marks Kit. Footprints and tire tracks sometimes can lead to a suspect's identity. In this kit, the detective will find plaster casting material, casting frames, silicone rubber putty, dust and dirt hardener, oil coater and other important materials for completing this process.

Document Evidence Collection Kit. An important document should never be folded, crumpled, or carried unprotected in a pocket. The document should be placed between transparent protective covers or in paper envelopes. In humid weather, some documents may stick between plastic covers and transfer type imprint to the cover. In such cases, heavy paper protectors are used. If a document is torn, it is not restored, except to place the pieces in the protective cover in their most obvious and logical positions. The detective should not subject a document to strong light for prolonged periods, should not add or destroy indented marks, and should not remove the document from its protective covers to make copies of it. The document kit contains plastic sheet protectors, solid containers for fragile evidence, paper envelopes, tweezers, a magnifying glass and a hard briefcase.

Rape and Sex-Offense Evidence Collection Kit. This kit contains a cervix scraper, a slide holder with two slides, plastic comb for pubic hair collection, seminal fluid reagent packet, white gummed envelopes and police evidence seals.

Post-Mortem Fingerprint and Cadaver Taking Kit. Left- and right-handed post-mortem cards, inking tool, tissue builder solution and tissue cleaner, 3cc molded hypodermic syringes and surgeon's gloves are found in this kit, as well as other equipment.

Arson and Explosives Kit. In this kit, the detective carries a variety of tools, including an axe, hatchet, shovels, hammer, clawhammer, wood saw, pliers, wire cutters, wood chisel, and a drill with assorted bits for wood, masonry and steel. Containers such as gallon and quart cans, glass jars and sealable bags are used to store the often charred and fragile evidence. The photographic kit is also used extensively when searching a fire or explosion scene for evidence of arson.

Clothing and Safety Items Kit. This kit is frequently used in a variety of investigative situations. It includes safety goggles, work gloves, coveralls, heavy-duty workboots and rubber boots, baseball and construction hat, a flashlight and electric lantern.

To best manage a crime scene, the detective is wise to carry, along with the above kits, police line barrier tape, crime scene notice signs, witness statement forms, Miranda warning cards, suspect statement forms, consent to search forms, a basic first aid kit, a dust and particle face mask, and crime scene, traffic, human body and furniture templates, as well as plenty of pens, pencils and paper.

T H R E E

THE ART OF DETECTION

In the police detective's search for the truth, he employs many techniques, styles and arts. The hundreds of thousands of criminal investigations conducted by police detectives across the country and around the world each year leave an indelible impression on society. Almost all basic investigative problems are similar in method of approach. In chapter three, I'll show you the diverse methods, problems and solutions used by police detectives universally.

The Rules of Evidence Impact

When a police detective begins to investigate a crime, she is guided by a basic working knowledge of the rules of evidence. Despite an offender's arrest, unless a conviction or guilty plea results, the investigation has been unsuccessful. The detective must "nail down" her case. If evidence accumulation and preparation do not lead to a conviction, the case and the work performance of the detective are tainted. Criminal investigators must always remember that making an arrest simply for its own sake, without following prescribed constitutional requirements for evidence gathering, is nonproductive.

The arrest of a suspect is only a small fragment of the entire process of bringing the suspect into the criminal justice system. Other responsibilities remain for the detective, one of which is to identify admissible evidence. Once this identification has been accomplished, the particular evidentiary items must link with the elements proving the crime happened and further linking the suspect to the crime. Many investigations that appear solid on the surface are devastated when presented at trial. The prosecutor remains accountable for the interpretation and presentation of evidence, but justification for assembling the indicting proof remains a responsibility of the police detective.

Justification pertains not only to the reliability of the evidence but also to the means by which it came into the possession of the detective. Although an arrest occurred based on substantial incriminating information, no punitive action will result if the method of obtaining the information was contrary to the rules of admissibility.

The fact that there are no established statutes governing evidence is, in itself, an impediment to the detective, who is influenced instead by rules, procedures, court decisions and interpretations specifying the manner that investigatory efforts must follow. A detective must remember that the means of obtaining evidence must be acceptable to the presiding justice. Evidence that was admissible in a prior criminal case, according to the interpretation and decision made by the judge that presided, might not be acceptable to the judge before whom the present case is pending.

When I was a young criminal investigator, the first case given to me after a lengthy apprenticeship involved a series of armed robberies in which the assailant often shot and wounded his victim. With youthful zeal (and I'm sure a good measure of luck), I tracked down the criminal but had little physical evidence to link him to the robberies. I needed the gun used in the robberies to match the slugs removed from the victims' bodies. I had enough circumstantial evidence to obtain a search warrant but did not find the gun among the suspect's personal belongings. To my surprise the suspect decided to waive his right to consult with an attorney during questioning and confessed in a lengthy statement that took hours to prepare. In that confession, the suspect revealed details about the gun including where he hid it. After recovering the gun and having the laboratory process and verify it was the robbery weapon, I believed I had arrived. However, my balloon was popped abruptly in court by a skilled (and well-known) defense attorney who grilled me endlessly during cross-examination. Unfortunately, the prosecutor was as young and inexperienced as I was and did little to protect me from relentless questions, especially about the confession, then about the suspect's verification in another confession that the gun belonged to him. The suspect then claimed he was coerced into making a confession and had not committed any crime nor had any knowledge of the gun that became the centerpiece of our evidence. The next blow came when witnesses and victims were intimidated by the defense lawyer and wavered on their previously solid identification of the suspect. The confession was eventually thrown out as inadmissible evidence and all that followed it — the recovery of the gun, verification, some witnesses and other facts — went with it because that information and evidence resulted directly from the confession. I learned quickly not to rely on or even try to get a confession and could fill a book with other horror stories involving detectives who learned, as I did, that confessions normally lead to the criminal being set free.

I learned that a confession alone (contrary to popular belief and to many police shows, films and novels) means nothing, and that if a suspect reveals information in it that leads the detective to strong supporting evidence, it becomes the goal of a good defense attorney to create reasonable doubt about the validity of the confession and the procedures used to obtain it. When the defense has convinced a judge or jury of that, the evidence that can be traced to no other source than the confession will normally go out the window with it. Some courts have allowed certain evidence to stand, but normally the detective loses either in that court or on appeal.

Police detectives must be fully aware that the acceptability of this evidence and its later admissibility in a court of law depend largely on their method of seizure, preservation and subsequent positive identification. Detectives must contend with the fact that their particular investigation might be making evidentiary rules history in itself because it is subject to review by higher courts. A detective's actions could lead to a future decision that will affect not only that case but those with similar circumstances throughout the criminal justice system. This thought remains uppermost in the mind of a police detective. The method in which he applies the rules of evidence to his investigation will contribute to or detract from the ultimate success of his work.

Evidence a police detective collects must overcome two obstacles before it's offered as trial evidence: (1) common-law and statutory rules of evidence (there are libraries of case law, and it changes almost daily); (2) constitutional protections implemented through the exclusionary rule. The exclusionary rule was developed primarily by case law from the U.S. Supreme Court. Its purpose is to exclude from use at trial evidence obtained by police officials in ways that violate a defendant's personal constitutional rights.

One of the tools a detective depends on is garnering information about the instruments or fruits of a crime. That involves "developing" suspects and legally "searching" their home, car or other area over which they have control and finding a key item or items linking them to the crime. To keep within the legal boundaries and successfully investigate a case, a detective must do the preliminary work described below.

Probable Cause

The Fourth Amendment of the U.S. Constitution protects citizens from unreasonable searches but provides for search warrants issued by a judge or magistrate who is satisfied that there's sufficient "probable cause." A request for a search warrant must be supported by a police oath or affirmation describing the specific place to be searched and specific items to be seized. Illustration 3-1 (pages 59-60) shows a sample search warrant form used by federal law enforcement officers. Each state has a similar form, with some variation in wording depending on state search warrant statutes.

"Probable cause," as defined in several cases and most notably by the Supreme Court, is "a reasonable ground for belief, less than evidence justifying a conviction, but more than bare suspicion. Probable cause concerns circumstances in which a person of reasonable caution would believe an offense has been or is being committed."

Obtaining a Search Warrant

When a police detective believes she has sufficient "probable cause" in a criminal investigation, she prepares an affidavit and takes it to a judge. The affidavit's purpose is to show the judge the detective's reasons, or probable cause, to believe an object or objects related to the crime under investigation are at a specific place she wants to search. In the affidavit, the detective must include personal

Search Warrant

United States District Court

FOR THE

UNITED STATES OF AMERICA

vs.

Docket No.

Case No.

SEARCH WARRANT

Affidavit(s) having been made before me by

that he has reason to believe that { XXXXXXXXXXXX
on the premises known as }

in the   District of

there is now being concealed certain property, namely

here describe property

and as I am satisfied that there is probable cause to believe that the property so described is being concealed on the person or premises above described and that grounds for application for issuance of the search warrant exist as stated in the supporting affidavit(s).

You are hereby commanded to search within a period of -
(not to exceed 10 days) the person or place named for the property specified, serving this warrant
and making the search { in the daytime (6:00 a.m. to 10:00 p.m.)
XXXXXXXXXXXX XX XXXXXXXXXXXX } and if the property be found
there to seize it, leaving a copy of this warrant and receipt for the property taken, and prepare a written
inventory of the property seized and promptly return this warrant and bring the property before
- as required by law.
   Federal Judge or magistrate

Dated this   day of   , 19

- -
Judge (Federal or State Court of Record) or Federal Magistrate

*The Federal Rules of Criminal Procedure provide: "The warrant shall be served in the daytime, unless the issuing authority, by appropriate provision in the warrant, and for reasonable cause shown, authorizes its execution at times other than daytime." (Rule 41(c)). A statement of grounds for reasonable cause should be made in the affidavit(s) if a search is to be authorized "at any time day or night" pursuant to Rule 41(c).

RETURN

I received the attached search warrant   , 19   , and have executed it as

follows:

On   , 19   at   o'clock   M, I searched the person or premises de-

scribed in the warrant and

I left a copy of the warrant with _____
                                                    name of person searched or owner or "at the place of search"

together with a receipt for the items seized.

The following is an inventory of property taken pursuant to the warrant:

This inventory was made in the presence of

and

I swear that this Inventory is a true and detailed account of all the property taken by me on the

warrant.

_____

Subscribed and sworn to and returned before me this   day of   , 19

_____
                                                            Federal Magistrate

observations, details of the investigation, hearsay received from other persons, and often information supplied by a reliable informant. Upon finding that probable cause exists, based on the sworn affidavit, the magistrate or judge signs the search warrant giving the detective the authority to conduct the search requested. In assessing probable cause, the information provided in the affidavit must also be current. For example, say a detective's affidavit cites an informant (already established in some way as reliable and credible) who claims to have seen about one hundred kilos of cocaine in John Smith's bedroom; if the detective tried to obtain a search warrant a month after seeing the cocaine, the information would be stale. There would be no "reasonable belief" the cocaine would still be there. However, if the affidavit is submitted on the day after the informant said he saw the cocaine, and considering the amount alleged to be on the premises, it would be highly probable that all or part of the cocaine would still be on the premises. Illustration 3-2 (page 62) shows a typical affidavit form used for many purposes, including a request for a search warrant based on probable cause.

Language of an Affidavit and Search Warrant

Affidavits supporting probable cause for a search warrant and the warrant itself (normally prepared by the detective or a prosecutor) must contain specific language. The language depends on what the detective wants to look for. If a detective is looking for an automobile, the search warrant cannot authorize searching anywhere on the premises that could not possibly conceal an automobile. For example, the warrant would not give the detective authority to search the house, looking in drawers and closets. The search would remain restricted to places where the suspect could place an automobile. However, when the investigator is looking for a small handgun linked to a crime, there's more latitude in the language and authority given in the warrant. He can look anywhere on the premises where the suspect could conceal a small gun.

The warrant must also contain specific language about the location. A detective may not show the premises as John Smith's house on Elm Street, Any City. He or she must specify "a free-standing house at 10 Elm Street, Any City and shown by public record as owned by John Smith." I like to visit the courthouse before preparing an affidavit and warrant, copying the exact information about an address from the registry of deeds book. That tells the judge

General Affidavit

State of
County of ....

Before the undersigned, an officer duly commissioned by the laws of   on this
....day of.., 19......, personally appeared..

who having been first duly sworn depose.... and say...:

....
....
....
....
....
....
....
....
....
....
....
....
....
....
....
....
....
....
....
....
....
....

Sworn to and subscribed before me this....................day of........................, A. D. 19......

(SEAL)
....
....

signing the warrant and later the court that considerable care was taken to ensure the reliability of the address. The warrant will be good only at the specific address, and if the detective inadvertently gets the wrong address on the warrant, it's technically worthless. For example, if the warrant says the detective has authority to search Apartment 14C, and on arrival he finds the suspect lives in 14D, the warrant's authority ceases. Since the person and reason cited in the affidavit and warrant do not apply to the person or circumstances of Apartment 14C, a search of that location would violate the occupant's constitutional rights. The warrant does not give the detective the right to search 14D, even though it does fit the affidavit and warrant. To continue the search, the detective must return to the judge and have the warrant corrected or reissued. A new affidavit may also be required even if it only cites a correction of address. Once in Florida I obtained a search warrant to seize business records of a small company in an industrial park made up of small office spaces, some filled, some vacant. I went to great lengths to learn exactly where the company kept their business records. However, upon serving the warrant on the following day, I learned the owner innocently moved the records during the night to the office across the street as part of a business expansion project. Although the office belonged to the same company (and person) I had to prepare a supplemental affidavit and a new warrant. When possible in these circumstances, it's common practice to leave an officer (often a patrol officer) posted outside the premises to ensure that the suspect doesn't try to dispose of the evidence. In the case above, I asked a deputy sheriff to watch the premises. When the suspect, now aware of the investigation, decided to load the records into a company van, the deputy sheriff, who observed the act, arrested the owner and impounded the van under another statute that allowed him to do so with probable cause to believe the person was trying to conceal possible evidence in a criminal investigation. After preparing the third affidavit and obtaining the third warrant, I searched the van and was finally able to seize the records I needed to use for evidence.

Other language the detective needs to use in the affidavit and search warrant includes a specific description of what she intends to seize as possible evidence should she find it on the premises authorized for search. For example, a detective looking for stolen property would not want to list a "twenty-one-inch Sony color television set." Anyone could have one, and if a judge issued a search warrant, a court would later find it invalid. However, if the detective shows in the affidavit and on the warrant that she is looking for a "twenty-one-inch Sony color television set, console model 456, with a brown wood case, serial number 00000000," a defense attorney would have a hard time proving in court the warrant contained an inadequate, vague or questionable description. The reason for this rule stems from the valid argument that a police officer could "manufacture" evidence to fit the crime. For example, John Doe reports a burglary and says the theft included a "twenty-one-inch color television set," but he doesn't have the serial number. An informant tells the police detective that John Smith, a known burglar, pulled the job, and a judge issues a search warrant. When the detective serves the warrant, he finds a television set that matches Doe's description; however the owner cannot positively say the set is his since anyone can buy the identical TV set. Without conclusive evidence the set is returned to Smith, the arrest for burglary is dismissed, and the detective and the police department are now open to civil liability for illegally seizing Smith's property. Since the detective found no other evidence linking Smith to the Doe burglary or other crimes, seizing the TV set normally would be viewed as "exceeding authority" based on the language of the affidavit and warrant authorizing the search.

Executing the Search Warrant

Depending on state law, detectives may have to inform the judge whether they expect to serve the warrant during daylight hours or at night. If at night, the detective generally must explain the necessity of serving the warrant then. Unless a detective can convince a judge that night service has to happen to prevent destruction of evidence, to prevent another crime from happening, or some other urgent reason, the search warrant will normally state its authorization applies only for daytime execution. Night searches, when unnecessary to prevent the probable destruction of evidence, lead to accusations of harassment, embarrassment and unreasonable use of police powers, especially when no evidence is found during the search.

Some circumstances will necessitate executing a search warrant suddenly without detectives or officers announcing their authority ("no-knock") or the use of forcible entry. The courts allow such action only when the detective shows that forced entry is necessary to avoid endangering law enforcement officers or when there's persuasive reason to expect an attempt to destroy evidence before officers can seize it (for example, flushing drugs).

When judges issue or sign search warrants, they will always set a limit on how many days the warrant remains valid. After that time, the warrant has no authority, and, if used to seize evidence, can result in an illegal seizure, which is worthless for prosecution and may subject the detective to disciplinary action such as suspension, termination of employment and criminal charges. The victim of an illegal search can also bring a civil suit against the officers and the police department and will probably have a good chance of winning damages.

Search Incident to Arrest. One exception to the search warrant requirement occurs during a lawful arrest. For example, when a law enforcement officer, including a police detective, makes a valid arrest, he may search the person and an area within an arm's reach of the suspect without a warrant. Officers have the right to protect themselves and a duty to ensure that the arrested persons do not harm themselves with concealed weapons. When an arrest occurs within a home and officers have reason to believe others might also be in the apartment or home, they can make a warrantless "protective sweep" of rooms, closets and other areas where a "person" might hide (that doesn't include drawers or places impossible for a person to fit into). They cannot, however, legally "search" the premises for evidence without a search warrant. Should the officer making a reasonable protective sweep open a closet and see boxes of items believed to be stolen (or drugs), he must not touch them. Instead, having secured the arrested person in jail with proper booking procedure, the officer will prepare an affidavit and attempt to obtain a search warrant to return to the location and seize the suspected contraband. If an officer does not follow this procedure, the items seized are not admissible in court.

Motor Vehicle Warrantless Searches. Motor vehicle searches have always caused law enforcement officers problems in the courts. Generally, officers must limit their legal search of a motor vehicle without a warrant to what they can see looking through a window. Other searches require a warrant. Normally, when an officer or detective arrests a suspect operating a vehicle, he has the vehicle impounded and then obtains a search warrant according to probable cause available. When there's reason to believe the evidence in a vehicle might deteriorate or otherwise become lost, the officer might conduct a search incidental to the impounding and establish an inventory of its contents. However, the prudent detective will look at the inventory sheet and, upon seeing items of possible evidence, have probable cause to ask for a warrant authorizing seizure of it as evidence of a crime.

Plain View Doctrine. The plain view doctrine for an evidence search relies on the presumption that a detective has a right to be where she observes evidence or contraband in an area open to plain viewing. An example would be when the detective is investigating a crime and sees on a table, in the corner of the room, a sawed-off shotgun. The officer is legally on the premises and can seize the weapon. If the view resulted from an officer walking by on a sidewalk and observing contraband through an open window, the officer would, without exigent circumstances, have to obtain a warrant before entering the house and making a seizure. The key to this doctrine involves a decision that the detective has a legal right to be able to see, in plain view, the illegal item or evidence.

When a Search Is Not a Search in Technical Terms. When police detectives need to search for evidence in abandoned property (for example, a house no longer occupied by the suspect or other persons, or a motor vehicle left in a public place for so long that it is assumed abandoned by the owner), an open field or a public place (a park or public building common areas) they do not need a search warrant to make the search and seizure legal. All of these exceptions operate on the premise that no constitutional protection can be asserted by anyone over objects that anyone may see or use. Open fields include any unoccupied or undeveloped area that lies outside the "curtilage of a dwelling." Curtilage means the area around the home to which the activity of home life extends. When the search and seizure do not violate the Fourth Amendment, there's normally no warrant needed for the search and seizure of evidence.

Consent Searches. Situations may arise during an investigation which lead a police detective to believe an individual may consent to a search of the premises. In these instances, the detective must secure proper consent from the person. A person who consents to a search waives his Fourth Amendment right to be free from search without a warrant. The validity of a voluntary search remains at the discretion of the court. For a search to have validity, the detective must show from a "totality of circumstances" that the consent was voluntary. Illustration 3-3 (page 68) shows a typical voluntary consent to search form used by police departments and detectives.

Sources of Information for Police Detectives

As we've seen, a successful police detective must possess many abilities. By far, their most important attribute is the ability to obtain information. Just as observation is the descriptive word used for the police patrol function, information is the descriptive word for the police detective function. Obviously, the detective must be able to derive information from crime scenes and the victims and witnesses that each case will inherit. The master detective knows where to go to obtain knowledge required but not immediately available. There are three general information-gathering processes: (1) searching international, federal, state, county and local government records; (2) searching private and public records; (3) developing information sources through the use of confidential informants.

International Information Sources

International Criminal Police Organization. INTERPOL has long been wrapped in mystique, but its real purpose is to supply information, not enforce the law. The following describes this valuable information source for police detectives:

- More than 125 countries are members of INTERPOL.
- The General Secretariat is at 26 Rue Armengaud, St. Cloud (Paris), France.
- The annual General Assembly is hosted by a member country each year. Top police and enforcement officials of member countries attend.
- Symposia are held almost monthly in various countries, attacking particular crimes by given geographic area or worldwide.
- No international criminal law exists. Each country maintains its own sovereignty and operates only within its country's laws.
- The constitution of INTERPOL forbids its involvement in political, religious, racial or military matters. If a criminal offense

• CONSENT TO SEARCH •

MI No. _____

I, _____
(Name, Address and Date of Birth of person consenting to search)

having been informed of my rights under the Fourth Amendment of the Constitution of the United States of America, hereby state the following:

(a) I fully understand my right to refuse a search of the property listed herein without a search warrant; and I have the authority to consent to this search.

(b) The person(s) listed below have satisfactorily been identified to me as state law enforcement officer(s).

_____

_____

(c) That I hereby freely and voluntarily give my consent for a search of:

_____

_____

located at _____

(d) That I hereby freely and voluntarily authorize and give my consent for the above named officer(s) to seize and take from my possession the items listed below.

_____

_____

_____

with the understanding that I will receive a receipt listing all property which was seized under the authority of this release.

(e) That I understand that I may withdraw this consent and authority to search at any time, and said law enforcement officer(s) will immediately stop their search; that I may limit the scope of their search, including the area to be searched and articles subject to seizure.

(f) That this written statement, authorization, and consent has been made by me without any threats or coercion by any law enforcement officer(s), including the threat of obtaining a search warrant, and is freely and voluntarily given.

(SIGNED): _____
(by person authorizing search)

WITNESSES _____   DATE & TIME _____

_____

_____

DATE & TIME _____

involves a person/organization of this type, INTERPOL will help on basis of the criminal act.

- The National Central Bureaus of the member countries have established facilities to communicate with member countries through radio, cable, telex and fax.

- The National Central Bureau in most countries is located in an office within the National Police. In the United States, the office is under the control and direction of the Departments of Justice and Treasury and is staffed by personnel from federal law enforcement agencies within Justice and Treasury, including the Drug Enforcement Administration; Secret Service; Federal Bureau of Investigation; Customs; Bureau of Alcohol, Tobacco and Firearms; and Immigration and Naturalization Service.

How INTERPOL Assists Law Enforcement (Local, State, Federal). The U.S. National Central Bureau can help when a police agency or detective requires a criminal investigation in any of the INTERPOL member countries. Investigations may be of the following types:

- Criminal history check
- License plate and driver's license check
- Full investigation leading to arrest and extradition
- Location of suspects, fugitives and witnesses
- All Points Bulletins to any or all member countries
- Issuance of International Wanted Circulars
- Tracing of weapons and motor vehicles abroad
- Other types of criminal investigation

Federal Sources of Information

Sources of criminal justice information from federal agencies are invaluable to the police detective. For example, the Federal Bureau of Investigation can help a police detective tap into the National Crime Information Center (NCIC), which receives and dispatches computer information on felons, stolen vehicles and stolen weapons. The FBI crime lab is the finest in the country and has countless records and fingerprint cards on file. Local agents often help local police departments and detectives. Criminal justice information is not available to anyone except a certified or accredited law enforcement officer and department, and then only for official use related to an investigation. Obtaining the information randomly or personally without a valid reason, even by law enforcement officers, violates a federal statute controlling access to it. Other federal agencies that can supply specialized information include:

Department of Justice — Office of the U. S. Attorney General. Washington, D.C., has massive information sources and police liaison offices.

- Federal Bureau of Investigation (FBI), U.S. Department of Justice. The NCIC (National Crime Investigation Center) today contains more than 35 million names. Input for the NCIC comes from local, county, state and federal law enforcement agencies. Files are indexed under wanted persons, stolen vehicles, stolen license plates, stolen articles with serial numbers, stolen guns, stolen securities, stolen boats, criminal histories and missing children.

- U.S. Marshal's Service. This service supplies extensive information about fugitives and other missing persons.

Federal courts.

- Like state municipal and superior court systems, federal courts can be indexed and their files examined. Federal courts rule on all federal law and on any interstate issues.

- Bankruptcy Court. This court provides information on Chapter VII, a standard for business bankruptcy; Chapter XI, the reorganization plan for debtors who own a business or are self-employed professionals (also known as reorganization); and Chapter XIII, the readjustment of debts of a person with regular income.

Federal Communications Commission (FCC). The FCC licenses all forms of communication including telephones and computer interface systems.

Alcohol, Tobacco and Firearms (ATF). The ATF administers and regulates any business dealing with alcohol, tobacco or firearms. It controls alcohol and cigarette stamps, issues federal firearms licenses, and maintains records of guns purchased through licensed dealers.

Internal Revenue Service (IRS). Although most IRS information remains confidential even to law enforcement investigations, the IRS will supply anyone with the date of a person's last return and include the address from which the filed return was sent.

Interstate Commerce Commission (ICC). This office regulates and licenses all forms of interstate commercial transportation. It can help detectives find truckers or trucking companies.

Civil Service Commission — Bureau of Retirement and Insurance. An excellent source of information about retired civil service employees.

State Sources of Information

State bureaus can be valuable sources of information. The type and number of state agencies vary by state but the following is a typical list:

Department of Motor Vehicles. An excellent source for photographs of a person and other identifying data, including addresses, as well as records of vehicles, license numbers, ownership of vehicles observed, and other information. In some states, motor vehicle information is open to the public.

State Board of Corporations — Secretary of State or Commerce. Here the detective can find names of corporations formed or doing business in the state plus the incorporators, their addresses, phone numbers and often other officers. This agency may also provide information on partnerships and, in some states, sole proprietorships. This information is public.

State Tax Departments (Franchise Tax Board, Board of Equalization, Sales Tax and Others). Although this information is often confidential, police detectives can get it with a subpoena or court order but only if supported fully as necessary to further an official investigation. Persons outside law enforcement departments cannot legally obtain any type of tax information.

State Licensing Board. All states regulate trades and professions within their boundaries. Listings of types of professions or categories can run pages and supply the detective with the information on applications to the state for a license to work in a profession. Licensing information will normally be provided or verified to any person requesting the information.

Vessels and Aircraft. States call for registration of watercraft (vessels) and aircraft just as they do motor vehicles. The information might identify ownership and location or other data for the detective. Some of the states and federal agencies allow the general public to obtain all or parts of this information.

Worker's Compensation Board. All legal employees have coverage under some form of worker's compensation to cover job-related injuries. These records can be a source of information for the police detective.

Other Agencies Supplying Information a Detective Might Use Include.

- Alcoholic Beverage Control
- Fish and Game Commission
- Agriculture Commission
- Insurance Commission
- Department of Justice—Office of the Attorney General
- State Bureau of Investigation
- The State Police or State Highway Patrol
- Highway and Transportation Department

County Sources of Information

Besides obtaining valuable data from the county sheriff's office, a police detective who knows what to look for and where to look can find volumes of information in the local county courthouse. Some valuable information usually available includes:

Court Proceedings.

- Superior Court: This court has two divisions. Criminal and Civil Superior Criminal Court handles all felonies (minimum of one year in jail to capital crimes) while Superior Civil Court handles all civil matters, usually involving claims over $2,500 and other types of lawsuits, including divorce.
- Municipal or District Court: This court also has two divisions: criminal and civil. Normally it handles misdemeanors (maximum sentence less than one year in jail) and small claims ($2,500 or less).
- Probate Court: This court administers estates.

Court records, except juvenile records or those legitimately sealed by the court, become public records and are open to anyone requesting them.

Register of Deeds and Grantee/Grantor. These county files and records show all real property exchanged, deeds, trust deeds, ground liens, power of attorney exchanges, judgments and other types of business transactions. These records will also be open to the public.

Vital Statistics. These records document all births and deaths within the county. Records include marriages and other information, depending on the county and state. Normally, states will only supply this information to the subject of the record, a person with a power of attorney representing him, or a law enforcement agency.

Fictitious Business Name Filing — Business Licenses. This information can identify persons operating a business, partners, corporate officers and other important information. This information is also open to the public on request.

Probation, Welfare and Unemployment Information. This information is normally available to the police. Other data may be available with a court order that verifies a need and as part of an official inquiry.

Property Tax Records. These records show who really owns property by who pays the taxes on it. This information in most areas of the country is open to the public.

Voter Registration. This office can help find victims, witnesses and suspects who have moved since a case began. This information may also be accessed by the general public. In many areas of the country, especially small towns, the voter registration list will be found in post offices on the public use counters.

Private Records

Information is available through various private sources. Many of these sources have invaluable data and most share information with police detectives if asked. Police detectives might look for victims and witnesses as well as suspects using these sources. Often, a case comes up in court months or even years after a crime was committed. Locating key witnesses and victims after a long time can be challenging for detectives. These private records often help in that type of search.

Insurance Companies. Much personal information is available through the data sheets of policy holders.

Airlines.

- How a ticket was paid
- Which airline flown
- Destination
- Point of departure
- Time of flight

Auto Rental Agencies.

- Driver's license information
- Where person will be staying
- Phone number to reach the person

Bank Records.

- Safety deposit box records
- Other individuals having access to safety deposit box
- Dates frequented
- Date of birth
- Savings account information
- Checking account information
- Identification of payees and banks used
- Money transactions
- Loan activity

Better Business Bureau.

- Complaints against a business
- Owners of a business

Unions. Hundreds of thousands of workers are members of national and local unions. Union files not only have valuable information, but a trip to a union hall may net personal knowledge gathered from co-workers who know the person under investigation.

Private Investigation Firms. Often, private investigators have in their files the information needed by a police detective. Most of these firms will cooperate with a police request.

Private Utility Companies. Although a great amount of information is not available through utility companies, items such as turn-off dates, payment record, and often a forwarding address might help the police detective.

Company Personnel Records. Employees who work for medium to large companies usually fill out extensive application for employment forms. These often hold information that can be valuable to a police detective.

Telephone Company. The telephone company often proves helpful in tracing phone numbers and keeps excellent records on their customers.

Private Collection Agencies. These agencies often help police detectives trace people.

Rental Agencies. Besides the basic information needed for the rental of small items, rentals of larger items such as trucks and trailers will have a destination and point of turn-in listed. This helps detectives locate persons who have left an area, including suspects, victims and witnesses.

Newspaper Indexes. Most newspapers maintain a depository or morgue with an alphabetical file indexing people and organizations with particular issues in past editions.

Service and Professional Organizations. Application forms for these organizations often note relationships and associations that can be valuable aids in tracing subjects.

Bonding Companies. Many types of occupations require a bond. Bonding companies have detailed information on persons presently and previously bonded with their company.

Transportation Facilities. At one time or another, every person will use an airplane, train, ship, bus or taxi. Railroad, steamship, airline and even taxicab companies maintain record systems that are often a good source of information.

Merchandising Firms. Large merchandising firms usually have security units. Investigators for these firms often have processing methods more advanced than local police departments or access to other types of information.

The Secrets of Social Security Numbers

Police detectives can obtain a lot of information from a social security number. Although the Social Security Administration remains secretive about social security accounts, it has publicized ways commonly known in law enforcement and private circles to learn much from that number.

The social security number has nine digits divided into three parts and separated by hyphens (for example, 000-00-0000). The three parts are the Area of Issue, the Group or Year of Issue, and the Sequence of Issue for that period.

Area Numbers

The first three digits, except in the 700 series, identify the geographic area of issuance. Initially, the continental United States, Alaska and Hawaii were divided into 579 areas numbered from 001 to 579. The number of areas allotted to each state depended on estimates of the number of people within the state who were covered by the program. When the initial registration for SSNs began in 1936, the New England states were allocated the lowest area numbers. The area numbers were progressively higher for the Middle and South Atlantic states with the Western states receiving the highest area numbers. Since this original allocation, the geographical-numerical relationship has been disrupted somewhat by the need to allocate added area numbers to certain populous states and other territories.

- Numbers in the 700 series were assigned only to railroad workers through 1963, after which social security offices assigned numbers in the regular series to newly hired railroad workers. The Social Security program began during the mid-1930s, and at that time the railroads enjoyed a special position in society and commerce as the primary means of transportation of freight and people. The railroads had become the country's largest employer, so a special block of social security numbers identifying the workers was created. However, as the influence and workforce of the railroad systems diminished, so did the need for distinction, and the practice of assigning special numbers was discontinued.

- The 800 and 900 series of area numbers have never been issued on a permanent basis. However, in the early phases of the Social Security program (1940s), some temporary 900 numbers were used in a Supplemental Security Income program. The practice of using temporary "pseudo" SSNs in the SSI program was discontinued.

Group Numbers

The next two digits break the numbers within the geographic areas into groups. Within each area, the odd groups 01 through 09, and the even groups 10 through 98, are issued first. Then groups 02 through 08, and the odd groups 11 through 99, are issued. For example, SSNs with area and group 223-02 were issued in 1974; those in area and group 223-40 were issued in 1951. Higher numbers within areas do not necessarily indicate later issuance than lower numbers within the same areas.

Serial Numbers

The last four digits are a straight numerical series from 0001 through 9999 within each group.

Impossible SSNs

No SSN has ever been issued with a 0000 serial number or 00 group number. Any alleged SSN showing these numbers would not be valid.

Pocketbook Numbers

SSN 078-00-1120 was the first of many "pocketbook" numbers. It first appeared on a sample SSN card in wallets sold nationwide in 1938. Many people who bought the wallets assumed the number to be their own personal SSN. Since then, the number has appeared thousands of times on employers' reports of wages, and often on taxpayer returns. There are over twenty different "pocketbook" SSNs, each made by some organization displaying an actual number in its advertising.

Authorized Uses of the SSN

The social security card wasn't intended as an identification document. It identifies a particular record only, and the SSN card matches the person's record identified by that number. The SSN is used for keeping records of a Social Security account; however, it has become as widely used for identification as driver's license numbers (in some states), and as the means of recording credit at stores with credit bureaus. Few organizations do not now use the social security number for accountability. Some other agencies that use the SSN extensively are:

- State unemployment insurance agencies
- Office of Personnel Management (Civil Service Employees)

- Internal Revenue Service (IRS)
- School data processing systems
- Department of Defense (since 1967, the SSN has served as the military serial number)
- Veterans Administration (VA)
- Indian Health Service
- Parent Locator Service
- Aid to Families with Dependent Children
- Food Stamp Program
- State governments

Advantages of Social Security Numbers for Police Detectives

Police detectives looking for suspects, victims or witnesses can use the social security number as a lead to a person's whereabouts. Fugitives often will return to where they grew up, even if they have not lived there for years. Using the clues supplied by a social security number, the detective learns the state where the number was issued and from the second set of digits can learn the year that number was issued. Often, using the last set of numbers, the detective can learn in which county the person claimed residence when the number was issued. From that information, the detective can estimate the age of the person and maybe narrow the search to a county where other leads will develop. The following list shows how the first three digits of the SSN lead the detective to the state where issued.

001-003	New Hampshire	449-467	Texas
004-007	Maine	468-477	Minnesota
008-009	Vermont	478-485	Iowa
010-034	Massachusetts	486-500	Missouri
035-039	Rhode Island	501-502	North Dakota
040-049	Connecticut	503-504	South Dakota
050-134	New York	505-508	Nebraska
135-158	New Jersey	509-515	Kansas
159-211	Pennsylvania	516-517	Montana
212-220	Maryland	518-519	Idaho
221-220	Delaware	520	Wyoming

223-231	Virginia	521-524	Colorado
232-236	West Virginia	525-585	New Mexico
237-246	North Carolina	526-527	Arizona
247-251	South Carolina	600-601	Arizona (cont.)
252-260	Georgia	528-529	Utah
261-267	Florida	530	Nevada
589-595	Florida (cont.)	531-539	Washington
268-302	Ohio	540-544	Oregon
303-317	Indiana	545-573	California
318-361	Illinois	602-626	California (cont.)
362-386	Michigan	574	Alaska
387-399	Wisconsin	575-576	Hawaii
400-407	Kentucky	577-579	Dist. of Columbia
408-415	Tennessee	580	Virgin Islands
416-424	Alabama	581-584	Puerto Rico
425-428	Mississippi	596-599	Puerto Rico (cont.)
587-588	Mississippi (cont.)	586	Guam, American
429-432	Arkansas		Samoa & all
433-439	Louisiana		Pacific areas
440-448	Oklahoma	700-729	Railroad Employees

Other Information Sources

Good police detectives must remain resourceful and creative in their thinking when all the usual sources of information lead nowhere. The detective often has to look for leads in places like the city library. Most libraries issue and maintain library cards, and the application form completed by the cardholder supplies home addresses, telephone numbers and other information that might supply a beneficial investigative lead. Newspaper and magazine subscriptions, even mailing lists easily obtained from commercial companies (for a fee) might help locate someone or supply a valuable lead. When a police detective runs out of ideas or cannot access information herself, another most important source of information emerges: the informant.

Informants—How Detectives Rely on Them

A person who gives information to the police and police detectives with no intention of providing subsequent information is referred to as an "incidental informant." A person who is selected, cultivated and developed into a continuous source of information for the police is a "recruited" or "confidential informant."

Informants are important to most areas of police service. Even patrol officers will find their arrest percentages and crime prevention records improving when they have aggressively recruited informants in their zone or beat. Dealing with informants involves nine key factors:

Selection. In choosing potential informants, the detective has to consider availability. Even if a person is willing to become an informant, he is only as good as his ability to obtain information. The detective needs to look for people whose jobs or positions in society give them access to information. The following types of people and occupations make potentially good informants for police detectives:

Local prostitutes

Newspaper reporters

Newspaper stand attendants

Taxi drivers

Barbers

Insurance investigators

Private investigators

All-night gas station attendants

Managers of transient motels, hotels and boardinghouses

Criminals who are on probation or parole

Newspaper delivery persons

Early or late delivery truckers

Local business persons

Bartenders

Parking lot attendants

Security guards

All-night convenience store clerks

Motives of Informants. Before recruiting an informant, the police detective needs to identify an individual's motives for assisting the police. Although there may be many reasons for a person to become an informant, the three basic reasons are:

- **Fear of arrest.** Prostitutes, minor criminals, and some business persons engaged in minor violations of the law and subject to arrest may be looking for some way out. To catch bigger fish, the police detective must often use smaller fish. For example, an investigator must weigh the value of a prostitution arrest—

or a parole violation, a minor drug arrest, or an alcohol beverage control violation—against information that leads to the arrest of a murderer, drug trafficker, arsonist or other major crime offender. Truly, this type of informant barters his freedom for the freedom of those engaged in major crimes.

- **Payment.** Some people will sell information for money. Although most police agencies do not have abundant monies available for informant fees, some provision is usually made for that purpose. Often the price is very low; for example, enough money for a few drinks or for bus fare.

- **Civic participation.** Honest business persons, security guards, mail persons and others not regarded as criminal or fringe criminals will often become reliable sources of information because they feel it is the right thing to do. There is no threat of arrest, and the offer of a few dollars would probably insult them. The detective can size up honest persons in good locations for getting information or making reliable observations and recruit their services using plain gratitude for their interest in civic participation.

Recruitment of Informants. Once the detective evaluates motives and reliability, recruitment should be a simple task. The criminal and fringe criminal realize that it is better to have the police chase someone else. The person who needs a few dollars now and then for a "drinking habit" knows she can sell information to the police and often takes considerable risks to obtain valuable information. If recruited properly, the honest citizen normally recognizes that his knowledge of a probable or actual crime will be important to police and will supply it freely.

Testing and Evaluation of the Informant. Before a detective can trust a potential informant, he must test the informant's reliability by requesting information that the detective already knows or can verify through other sources. If the informant cannot obtain information that is easy to get, or if he lies during the first tests, he is dropped.

The detective also can evaluate the informant. Is he or she intelligent? Lazy? Trustworthy? This evaluation is a critical part in the informant process.

After a successful early testing and evaluation, the detective asks the informant to get information the detective doesn't know.

Occasionally, however, the detective should retest the informant and be wary of his reliability and trustworthiness.

Throughout my law enforcement and intelligence career I have relied on informants often. However, I learned early that much wasted money and time can result from relying on them. Once, in Virginia, I worked on a case that involved massive fraud against the government. I needed inside information either directly or through another party to develop enough details to avoid tipping my hand and risking the destruction of evidence. I met a man who seemed like a natural. He needed money and appeared intelligent and adept. Unfortunately, he turned out to be the most remarkable con man I ever encountered. The man was so convincing that even later, when I knew the information was fabricated, I wanted to believe him. Finally, after wasting much time and money, I found another informant to follow this man to one of the meetings he claimed to have regularly. It turned out the con-man informant went to a movie and sat through it alone, then returned to me with a long and detailed set of notes about his secret meeting. After that test, the money was stopped and the con-man informant disappeared, moving from his frugal apartment and leaving no forwarding address. My guess is that he went on to bilk someone else new at law enforcement in a distant city. After that, I used informants to check on informants regularly and found it worked well.

Methods of Contacting Informants. Unless a police detective takes precautions, the informant may become "known" as a police informant by the people she is informing on. If this happens, it creates two problems: The personal safety of the informant is jeopardized, and the informant will no longer be useful as a source of information. To prevent this from happening, detectives should follow these basic rules:

- Do not meet at the police station.
- Do not meet at the same locations or at the same time.
- The detective sets the time and place, not the informant.
- When a detective must call an informant, he must use a cover story so the informant can convincingly explain the caller and the reason for the call.
- If the informant calls the detective, he should use a telephone outside the regular police business line.

- Caution must be observed in using any correspondence, such as letters or messages.

Payments to the Informant. Although it would be good to receive free information, police administrators realize that most information will have a dollar value. Usually, the goals of the police determine the price. Informants must understand that local police department funds have limits. Larger sums of money for major narcotics or organized crime information usually come from federal agencies that have more funds available and a considerable interest in these crime categories. Basic rules most detectives follow when considering informant payments include the following:

- The payment should not be overpriced.

- The payment should not be too low for the quality of information and the risk factor involved in obtaining it.

- Cash payments, as opposed to a check, are traditional and are made on delivery of information.

Security of the Informant. Under most circumstances, the security and protection of the informant receive critical attention by the detective. The informant's identity is not disclosed during any conversation, and a code name or number is used in the detective's notes and reports. The informant's actual name and other personal data must always stay in a secure file opened only on a need-to-know basis. There could be some discussion of whether informants are the personal "property" of the detective who selected and recruited them or whether they belong to the police agency, but there can be absolutely no disagreement about the importance of each informant's security.

Continuance or Dismissal. As long as the informant delivers quality information in a "reasonable" quantity, he or she will continue as an active source of information. If an informant is in a position where her personal safety may be compromised, she's released—at least temporarily. The death or injury of one informant, once his status becomes known on the streets, affects the mental well-being of all informants.

After a time, an informant may not produce the amount or quality of information expected of him by the detective. Because dealing with informants is a time-consuming task, only the best can continue as a source of information on an active basis. Attentive tact remains the rule when dismissing an informant who is not meeting the detective's standards. If the informant feels that his release is caused by too much work from the detective, or because the detective feels the informant should drop out for a while for security reasons, the dismissal will leave the informant in a good frame of mind. Accusing the informant of being lazy or stupid only results in the possible loss of good future information. The prudent detective tries not to destroy any possible information source.

Treatment of the Informant. The treatment of informants will vary with the reasons each became an informant. With the paying informants, it is a business relationship, though the monies may not be substantial. The informant who is dealing information in an effort to stay out of jail needs the detective almost as much as the detective needs him.

The person who is an informant because she feels it is her civic duty to help the police is yet another matter. The relationship between detective and informant will also depend on the education level and the basic personality of both parties. Although there will be differences in the handling of various informants, the successful detective follows some basic rules:

- Never degrade or use derogatory terms about informants.
- Consider information given as valuable until proven otherwise.
- Do not overreact to the information received and stay noncommittal about its value.
- Tell the informant that his information helps with the case but do not make comments such as "I could not have done it without you."
- When agreeing to pay for information, do so, and use cash.
- Be punctual for meetings. It is often a good policy to be early.
- Don't be overanxious. Unless time is really being wasted, be patient with the informant.
- If the informant is a female, a male detective must protect himself from false accusations of misconduct.
- Stay in control of the investigation. Often an informant will try to take over if he feels he knows more than the detective.
- Don't supply information unless absolutely necessary. Never become an informant's informant.

- Never permit an informant to violate the law or issue him "police" identification.
- Always be on the alert for the informant who takes on an equal role with the police. When this happens, the informant will often "brag" to other individuals that she is working "undercover" for the police.

F O U R

LARCENY, BURGLARY, ROBBERY AND ASSAULT

Four types of crime against property and persons create most of the day-to-day work for police patrols and the detective division. Larceny (theft) is the wrongful taking of property with the intent of maintaining permanent possession of that property. Burglary is breaking into and entering the building of another with the intent to commit a crime inside that building. Robbery is the taking of a person's property while in his presence, by force, violence or intimidation. An assault happens when someone attacks another person in some way and the attack results in bodily harm. These crimes often are linked to more serious crimes involving drugs, arson and homicide.

Crimes fall into two criminal justice categories: misdemeanors and felonies. A misdemeanor in each state brings a maximum jail term of one year and normally a maximum fine of about $5,000 (fines vary in each state while the jail term remains consistent). A felony brings a minimum jail term of one year and fines above the lower court levels. Felonies also include capital crimes. The process for determining whether a crime will become a misdemeanor or felony depends on state or federal statutes. Normally, the value of property stolen will determine if a larceny will be a misdemeanor or felony. Most states set misdemeanor value limits between $500 and $2,500. Armed robbery and most burglaries are felonies because the crimes themselves are separate from the value of the theft. An armed robbery, for example, that nets fifty cents will qualify as a felony because value of items or money stolen has no real bearing on the crime. The same rule normally applies in burglaries. Assaults, like larcenies, can fall in either the misdemeanor or felony categories depending on seriousness, injuries and whether or not the assailant had a weapon. Some assaults can happen without contact, and they normally go to court as a misdemeanor.

Larceny

Larceny is one of the most frequent crimes confronting the police and police detectives and is responsible for a large part of the detective's daily workload. Larcenies create difficulties for detectives assigned to investigate them. Often, discovery or reporting of the theft is delayed. Victims may be unable to accurately describe the property taken or prove it's theirs when police recover it from a suspect. All of this adds to the detective's investigative headaches.

Legal Considerations

The crime of larceny includes several different offenses that police detectives have to consider before starting their investigation. The detective must consider that all larcenies have in common a wrongful acquisition of (or assumptions or exercise of dominion over) the property of another coupled with the offender's intent to permanently deprive the owner of the property. The element of intent will prove the greatest challenge for the police detective during his investigation of this crime. Detectives attend to the following guidelines:

Common Law Larceny. This offense is defined in common law (as opposed to statutory law) as a taking by and felonious carrying away of property belonging to another, with the intent to deprive him or her of that property permanently.

False Pretenses (Fraud). This offense contains all the elements of larceny, plus the taking of property must happen by a designed misrepresentation that causes a victim to transfer custody of his or her money or property to the perpetrator. This can involve lawyers, accountants or con persons who gain control of a person's property, money or possessions.

Embezzlement. This larcenous act happens when a person lawfully receives the property of another through his or her position of trust and then intentionally withholds that property unlawfully. For example, a bank teller receives money to pay customers, retains part of the money, and then alters the records to cover up the amount he has taken for personal use.

Elements of Proof for Larceny. Whenever a police detective begins any investigation, he needs to know firsthand the elements needed to prove the crime happened, and when a suspect becomes known, to prove that the suspect committed the crime under investigation. To prove the crime of larceny, the detective must satisfy the following elements of proof:

- The offender wrongfully took, obtained, or withheld from the possession of the true owner or any other person the property described in the complaint. Generally, any movement of property or any dominion over it with the intent to deprive the owner of the property without the owner's consent will establish this element of proof. However, not included in this element are the offenses of receiving, buying, or concealing stolen property or otherwise being an accessory after the fact.

- The property belongs to a certain person named or described in the complaint. The offender might have taken, obtained or withheld the property from the true owner or from a person who had greater right to possession than the offender.

- The property reported stolen has the value alleged or had some value. As a rule, determining the value of stolen property stems from its legitimate market value at the time and place of theft. For example, a television set may have cost $500 new, but when stolen three years later might have a value of $150. Although stealing something with no value (like a common rock from the yard of a neighbor) might have moral implications, no larceny has been committed unless the owner of the rock can establish legitimate monetary value.

- The facts and circumstances of a larceny case show that by taking, obtaining or withholding the offender clearly had intent to permanently deprive or defraud another person of the use and benefit of the property involved or to take it for his or her own use or the use of any person other than the true owner. These intents collectively establish the "intent to steal." Establishment of an "intent to steal," in most crimes, often arises from an inferred or implied intent developed from proven circumstances of the crime or the behavior of the offender before, during and after the crime.

Basic Investigative Techniques for Larceny Cases

Larceny takes many different forms, ranging from the once-in-a-lifetime theft by a person who needs money to safecracking and theft by professional thieves. The police detective knows that effective investigative techniques vary with the type of larceny they confront, the geographical area of their jurisdiction, and a variety of other circumstances. However, many basic investigative techniques apply to all types of larcenies and are discussed in the following sections.

Initial Investigative Actions

Before a police detective leaves the station house for a larceny crime scene, she obtains all the available facts from the complainant, the person receiving the complaint, and the report written by the desk sergeant or patrol officer. Using that information, the detective can formulate an investigative plan and select, as applicable, the equipment needed to process the scene from the list of items shown in chapter two. When approaching the crime scene, the police detective always stays alert for any suspicious persons hanging around or among onlookers. Often, especially when a larceny involves neighbors, employees, juveniles or amateurs, a perpetrator may stay in the area to see what actions the police take. Detectives also know that witnesses will join other onlookers, wanting to tell what they know but uncomfortable about coming forward. That crowd of people can often supply valuable information otherwise overlooked.

Procedures at the Crime Scene

After following the general procedures of photographing, developing latent fingerprints, and other crime scene processing, the police detective will question the victim to find out the following information:

- Detailed description of the stolen property, including serial numbers, make and type of model, size and color, and personal marks such as initials and alterations.
- Names and addresses of persons able to verify ownership or possession of the items and corroborate the location of the property as stated in the victim's complaint.
- Nature and location of documentary evidence (for example, sales slips, invoices, or other proofs of purchase or acquisition) that will help the detective establish ownership, possession, and value of the stolen property or aid in its identification when recovered.
- Description of situations, conditions, incidents or statements that may tend to cast suspicion on any persons including:

  Names and addresses of possible witnesses.

  Names and addresses of persons having access to the stolen property.

  Any other relevant information the victim can furnish.
- Names and addresses of persons at or near the scene so that the detective can question them to find possible witnesses.

The type of articles taken may provide a lead to the offender. For example, if the theft involved only toys, the offender may be a child or a person who has children. To aid in identifying the offender, the detective asks the following questions:

- What was stolen? The detective obtains complete descriptive information.
- From where were the articles stolen? A detective demands the exact location, avoiding generalizations. For example, department time and money may be wasted if, in the end, an alleged victim realizes the property wasn't stolen after all, just borrowed by a friend or misplaced.
- What valuables were present but not stolen? For example, the alleged thief stole a typewriter but did not steal a diamond ring and gold bracelet or valuable coin collection in plain view within the same room as the typewriter.
- How could the offender change, alter or disguise the stolen

items to permit their resale, reregistration or open use? When an offender steals items to resell them, he will try to make them untraceable.

- What required materials, equipment or facilities would the offender need to disguise the stolen articles?

Investigative Procedures After Leaving the Scene

After leaving the scene of the crime, a police detective must create leads from definitive descriptions of the stolen property, find the property, and link the suspect to the offense. The following information may supply those leads:

- Description of the property by the owner or witnesses. This description is strengthened when owners or witnesses can point out peculiarities, modifications or adjustments made by or known to them.
- Photographs or sketches of the stolen items.
- Serial numbers, laundry and dry cleaning marks, jeweler's marks, monograms or other personalized markings.
- Manufacturer's data labels and peculiarities of manufacture or design.
- Trace materials placed by the owner on items believed targets of theft. In cases of repeated thefts, materials or objects may be marked in ways enabling subsequent positive identification.
- Presence on stolen items of identifiable contaminants or materials from the scene of the offense; for example, traces of machine shop dust inside cracks on a piece of expensive stolen equipment.
- When the owner of stolen property has insurance, the amounts, policy number, names and addresses of the insuring companies and beneficiaries of the policy or policies. Often, an insurance company may be able to furnish a detective with a detailed description of the stolen property, including sketches and photographs obtained from the victim when insuring the property.

Questioning Witnesses

The police detective makes every effort to find witnesses and question them to get additional information, leads and corroborating proof of ownership and theft. The common guidelines used by police detectives when questioning witnesses are as follows:

- Verification, by documents or statements, of the victim's ownership or possession of the property stolen and its location before the theft. Often, skilled detectives find witnesses in unlikely places or positions that can supply valuable information in this category. That information comes from the detective asking the right questions and remaining consistent even when logic would dictate that the interviewee would not have such knowledge. Much of that acumen stems from experience and instinct. Sometimes, informants have told police of a person who planned to obtain money by reporting a theft and using the police report to file an insurance claim. Later, the person might sell the same items to a backstreet dealer or fence.

- Presence at the crime scene of any persons acting suspicious. These persons often seem to be suspects at first observation. Detectives often learn that suspicious behavior stems from nervousness about having information and apprehension about revealing this knowledge to the police and becoming involved.

- Presence at the crime scene of any persons known to have committed or been involved in larceny. This information is particularly important if the stolen property is of the same or similar type as property taken in other cases involving the known suspects. Often, detectives find that former offenders know the perpetrator of the crime under investigation or may have in some way participated in the crime.

- Presence at or near the crime scene of a motor vehicle and a description of the vehicle from witnesses, security or police patrols who noticed it before learning about the larceny. This information often comes from a note in a beat patrol officer's logs or from field intelligence furnished by a neighborhood watch or informant.

Other Investigative Actions

- Detectives regularly notify other law enforcement agencies about a larceny and supply a detailed description of the stolen property.

- Detectives check modus operandi files when available at their department and adjacent jurisdictions. This step often leads to valuable information, especially when the larceny appears to have been the work of a professional thief. Depending on what items were stolen, the detective might be able to discover probable perpetrators.

- Detectives make inquiries about any unusual activities at or near the crime scene before or during the estimated time of the larceny. An observant mobile canteen operator, for example, might have noticed two men in the area of a major commercial larceny during the days before the crime and may supply excellent descriptions.

- The detective checks possible and likely places of disposition of stolen property including:

  1. Pawnshops.
  2. Secondhand stores.
  3. Known fences (dealers in stolen property—often, police allow some of these people to continue in business, and in return for the police looking the other way on minor deals, the "fence" agrees to serve as a reliable informant, especially on major larcenies).

- When a detective finds stolen property in the above locations or elsewhere, he will try to obtain added leads with a detailed description of the person who sold or pawned the items.

Evaluating Evidence

An evaluation of collective evidence may lead the detective to a suspect or suspects. Logical suspects include:

- Persons having a motive for taking the property, or professional thieves who deal in a particular type of property.
- Persons having easy access to the property.
- Strangers or loiterers at the scene about the time the offense happened.
- Unusually inquisitive or solicitous individuals (this is often a masquerade).
- Individuals who have large gambling losses or excessive spending habits.
- Drug users.

Establishing the Motive

Establishing the motive for the offense will help the detective solve the crime. The motive may not be solely the desire to possess the stolen property or professional interests. Motives often include spite, vandalism, lucrative opportunity or the desire to deprive a person of his property. The stolen articles may suggest an obvious motive instead of the actual motive. The offender, failing to find the property he or she planned to steal, may take other items instead. When certain of the motive, a police detective tries to identify persons who probably had that motive and fully investigates their activities.

Questioning Suspects

When a police detective interviews the victim and witnesses, makes an evaluation of the evidence collected, and develops the identity of a suspect, the next step is usually to question the suspect. A skilled detective will not approach a certain suspect until there's almost no need to question him. A novice detective tends to move too fast and approaches a suspect early on. Suspects, having intimate knowledge of what they did when committing the larceny, will quickly recognize the detective either has them cold or is fishing for a confession. I always approached suspects by first explaining that it made no difference to me if they wanted to talk or confess, that I already had sufficient evidence against them. I also showed them the evidence (verbally) and then told them what they did at the scene and later. After this explanation I would advise them of their rights and offer them an opportunity to tell their side of it. During three decades of criminal investigations, I can recall only five or six, out of hundreds of criminals, who didn't confess. It seems to be human nature to confess, especially when the perpetrator believes there's a chance that cooperation might ease the penalty later. However, remember the warning in chapter two regarding confessions. A detective should not approach a suspect for a confession unless it's not needed. Suspects may try to beat the charges against them in court; their defense attorneys may attack the credibility of the confession and allege coercion or failure to advise the suspect that he or she did not have to say anything, etc.

The detective attempts to obtain the following information:

- Where was the suspect when the larceny happened?
- Who can verify the suspect's statement and whereabouts? The detective must decide if these persons do corroborate information received from the suspect.

- Is the suspect believed or proven involved earlier in larceny?
- Is the suspect employed or working recently in the establishment where the offense happened?
- Did the suspect have access to the place where the offense occurred?
- Does the suspect have friends employed in the establishment where the offense was committed?
- Is the suspect friendly with persons known to have committed or are suspected of having committed larceny?
- Does the suspect have any grudges against the owner or management of the establishment where the offense of larceny was committed?
- Is the suspect living above his or her normal income?

Searching a Suspect's Premises

When circumstances warrant, the detective may legally search the premises of a suspect with a warrant. The detective must obtain proper search warrants before conducting a search, and only that property specified in the warrant can be seized. If the detective finds stolen property on the premises controlled by a suspect, some prima facie evidence to associate the person with the offense may exist. This may involve questioning the suspect, witnesses, and the persons who supported or confirmed the suspect's original statement about his whereabouts when the offense was committed. Also, to strengthen evidence of identity and motive, it may be desirable to conduct a more intensive investigation of the suspect's background to uncover a previous involvement in larceny or evidence that he's engaged in activities or circumstances that need more funds than his normal income provides or special requirements for use of the goods taken.

Study of Security Measures and Supply and Accounting Procedures and Records

A study of security measures and supply and accounting procedures where offenses happen may help the detective's investigation. Weaknesses in security measures and accounting procedures may provide leads about the offender, as well as about the methods used to commit and conceal the offenses and to remove, transport and dispose of stolen items.

Background Investigation of Supply Handlers, Clerks and Custodial Personnel

Persons having access to or custody of property will be investigated by the police detective, especially when repeated larcenies happen at the same location. Complete investigations into their backgrounds may reveal who has a motive for the offenses.

Check of Welfare Agencies

A police detective might find leads in information from welfare agencies concerning persons who have recently sought aid for personal or family financial problems or who have recently repaid loans to the agency. Persons whose financial circumstances provide motives for offenses may become suspects. However, the detective must avoid casting suspicion on persons simply because they have financial difficulties.

Check of Personnel and Financial Records

The detective might find important leads through investigation of personnel and financial records. An individual may have no legitimate income or be financially committed beyond the limits of his or her income. While checking these records and during follow-up investigations, a detective needs to be discreet to avoid discrediting innocent persons.

Use of Evidence

Evidence the police detective gains through questioning persons or from other leads must be thoroughly evaluated. Investigative evidence, properly handled and thoroughly evaluated, may help accomplish the following:

Place a Suspect at the Crime Scene. This might happen by establishing that the suspect or his vehicle was observed at the scene by a witness or the victim, that he left fingerprints, palm prints or footprints, or that his vehicle left identifiable tire tracks. Other techniques for placing the offender at the scene include identification of soil or rock particles found on the suspect's clothing or vehicle that correspond to the type of soil or rock present at the crime scene, identification of property or tools left at the scene and traced to the offender, or the determination that other materials found at the scene can be traced to the suspect.

Find the Stolen Property. Finding the property or evidence of the property in the possession, custody or control of a suspect is not sufficient to convict an offender of a theft. The detective must obtain evidence to show the suspect knowingly and illegally deprived another of the possession of the property. One way to prove this is through evidence — often a witness — that the suspect sold or attempted to sell the stolen property without the permission of its true owner.

Show That a Suspect Profited by the Offense. It helps the case to show that the suspect benefited from the larceny or came into money under suspicious circumstances directly related to certain facts of the offense, especially if the suspect cannot show that the funds or credits were obtained in a legitimate manner. Such information may lead to the identification of offenders, receivers of stolen goods, or associates of an offender carrying out a felonious scheme.

Specific Larceny Offenses

Motor Vehicle Thefts

Motor vehicle thefts have become a common problem and often call for special sections and teams working out of the detective division. Reasons for the thefts including joyriding, use in a crime, or professional auto theft to supply "chop shops" where newer cars are disassembled and their parts sold or entire cars are shipped intact out of the country.

When investigating a motor vehicle theft, the police detective uses nine key elements to develop leads:

- Obtains a full description of the vehicle, including VIN (vehicle identification number), motor and body numbers.

- Determines the time and date of the theft and the vehicle's location when stolen (first assuring the vehicle wasn't repossessed by a finance company).

- Notifies and gives all pertinent information to the FBI, especially when near a state line or when there's indication the vehicle crossed a state line or was stolen for shipment to a foreign country.

- Determines who had access to the place where the vehicle theft happened. These persons are interviewed to determine if any of them were involved in the theft.

- Determines what personnel are missing who may have had a motive or cause for stealing the vehicle. The detective checks to determine if these persons show involvement in the theft.

- Contacts municipal, county and state law enforcement agencies for help in finding the vehicle and offender.

- Gives data, including VIN to the NCIC (National Crime Information Center). This step is important because it allows law enforcement officers throughout the country to determine whether a stopped or abandoned car was stolen. When police want to check a license number, VIN or a serial number on any other stolen property, they routinely conduct a computerized search through the NCIC.

- Conducts necessary investigative actions after recovering the vehicle, such as searching it, trying to develop latent fingerprints, taking photographs of interior and exterior, and other actions as needed.

- The National Automobile Theft Bureau (NATB) supplies law enforcement with guides to help detectives with information about vehicle ID numbers and their location on a variety of motor vehicles.

Larcenies Involving Safes

When a larceny involves a safe, a police detective performs the following procedures:

- Determines the modus operandi used in opening the safe (often identifies methods of known professionals).

- Forwards samples of explosive residue, if applicable, and of the safe dust to the department, state or FBI crime laboratory for analysis. (Use of certain types of explosives may also identify the professional.)

- Sends safe, when feasible, to a law enforcement crime laboratory for examination. When removal of the safe is not possible, the investigating detective photographs it and makes casts or molds of toolmarks to send to a laboratory. Often, amateur and professional safecrackers alike will "peel" the door of a safe using distinguishable techniques. When possible, examination of the door or the entire safe by laboratory technicians will identify the type of tool used and what the detective should look for during an investigation. If the detective later finds the same type of tools in a suspect's possession, the laboratory can match those specific tools to the marks and provide expert testimony in court.

- Sends suspect's clothing to the crime laboratory to have it examined for explosive residue or safe dust. When a police detective finds suspicious clothing during a legal search of the suspect's home or vehicle, crime laboratory technicians may match residue from clothing to that from the safe.

- Questions known safecrackers and checks their alibis thoroughly. The "breaking" of a safe requires skills limited to a few persons. Investigation of the crime scene and other information often leads a detective to persons with a record of safecracking larceny. The development of intelligence on known "rings" of professional thieves is important in investigating safecracking cases. Such professionals may have the help of apprentices; younger people may also aspire to reaching professional status by undertaking jobs a professional might not try. The modus operandi of known professionals in the area, coupled with an evaluation of techniques applied in any given instance, can greatly help detectives during their investigation.

Burglary

Burglary is a crime of stealth and calls for meticulous investigative procedures to identify and prosecute perpetrators. Unlike assaults and robbery or other crimes of violence, burglary often is discovered long after it happens. However, burglaries are often linked to other crimes, including crimes of violence such as murder or arson. The Uniform Crime Report produced by the FBI each year discloses that victims report about five million burglaries each year, of which only about 18 percent are solved. Of burglaries solved, few lead to successful prosecution because evidence collected often cannot prove complicity in the crime. Many victims never report burglaries to the police, especially businesses or persons who have no insurance or victims of previous unsolved burglaries.

Key Points About Burglary

Every burglary contains the signature of the perpetrator; the police detective's job is to find it. That signature includes a variety of clues extracted from the crime scene, witnesses, motives, actions of suspects and other aspects that a skilled detective pieces together to bring about a successful conclusion to the case.

A common myth about investigation involves gathering evidence that taints public opinion about law enforcement capabilities and performance. In television and motion picture portrayals of law enforcement efforts, crime laboratory technicians play an important role, swarming over a crime scene of any kind and supplying detectives with a wealth of information leading to immediate arrests. In reality, there are few crime laboratories and limited technicians, and those existing have the same budget problems as departments. Detectives largely must process the crime scene, develop leads and investigate this crime nearly single-handed in most departments.

Important Definitions

In common law, the crime of burglary is the breaking and entering of a dwelling house of another in the nighttime with the intent to commit a felony therein. Modern statutory definitions of the crime are much less restrictive. For example, laws now commonly require no breaking and specify no time of day or night, nor do they exclude other kinds of structures. Also, certain state statutes classify the crime into first-, second- and even third-degree burglary to provide latitude for prosecution efforts.

Burglary and Lesser Included or Related Offenses

Included in the crime of burglary are lesser offenses. Depending on a state's statutes for this crime, a variety of different circumstances might apply. Besides the offense of burglary, some lesser included or related offenses are:

Breaking and Entering. There must be a breaking, either actual by physical force or constructive by trickery. To enter through a hole in a wall or an open door does not establish a "breaking." Removal of any part of the structure, such as a screen or window glass, does establish "breaking." Entry is accomplished when any part of the body enters the structure (building). An instrument such as a pole inserted into the structure to extract property from the dwelling also is entry.

Unlawful Entry. Entry upon lands or structures thereon that is effected peacefully without force and done through fraud or some other willful wrong is usually unlawful entry. It's closely related to burglary and breaking and entering. It is an entry accomplished through fraud or willful wrong by the offender. The intent to commit an offense within the place entered is unnecessary to establish this offense.

Housebreaking. Generally, housebreaking is a burglary, calling for breaking and entering a dwelling house with intent to commit any felony there. Under some statutes, housebreaking may include "breaking out" of a house after access was gained without breaking.

Criminal Trespassing. Criminal trespass occurs when a person enters or stays on or in any land, structure, vehicle, aircraft or watercraft when he or she is not authorized or privileged to do so. The crime involves entering or staying in defiance of an order not to enter or to leave the premises or property that is personally communicated by its owner or other authorized person; or entering such premises or property when posted in a manner likely to come to the attention of intruders or when fenced or otherwise enclosed.

Constructive Breaking Into a House. A breaking that might happen over time. For example, a yard worker removes screws from door hinges over time or uses his position to enter the building and create a situation making breaking into the house easy. Also when a burglar gains entry into a house by threats, fraud or conspiracy.

Types of Burglary

The two basic types of burglary include commercial and residential. Both have an alarming rate of increase and create serious concern to both police patrol and detective divisions. Often, the burglary rate determines the amount of confidence the police department can expect from its community. When beginning the investigation into both types of burglaries, the police detective always considers the possibility of an insurance fraud. Often, the victims of commercial and residential burglaries are also the perpetrators.

Commercial Burglary. Because commercial establishments often have better protection than residences, burglars may become expert in many methods of entry. He or she may also breach elaborate burglary alarm systems. Sometimes, information a police detective receives from an informant alerts the police to a burglary that has yet to happen. That type of information often leads to a surveillance of the building slated for burglary.

Residential Burglary. Expensive homes are the primary targets for residential burglaries; however, every home is a potential target. Beside the millions of dollars taken in residential burglaries each year, the potential for personal harm, even homicide, to inhabitants exists each time a family home is burglarized.

Profile of the Burglar

Because most burglars prefer to commit their crimes under cover of darkness and not to meet the victims, many people believe that burglars are cowards. Although a burglar may lack the outward confidence of an armed robber, never underestimate the capability of harm or threat he poses. Kidnappings, rapes, serious assaults and homicides often supply the motive or conclusion of a burglary.

When investigating a burglary, the police detective always deals with the intelligence of the burglar, which can vary from one extreme to the other. The higher the intelligence of the burglar, the more difficult the investigation confronting the police detective.

Intent and the Essential Elements of Proof

The crime of burglary, like all criminal offenses, calls for proving clear intent by the offender. Some crimes, by their commission, establish clear intent by the offender, such as robbery and assault. Burglary, however, is not as clear-cut.

For example, a former maid or gardener who received a key to a house during employment and was not required to relinquish it upon ending employment returns two weeks later and enters the house while the owners are absent. The offender's defense to the charge of burglary is probably that he or she returned to the house to retrieve personal items. The owner may allege the former employee stole items from the house. Though the employee claims to own the stolen property, the employee may insist that the owner gave him or her the items earlier. Since entry was gained with a key, and the owner made no effort to change the locks or recover the employee's key, clear intent might be difficult or impossible to prove, depending on the items removed from the house.

It is also possible the former employee did not take all the items claimed. In such cases detectives determine how many others have keys, including current employees who may be taking advantage of the confusion.

Burglary Scene Investigative Procedure

Initial actions in burglary investigations include the following:

- Recording the location and description of the structure or area entered.
- Determining where the owners or occupants were during the crime.
- Finding out when the owners or occupants left the premises and whether all the doors and windows were secured.
- Determining who has keys to the structure.
- Trying to find out the time of entry by the offender.
- Photographing, sketching and processing the scene for fingerprints, which must have priority before and during the search. Entry points, pieces of furniture and other miscellaneous household items (or office or commercial building items) possibly handled by the perpetrator(s) should be dusted for latent fingerprints.

Approach and Entry Investigations

After completing the initial investigative steps, the detective must also:

- Look for evidence to determine whether the offender walked or rode to the crime scene (footprints or tire tracks showing the route or means of entrance to the real property involved). Make casts of tire tracks and footprints found at the crime scene.
- Determine who had approached the crime scene earlier. Security or police patrol and area residents or workers often have seen something that can identify persons in this category.
- Collect toolmarks made by the burglar from forcing entry into the building or office in original form if possible (for example, by cutting out parts containing the marks or taking a door from its hinges and retaining it as evidence or sending it to the crime laboratory for analysis). When it is impossible to collect original toolmarks, a detective makes casts or molds of them.
- Determine what equipment, if any, such as ropes, ladders or digging tools, was used in the breaking and entry.
- Establish where and how the offender gained entry. Examine the property carefully for broken or unlocked doors, windows, skylights or gates. Determine whether locks or fasteners were forced, picked, or if holes were sawed or hacked through walls,

floors, partitions or roofs. Laboratory examination of wood, glass or metal evidence found at the crime scene may disclose the direction of the breaking force or determine the general type of instrument used.

- Exercise caution to ensure he's not following a trail of misinformation established by the offender to mislead the investigation (for example, the suspect breaks a window to conceal entry with a key or lock picks). Examine all the possibilities without jumping to a conclusion about entry.

- Determine the size and shape of openings, if they're large enough to fit the offender or to permit removal of the stolen property, and the height of the openings from the ground or from where the offender stood.

- Establish whether bodily entry to the premises occurred or if only the offender's arm or some instrument was used to gain his or her objective, or whether it appears that someone inside the building may or must have helped in the offense by passing articles to the offender.

Reconstructing the Offender's Activities at the Scene

Often, a detective can simulate the offender's search of the scene. The detective's simulation may show whether the offender was familiar with the premises and if he or she knew in advance the location of the object or objects stolen. The manner of the simulation may show the detective the key characteristics of the offender's modus operandi.

A close examination of fingerprints and other evidentiary items at points where the offender searched the premises may reveal important information. An attentive study of evidentiary facts may suggest how long the offender spent in the premises, whether interrupted, the level of burglary skill, and how secure the offender felt during the crime. Detectives try to answer the following questions:

- Did the offender go directly to the objects he or she stole? This could show advance information and would suggest whether the detective needs to explore how the burglar obtained that information.

- Does the offender's search show signs of systematic, thorough, selective or haphazard characteristics? The manner of search may indicate the work of a professional or amateur.

- Did the offender replace objects after examining them?
- Did the offender close doors, windows and drawers? Such actions may show his or her choice of articles and motive, as well as his or her presence of mind and consciousness of detection. Items stolen may also aid a detective in determining whether the offender will sell stolen items or use them for personal or business use. For example, a professional burglar might "take orders" for specific items of jewelry, or business or professional equipment (for example, medical items, computers, dental equipment and the like).
- What did the burglar do to guard against detection while searching the scene? Did the offender close the window shades or blinds or lock the inside door? Did he or she plan alternate escape routes?
- Was the scene rearranged to delay discovery of the offense?
- Was evidence destroyed?
- Were fingerprints wiped off, gloves worn, toolmarks defaced, or footprints and tire tracks obliterated?
- Was evidence damaged by the offender, the victim or witnesses before police arrival?
- Were records in order, or was there an attempt to falsify, destroy or misplace them?
- Were added offenses, such as arson, committed to hide the offenses?
- Was the crime scene or evidence intended to be misleading or to draw suspicion from the offender?
- Is there reason to suspect the victim is the perpetrator?
- Was the crime staged in an attempt to collect insurance or make other kinds of claims?

Transportation

Evidence of the type of transportation used and the specific vehicles involved is important to the investigating detective. He or she will make casts of suspicious tire tracks found at the crime scene. Tire tracks and casts often enable the detective to determine the type and number of vehicles, direction of travel, places parked and materials dropped (gas, mud, oil or water) or picked up (soil or rock). Once a suspect vehicle is found, the crime laboratory can examine it and compare it with casts made at the scene.

Exit and Flight

Suspects sometimes leave clues during their exit and flight. Detectives consider the following:

- Did the offender prepare or use an existing escape route or break out?
- Did the offender unlock a door or window?
- Were toolmarks, footprints or fingerprints left at the scene?
- At what time was the exit made?
- Did the offender make more than one trip to remove stolen items?
- Was help needed to effect the removal of the stolen items?
- How many persons needed to handle the equipment used in committing the offense?

Burglary Investigation Profile and Pattern Guide

Police detectives find the following evaluation points helpful to create a profile and pattern (modus operandi) of a burglar or burglary ring when a series of burglaries happens systematically.

Location.

- Of the house, office or structure.
- Type of area (urban, suburban, rural).
- Of the owner during the burglary.
- Of the owner before the burglary.

Offender's Actions.

- Does evidence establish the offender's point of entry?
- What means or methods were used to enable the offender to gain entrance?
- How does the obvious entrance point relate to the size of objects stolen?
- Does the crime scene show ransacking or selective search?
- Were measures taken to guard against detection?
- How was the scene left?
- Does evidence show a definitive point of exit?

- What means did the offender use when exiting?
- Is there evidence of the offender returning to the scene to relock doors, close windows, etc.?
- What were the means of approaching (walking or riding) and leaving (escape route) the scene?

Property.

- What type of property was stolen?
- Can the owner supply identifying features of the property, such as serial numbers, damage, peculiar markings, etc.?
- Is there evidence of specific objects being taken such as guns, TVs, stereo equipment or professional items?
- Were some valuable items present but not stolen?
- What means were used by the offender to carry the property off the premises?

Physical Evidence.

- If a vehicle was used, can casts of tire marks be made?
- Are there toolmarks at the point of entry or elsewhere?
- Was any glass broken? Does it provide any trace evidence?
- Are there any fingerprints, palm prints or footprints?
- Is there any other evidence of equipment used in the burglary?
- Is there evidence that the offender tried to destroy any physical evidence?

Armed Robbery

The crime of robbery is a serious offense that detectives confront many times in their careers. In common terms, robbery is the taking with intent to steal anything of value from a person against his or her will, with force, violence, or fear of immediate or future injury to his or her person or property—or the person or property of a relative or a member of his or her family or of anyone in his or her company during the robbery.

Essential Elements of Proof

Investigation of robbery relies heavily on the elements of proof. The public perception of robbery varies, and often elements vary in state statutes. However, the following elements are usually called for as a minimum:

- A theft happened at a specific place and either personal or commercial property was stolen. This includes money or other property of value.
- The theft was from a person who would not otherwise surrender possession of the property of value. It is unnecessary for the property taken to be within any certain distance of the victim. For example, a perpetrator enters a house and forces the owner by threats of serious bodily harm with a weapon of some kind that is recognizable as having the capability to do so, and the owner discloses the hiding place of valuables in an adjoining room. If the offender leaves the owner tied, goes into that room, and steals the valuables, he or she has committed armed robbery.
- The property was taken against the victim's will by force or violence — the actual use of force or violence or engendering fear in the victim for personal safety. For example, a perpetrator may threaten with a gun, knife, club or other weapon capable of causing serious bodily harm. Any amount of force is sufficient to establish robbery if the force overcomes the actual resistance of the victim or causes him or her not to resist.

When a police detective investigates an alleged robbery, she must be alert to the possibility that robbery might not have happened, although a lesser included offense or different offense might have been committed. What appears to be a robbery could be only theft. Theft by taking is an integral part of robbery and may be the offense if there is insufficient evidence to prove the requisite force or engendered fear. Conversely, if proof does not support a charge of theft, and the force element is present, a charge of assault may be made.

Multiple offenses, such as when a group of people is threatened and property is stolen from each person, establish as many robberies committed as there are victims. The offense against the person (the assault element) is more serious than the offense against the property (the theft element). Therefore, each instance of taking becomes a separate offense. However, when several people are threatened but property is taken from only one victim, only one robbery has legally occurred, although all the others might be victims of assault with a deadly weapon.

Detectives use caution because sometimes victims were not robbed as reported. Victims may have reported a robbery as part of a scheme to defraud an insurance company. Robbery, like burglary and arson, is often falsely reported as prerequisite to insurance claims or to cover the negligent loss of property. For example, an employee entrusted with a costly item of equipment decides to use it at home to do company work over the weekend. After leaving it in his unlocked car to run an errand, he returns to find it stolen. If the employee reports the crime truthfully, the company will allege the employee was negligent and might fire him. Instead, the employee decides to report that during an armed robbery, the assailant took his money and jewelry plus the company's equipment. The company will be sympathetic to the employee, but this creates headaches for the police who begin investigating an armed robbery. During a detective's thorough investigation, she may discover the hoax simply through attentive questioning. It's always a good idea to interview a victim more than once, and a few days apart. It's difficult to remember an exact detailed description of a fictitious perpetrator and circumstances, especially when the victim doesn't know the detective will return for later interviews. If the robbery is real, the information will remain consistent, and a real victim may provide additional leads later. Certain information cannot change if it's accurate. For example, if a victim first says the perpetrator was bald and later describes his short brown hair, a detective can reliably assume that no robbery occurred.

Armed robbery can be difficult to investigate for other reasons, too. A robbery can involve intricate planning or be carried out as a spur-of-the-moment whim. In either event, a perpetrator is usually difficult to identify. Most robberies happen at night or under conditions where the robber's features are hard to distinguish. Often, a mask or disguise increases the difficulty of identification and creates significant problems in prosecution efforts even when the perpetrator becomes known. In situations where a robber directly confronts the victim, the emotional state created often intimidates the victim enough to prevent her from furnishing a detailed description.

The technique for theft investigation and many techniques for assault investigation are applicable to the investigation of robbery because elements of both offenses are lesser included offenses in the act of robbery. Normally, victims of a robbery will report it to the police soon after it happens. Law enforcement officers and investigators must respond immediately, because the possibility of finding the offender is often directly related to the length of time taken to begin and follow through with an investigation. Failure to identify a perpetrator immediately after a robbery reduces the probability of a successful prosecution.

Assault

Law enforcement officers deal regularly with assault. Each state has a statute addressing assaults. To help understand this crime and its relationship to the others in this chapter, a quick review of key court decisions and the model penal code follows. Although some statutes define assault with a deadly weapon as aggravated assault, the following information supplies a general overview of the various criminal aspects involved in these crimes and how police detectives investigate them.

- **Assault:** "Any willful attempt or threat to inflict injury upon the person of another, when coupled with an apparent present ability so to do, and any intentional display of force such as would give the victim reason to fear or expect immediate bodily harm, is an assault. An assault may be committed without touching or striking, or doing bodily harm, to the person of another." (State v. Murphy, 7 Wash. App. 505, 500 P.wd 1276, 1281)
- "Often used to describe illegal force which is technically a battery. For the crime of assault, victims need not be apprehensive of fear if the outward gesture is menacing and defendant intends to harm, though for tort of assault, element of victim's apprehension is called for." (People v. Lopez, 271 C.A. 2d 754. 77 Cal. Rptr. 59, 63)
- **Aggravated Assault:** "A person is guilty of aggravated assault if he: (a) attempts to cause serious bodily injury to another, or causes such injury purposely, knowingly or recklessly under circumstances manifesting extreme indifference to the value of human life; or (b) negligently causes bodily injury to another with a deadly weapon; or (c) attempts by physical menace to put another in fear of imminent serious bodily injury." (Model Penal Code, §211.1)
- **Assault With a Deadly and Dangerous Weapon:** "An unlawful

attempt or offer to do bodily harm without justification or excuse by use of any instrument calculated to do harm or cause death. An aggravated form of assault as distinguished from a simple assault, e.g., pointing a loaded gun at one is an assault with a dangerous weapon." (State v. Gregory, 108 Ariz. 445, 501 P. 2d 387, 390)

Generally, the crime of assault with a deadly weapon or other means of force (such as a hammer) requires that the weapon used will probably produce death or grievous bodily harm. It is unnecessary, however, that death or grievous bodily harm be inflicted. Almost any instrument or object can be considered deadly or dangerous. Courts have held that items such as a bottle, beer glass, rock and a piece of pipe could probably inflict death or grievous bodily harm. However, it's held that an unloaded pistol, when presented as a firearm and not as a bludgeon, is not a dangerous weapon or means of force able to produce grievous bodily harm, and this would be so whether the assailant knew it was unloaded or not. This is an important consideration during investigation of this crime. The underlying key element of proof is that the person responsible must be capable of committing the crime. In other words, if he threatens with a gun, it must be loaded. Or, for example, if a person threatens another with a large knife, if the assailant is on crutches and cannot walk without them, and if the victim remains capable of moving about or escaping and is not trapped in any way, the knife is probably not considered a deadly weapon because the capability of using it for assault is absent.

Assault Investigation Checklist

This checklist spans the entire spectrum of assault. Assault with a deadly weapon is usually the most serious form. Other lesser assault offenses are probably applicable when the police detective cannot prove the more serious offense.

Substantiate the Allegation. Upon receipt of information alleging an assault happened, first establish that the offense did happen. Detectives normally do that by questioning the victim, an attending physician and any available witnesses.

Question the Victim. Usually, police procedure calls for questioning the victim at least twice. Color photographs of the victim (with his permission) offer a true picture record of injuries. Another set of photos taken about three days later will often show the full effects of the injuries.

During early questioning, besides establishing the probability that an offense happened, the detective tries to determine the type of weapon used, if any, and whether the victim knows or suspects the identity and motive of the assailant.

The detective's first questioning is brief, particularly when a victim is seriously injured or if questioning delays the search of the crime scene. When a physician believes the victim may die from the injuries, the detective must quickly obtain as much information from the victim as possible. A skilled detective will use a tape recorder to record any dying statements or declarations.

After a search of the crime scene, subsequent interviews may provide investigative leads. Most assaults stem from clear motives. The detective's discovery of a person with a motive and the opportunity and capability to commit the assault may lead to the possible identification of the assailant. Detectives also know victims may have a reason for withholding the truth about the assault, especially when they claim to know the assailant or any reason for it to have happened. For example, a man assaulted by the husband of a woman with whom he is involved may deny any knowledge of why the assault happened and may conceal the identity of the assailant. Also, detectives understand that a victim may not know why the assault happened. In seeking investigative leads, a detective considers the possibility that the assailant made a mistake in identity, or the victim unintentionally or unknowingly interrupted some unlawful act of the assailant.

Search the Crime Scene. Detectives search the crime scene for evidence as soon after the incident as feasible. The search may often begin while the victim is still on the scene in cases where no immediate medical treatment is necessary. The crime scene search and collection of evidence will often make use of a well-planned field investigation kit selected from those items shown in chapter two. The detective gives special attention to objects, footprints, fingerprints, scuff marks and other traces that show activity or presence of persons at the scene. A commonplace item such as a button or piece of thread found at the scene may be of evidentiary value and provide a lead to the identity of the assailant. Detectives always look for physical objects that might have served as a weapon. If the victim was not present during the search, detectives usually revisit the scene with the victim after their initial crime scene search. This technique provides a better understanding of how the assault happened and may lead to the discovery of additional evidence and valuable leads.

Question Witnesses. Police detectives promptly find and question available witnesses to the assault. There is no legal requirement to caution witnesses of their rights. However, if, during the interview of a person a police detective considers a witness, that person says something that may make her a suspect, a prudent investigator stops the interview and informs her of her rights immediately. Although the Miranda decision (interpreting the constitutional Fifth Amendment rights by the U.S. Supreme Court) calls for rights to be explained to an "arrested person" or "person in custody," a prudent detective who wants to win in court will discuss the rights with suspects not yet arrested.

When detectives question a suspect not under arrest or otherwise in custody, the suspect's rights, although based on the Fifth Amendment, become a "noncustodial" caution. For example, until a suspect is taken into custody, the government has no obligation to provide an attorney. Before arrest a suspect can leave at any time and refuse to answer questions or cooperate with the detective. Police detectives always keep the following points in mind:

- Be aware that witnesses may be reluctant to answer direct questions because they fear they may have to appear in court, or because the assailant is a friend or acquaintance, or from fear of the assailant retaliating against them.

- Develop all information about any unusual activity in the area by questioning persons living, working or near the scene about the identity of the persons who were seen or believed to have been in the area.

Question Suspects. Detectives seek answers to the following questions when questioning suspects:

- Did the suspect have a motive, opportunity and capability to commit the assault?

- Was the suspect near the crime scene before the assault?

- Does the suspect own or have access to the type of weapon used in the assault (if known)?

- Can the physical evidence found at the scene be linked to the suspect?
- Does the suspect have a sound alibi?

Get Background Information. When a police detective's investigative effort does not identify the assailant, she often checks the victim's background, associates and activities; she reviews law enforcement and other records to determine the victim's involvement in any previous incidents; she questions relatives, fellow employees, neighbors and associates. Information from these sources may show the victim has a motive for withholding information.

Often, the detective must confer with the victim's attending physician to determine if the injuries sustained could have happened by the circumstances the victim claims. The detective wants to know the estimated age of the injuries and any related information that might show if the victim gave police an accurate account of the assault.

The physician responsible for the care of the victim may help the detective determine the type of weapon used to create the injury, the approximate time it happened, and the incapacity of the victim because of alcohol, drugs or physical disabilities that might affect the victim's accurate recall of the circumstances.

F I V E

ARSON

Chapter five explains the complexities facing police detectives as they tackle an investigation of a fire of suspicious origins. The police become involved, normally after the fire department and state fire marshal supply an opinion, for several reasons. First, arson is a serious crime, and although a fire department has some expertise in determining the cause, the fire department does not have investigative responsibility in most jurisdictions. In a few major metropolitan fire departments, investigators with limited law enforcement authority look for the arsonist; however, in most jurisdictions the task falls to the police department, which uses members of the fire department as expert witnesses.

Another reason a police detective will become involved, even in metropolitan areas that have fire investigators, is that arson is often used to cover up other crimes, such as murder, embezzlement and burglary. Whatever the reason, the police detective must have a working knowledge of arson investigation and often receives specialized training at various schools and seminars across the country.

The Police Detective's First Steps

A police detective fire investigation hinges on proving fire cause and origin, which are necessary to trace an arson to a perpetrator. People who commit arson fall in two distinct categories: amateur and professional. The amateur often splashes a structure with gasoline or some other accelerant and throws a lighted match into it. A professional uses a variety of accelerants and incendiaries but often has simple igniting devices. The professional arsonist, like other professional criminals, has a trademark or routine that an attentive detective will catalog. However, knowing the identity of a perpetrator and collecting conclusive and convicting evidence are two different matters. The detective cannot establish the crime resulting from a fire until all possible fire-causing factors except one have been conclusively disproved. Fire investigation requires a cautious process of elimination, and this process must squarely consider the various possibilities of natural or accidental causes, including the possibility of arson solely to collect insurance. It is probably among the most difficult investigations a police detective will undertake.

When a fire chief suspects a fire was arson, the state fire marshal's office is contacted and within hours a fire investigation specialist arrives at the fire scene. The state fire investigator accompanies the fire department chief or commander in a search to determine whether the fire started accidentally or as a result of arson. Although there is a tendency for law enforcement officers to rely on fire investigation experts, the police detective typically has the investigative responsibility. Usually, fire marshal representatives cover huge geographical areas and are unable to spend the hours, days and often months of investigation called for on only one fire, unless it involves the death of several persons.

Range of Fire Causes

Fires originating from electrical sources comprise a major category of accidental fires, and fires caused by improper or defective electrical wiring are a chief component of this category. Professional arsonists often create shorted electrical wiring to disguise arson.

Fires can begin in diverse ways. For example, fires can start from an open-flame device like a cigarette lighter, from a lit cigarette, or from a variety of incendiary devices—often accelerated with a flammable liquid such as gasoline, kerosene or charcoal lighter fluid. The arsonist may place gunpowder trails strategically within a structure and ignite them among combustibles. Chemicals can be combined to create fire, often with the aid of a time-delay device. (For example, a chemical-filled prophylactic may be suspended over another carefully situated chemical. Burning occurs when one chemical eats through the condom and falls into the chemical below.) Lastly, a simple lit match applied to paper can wreak great havoc in a room packed with combustibles.

A variety of human follies can lead to the onset of fire, such as when a person falls asleep while smoking a cigarette. Other fires begin when a person smokes in the immediate vicinity of a high concentration of gasoline vapor, leaves hot grease frying unattended on a kitchen stove, or burns wood in a fireplace without a screen to trap flying embers.

Dogs and cats can knock over hot lamps and portable space heaters, either by accident or because they were trained to do so by a devious human master. Rats can eat through wires unprotected by conduit, causing a short circuit, sparks and ensuing fire.

Long-term neglect of frayed electrical wiring and overloading of available circuitry with too many simultaneously operating appliances can cause a short circuit, arcing, and the spitting of flames into an open atmosphere. Natural gas lines, heating appliances, and electrical wiring components may have manufactured defects or improper installation that eventually leads to an explosion or fire.

Lightning can strike timber or other combustibles, causing an eruption of flames. Under certain environmental conditions, oily rags improperly stored in a confined unsealed space may spontaneously combust. Even the sun reflected through a prism can sometimes generate enough heat to make dry vegetation burst into flames.

Occasionally the cause of a fire is readily apparent to an investigator who may find, for example, two separate corners of wood paneling consumed by fire near the baseboard, in a V-pattern, with charred crumpled paper lodged against the wall in both locations, loose matches and a matchbox on the floor nearby. The obvious cause of this fire is arson; however, when fire fighters find a body with five bullet holes in that burning building, the police detective knows the arson happened to cover the murder. However, arson rarely has a readily apparent motive, and police detectives cannot allow themselves to assume the obvious, thereby neglecting a painstaking effort to eliminate every conceivable natural or accidental cause of the fire. Many arson fires escape detection, especially those started by skilled professionals.

A police detective preparing or presenting an arson investigation to a sitting grand jury or a trial judge and jury needs to consider their viewpoint. Judges and jurors invariably lack even rudimentary knowledge of fire investigation principles, and they depend on the credibility of the police and fire investigators. When a police investigation establishes all reasonable possibilities for the fire's origin and causes, including opinions of qualified and unbiased fire experts corroborating the detective's findings, the court or grand jury often supports indictment and later conviction of a perpetrator.

In an arson investigation, the detective seeks either positive physical evidence showing a fire's most probable cause or negative proof. A detective always looks for positive physical evidence, but a skilled arsonist knows how to create diversions, making the cause of a fire appear to be something other than it is.

Establishing negative proof requires evaluating fire causes by compiling circumstantial evidence about the fire scene. When a detective forms a theory based on negative proof, he must sort through and consider all circumstances and relate it to the physical evidence. Arrived at by the approach of negative proof, arson can often develop as the only plausible explanation for a fire's cause. For example, if there was no electric current or natural gas service into the structure when the fire happened, a detective has absolute negative proof the fire was not accidentally started by anything related to natural gas or electricity.

Electricity and electrical wiring regularly cause structural fires. Three of the most infamous and costly fires in America were caused by electrical malfunctions. The most recent, the MGM Grand Hotel fire in Las Vegas in 1980, killed eighty-five people.

Police detectives always have good reason to suspect electricity and electrical wiring in any structural or vehicular fire where electrical current was running through a circuit. However, electricity and faulty wiring too often become the whipping boys of fire causation and may be invoked to conceal disinterest or incompetence by fire departments, fire marshal investigators and law enforcement departments. Electricity is also a handy fall guy for desperate criminal defendants seeking to ward off blame where arson is alleged. It's a favorite obfuscating element for a professional arsonist or person who researches fires at the public library and recognizes the ease with which most investigators will accept electrical causes for fires.

Concept of Investigation

The police detective's investigation of arson or suspected arson, whether working independently or collectively as part of a team, includes two stages.

Stage One: During the Fire. Police officers responding to a fire in support of fire fighters play a key role at this stage. The patrol officers should collect valuable investigative information through careful observation of several aspects.

Stage Two: After the Fire. Investigation after the fire is often a tedious, dirty task important to gather evidence and reach accurate conclusions. Systematic checklists and techniques coupled with information collected by patrol officers during stage one will often lead a detective's investigative effort to a successful outcome.

Police Department Observation During the Fire

At the scene of a burning structure, the patrol officer or detective always seeks the advice and opinions of fire fighters and other persons familiar with the building. Fire fighters may have information about fire origin, intensity, duration and other valuable clues that could lead the police detective to a productive investigative effort. Persons familiar with the building and area can provide information about contents and interior arrangement before the fire.

Police officers or detectives arriving at a fire scene conduct an investigation much like the investigation of any other crime scene. However, because of the situation they often have several advantages. The detective at a fire scene can watch the crime of arson as it happens. Valuable investigative leads become available during the burning process, but officers collecting that information must usually move quickly. Fire fighters have a rigorous task and massive equipment. They are intent on knocking down a fire, not on investigative strategy. The fire fighters' activities, falling debris and smoke quickly destroy evidence. If possible, and according to the location of the structure, patrol officers and detectives look for evidence of activity outside the structure, such as prints of shoes, tire tracks, empty containers, cigarette lighters, matchboxes, tools or other items that may show the fire started from an incendiary device.

Examining the burning building is important while the fire is in progress. The detective notes if windows, doors or other openings were open, closed or locked when the fire started. She observes walls to note any suspicious conditions, such as a break-through that might have happened from an explosion or a burned-out section where the fire might have originated. Detectives walk completely around the building at a distance, observing the smoke patterns on the tops of the windows and doorways. The pattern will show the direction the fire is burning because of drafts and ventilation.

Detectives also note the location and extent of the fire, and whether it's concentrated in a specific part of the building. When there is more than one fire burning within a structure, the detective observes the fires' relation to each other if possible (for example, two fires within a building, each at opposite ends of the building). Two or more separate fires within a building often indicate arson. However, there might have been only one original fire, with other fires arising from circumstances such as drafts and combustible materials igniting from heat.

Observing the Burning Residue

- A fire scene detective must carefully note the color and location of flames. Flames may show the intensity of the fire and the type of materials that are burning in it.

- Steam and smoke, particularly at the start of a burning, may aid in determining what substances are burning and the type of substance that started or accelerated the fire. Attentive observation of the smoke can be of considerable importance because its appearance and odor, including its chemical composition, yield information that may be of definite value. However, even when a detective cannot see and smell the smoke, he will probably find witnesses including fire fighters who did, and their testimony is important.

- Smoke is largely made of carbon, mineral ash, and partly consumed organic materials, with a variety of invisible gases that give smoke most of its odor. Oil, gasoline, creosote, tars, paint and like organic materials having a petroleum base usually burn with a black, carbonaceous smoke. Black material in smoke indicates that some such organic material is being burned; this is important in investigating arson because of the common use of like materials in starting fires.

- Wood smoke is usually gray or white, although sometimes appearing black where the air supply is poor or the wood is green and the burning temperature low. It is unlikely that a dry wood fire will give off much black smoke.

- White clouds of smoke appearing before the fire fighting equipment begins extinguishing a fire shows a combustion of moisture-laden substances.

- Reddish brown or yellow smoke shows that the fire is burning nitric acid, nitrates, nitrated plastics, celluloid or products having a nitrocellulose base. The presence of reddish brown or yellow smoke in premises where materials of this type are seldom present suggests use of a similar substance to aid the spread of the burning.

- Grayish smoke stems from loosely placed substances, such as straw and hay, that give off flying soot and ash.

- Smoke odor supplies the detective with an added technique of identifying the substances being consumed by fire. Ammonia, often used by an arsonist to keep fire fighters away from the burning and to offset the odor of gasoline, is readily recognizable. Gunpowder, gasoline, rubber, alcohol, manufactured gas, linseed oil, turpentine, paint thinners and lacquers have distinguishable odors. Feathers, wood and hair give off a typical sulfurous odor because of their high sulfur content. Vegetable materials may produce acrid or aromatic odors, which may give a detective some indication about the fuel used.

- A fire scene detective must note the manner of burning, observing whether the burning is slow or rapid, and learn if the fire involves accelerants or highly combustible materials.

- On arrival at a fire scene the police officer or detective must immediately circulate through the crowd. She watches faces and actions of onlookers and takes note of any spectator who seems to be getting personal satisfaction from the fire. Pyromaniacs enjoy flames and excitement. The best place to look for them is at the scene of their own fire. If the fire happens late at night or early in the morning, the incendiary may be conspicuous by being the only fully clothed person in the crowd, especially in urban or suburban residential areas.

- A fire scene detective should note the weather during the burning, and later research the weather in the days before the fire. Warm, damp days are more conducive to spontaneous combustion than hot, dry days. During the period of burning, take notes on the temperature, humidity and air circulation. Also, detectives often check with the weather bureau to find out the exact conditions that prevailed when the fire started and in the days preceding the burning.

- It's helpful to take photographs and make sketches during the burning, after the fire fighters have extinguished the fire, and during the search for evidence.

- The skilled use of color photography at a fire scene, particularly during the structure burning, often supplies invaluable leads to a detective when analyzing information after the fire. Such photographs also often prove to be of great value during the late stages of investigation and in the courtroom. Photograph the spectators and the surrounding areas. Photographing suspicious persons at fire scenes can sometimes help the police identify a pyromaniac who stays to watch the fire. If the same person appears at more than one fire, the detective has a good lead in the case.

The Police Detective's Post-Fire Investigation

Investigation of a structure fire begins with an inspection of the exterior of the burned building. The fire may have originated on the building's exterior and consumed its way inside the structure. The condition of doors and windows may yield valuable proof of the type of fire. A splintered doorjamb or fresh pry marks noted around a door lock may tip the detective to suspect illegal entry and a likely arson — maybe to cover up a burglary. However, she checks to see if fire fighters caused the damage before reaching a conclusion. Often, fire fighters will note forced entry to a building when they first arrive at a scene; their observations and opinions are often invaluable and time-saving. For example, fragments of glass found outside the building and observed by fire fighters before their efforts make later observations difficult can help show whether an explosion happened; whether the fire was fast-moving or a slow, smoldering blaze; whether an intruder broke a window and made a hasty exit from it before any flames reached the windowpane; and whether the window was in place when the fire started.

Police investigations of suspected arson can become complicated, especially when it's necessary to sift through debris of a fire scene looking for physical evidence. The seasoned detective knows that fire investigation requires the correct attire, including boots, a jumpsuit or old clothes, gloves, flashlight, and a cap or hat. Trying to investigate this type of crime scene in a suit or street clothing will ensure that the detective's clothes smell like a chimney. Skilled detectives do not forget a shovel and other items for poking around in the debris. An arson evidence collection kit, including cameras, is a necessity. I suggest both a high-quality 35mm with color film and flash, and a Polaroid camera with color film. The Polaroid assures having a photograph if the 35mm film or specific shots do not turn out satisfactorily when developed, and the 35mm negative can be enlarged to produce exhibits in the detective's investigative report and for court presentations.

One of the biggest problems a detective faces is a lack of light. When available and possible, a portable lighting system is placed in dark areas where photographs are important. The Polaroid is a good way to test what the 35mm shot will look like when developed.

The police detective's preliminary investigation at the scene of a fire that's suspected to be arson most often will happen concurrently with the fire department and fire marshal's investigation. The general principles for examination of residues from fire will vary with the type of event and damage.

Three General Principles

All Combustible Material Is Destroyed. Any evidence that remains after an intense fire is noncombustible. It may be in considerable quantity, and of definite importance. For example, metal tools or other metal objects foreign to the premises might have been used in entering or part of a device to cause ignition. Similarly, objects known to be present at the locale might have been used by the arsonist and moved or changed by him in the commission of the crime. The investigator will normally begin investigating by looking for what is there that should not be there.

Only Part of the Combustible Material Is Destroyed. Fires extinguished in an early stage leave much of the combustible material intact. In these cases, not only will wood or similar combustible building materials supply valuable items for analysis, but they will also enable recovery of traces of hydrocarbon solvents used to set the fire and other paraphernalia used by the arsonist.

An Arson Attempt Is Unsuccessful. Occasionally, the arsonist arranges some device designed to ignite a building during his absence to establish an alibi. Early discovery or operative failure of the device may prevent the fire from starting. In this situation, a connection exists between the enigmatic fire-setting device and the likelihood that the crime will be solved. While nothing is so difficult to trace as a burned match, tracing a sophisticated timing device may be easy.

Important Tips for Police Detectives

- In cases of suspected arson, fire fighters should delay normal cleanup operation until the detective has an opportunity to complete an investigation of the premises.
- After securing the fire scene and before touching or moving anything, a detective observes and takes notes on items that appear material to his case. He also makes supplemental notes with scaled sketches and complete photographic coverage, making certain of sketch and photograph accuracy.
- The detective exercises great care in examining, collecting and preserving articles found near the fire that may bear fingerprints.
- Skilled detectives always check the gas and electric meters to learn if natural or propane gas and electric utilities serviced the building before and during the fire. If the building is connected to propane tanks, he checks the tanks to determine if they were in use and turned on. *Note*: Fire fighters often turn off gas, electricity and propane or other fuel feeds on arrival at the fire scene. A detective needs to talk with them first to determine if the items were turned off, which ones, and if they were operable when fire fighters turned them off. For example, a propane or fuel tank feed might have been turned off by fire fighters as a matter of routine, but their investigation may also show the tanks were empty at the time of the fire.
- The electric service panels need careful examination including photographs. The detective looks for tripped circuit breakers, blown fuses or overloaded protectors and examines them for signs of tampering before the fire. A detective will scrutinize the interior of a service panel later in his interior building in-

spection to correlate discoveries. The service panel interior should be photographed both with Polaroid and regular film, making certain the photographs are clear and easy to read. The reason for standard film is for later enlargement should evidence be linked to this panel.

- The Polaroid is useful while tracking circuits through the rest of the structure. For example, if a detective finds the origin or origins of fire, he notes the vicinity of electrical outlets, appliances and other connections and refers to the photograph to determine if breakers were tripped for that area of the building. If the fire was of electrical origin, breakers would trip or fuses blow. If they are not tripped or blown, the origin was surely not electrical. It's also wise to determine if the electricity was connected to outlets.

- Immediately before or during the exterior perimeter inspection, the police detective finds out what information is already known about the blaze and the circumstances surrounding its ignition, including important observations and discovery of physical evidence inside or outside the building by fire fighters. The color of smoke and fire witnessed by fire suppression crews and onlookers can be a valuable clue for a detective. *Note*: I always look for photographs and video footage. Good sources are neighbors, employees of a company, owners, television and newspaper reporters or freelance photographers. Many are on the scene immediately, and their photographs may be crucial for corroborating other physical and circumstantial evidence.

- Finding the point of origin of a fire is essential in most arson investigations. This area will prove most productive when a detective searches for any apparatus or device that might have been used to start the fire.

- A police detective follows the path of the burning to its source by observing the intensity of the destruction and charring of uprights. Once found, the point of origin is protected as necessary to permit cautious collection efforts.

Facts About a Fire's Point of Origin
- Fire that envelops a wooden beam tends to round the edges on the side away from the source of the flame.

- The surface of charred wood normally bears a pattern of crevices similar to the pattern on the skin of an alligator. The probable point of origin is normally where both the small checks in the alligator pattern and deep charring are found. Bear in mind that sometimes fire fighters might have been able to extinguish the fire at the point of origin in the first stages of their operations while the fire burned unchecked in other areas. In these instances, a detective may find that the most intense heat or prolonged burning happened at locations some distance from the point of origin, possibly where combustibles were stored.

- The point of origin of a fire will be close to the lowest point of burning or charring. Fire travels downward very slowly unless there is a downdraft. The collapse of a roof or floor will change the situation, since burning materials will be carried to a lower level where new fires will be set. In this instance, the second fire may well obliterate the point of origin of the first fire.

- Direction of flame propagation is influenced by the direction of drafts and winds. The pattern of the burned area will usually show their direction. Generally, the origin of the fire will be on the windward side of the burned area since the flame will travel in the direction of the wind or draft. If the fire is in the open, changes in the wind direction may turn the fire and obscure the point of origin. When there's no change in wind direction, a fire in the open, such as in a forest, will normally burn in a triangular pattern determined by the prevailing wind. The point of origin will be close to the apex of the triangle.

- The point of origin of a fire in a building will be close to the lower apex of the triangular pattern since fire normally burns upward with a lateral spread.

- Examination of electrical fixtures and burned wiring may show the fire's point of origin. Electrical wires burned through by fire will have a sharp point, while wires burned because of a short circuit will have a round bead on the end.

Investigating the Point of Origin

When a detective traces the origin of a fire with a complex pattern, she remembers that general rules still apply but must take into account variables such as availability of fuel, physical arrangement of the structure, chimney actions and similar factors.

Examination of debris at the point of origin must be made with great care. The detective looks for possible accidental causes and for proof of arson, such as traces of combustible substances, apparatuses or devices. For laboratory examination, she collects peculiarly colored ashes or soot, unusual formations of clinkers (the noncombustible remains of partly combusted materials and impregnated materials). When a pick and shovel must be used in an area, a systematic method of search remains important.

In a fire investigation, as in any suspected crime investigation, integrity of physical evidence is absolutely important. Samples of suspect liquids must be collected in proper containers, such as covered cans that have not been used, lest the liquids evaporate or become contaminated with residue of the container's previous contents. Fragile items such as sections of burned wiring or a suspected charred cigarette-matchbook device must be handled with the utmost care so that they do not break into pieces when picked up. Occasionally, an on-scene decision will have to be made about how a given item of physical evidence is to be handled. Specifically, a police detective may have to decide whether it is more important to preserve a delicate object for visual inspection by a jury at a possible future trial or to submit the article for fingerprint analysis or laboratory testing. A real possibility exists that a severely charred item will disintegrate during the testing procedures. Whatever their decision, detectives always take carefully thought-out photographs, in both Polaroid and regular film, making certain there is sufficient light and camera angles to clearly show the evidence in the place where it was found.

Special lacquer available to investigating detectives allows them to spray a delicate object and keep it intact, but doing so generally ends any opportunity to submit it to a lab for fingerprint analysis. Also, dusting an item for fingerprints may prevent further laboratory analysis for other purposes, such as detecting the presence of hydrocarbons that would show the fire was boosted by use of an accelerator. Wiring should generally be collected without the aid of a lacquer spray, so that it can later be examined in unchanged condition by an expert; objects such as suspected cigarette-matchbook devices, which rarely yield fingerprints or other helpful information on closer inspection, should be treated with lacquer spray to preserve them for use as potential trial exhibits.

Items to be removed from the fire scene for evidence must be photographed where they're found. This photographic record does two important things: (1) It supplies proof of evidence discovery at a specific location at the structure; and (2) it enables the detective to produce a photograph at the trial should the item be destroyed or damaged during retrieval, in transit, or in laboratory testing.

Each item a detective collects as evidence must be packaged in the proper container and tagged listing, at minimum, the date, time of recovery, place of recovery, a brief description, the detective's initials and the case number. A burned object is never tagged directly. A label on the can in which the object is placed will suffice. Anything too large for a can, such as a partially charred chunk of baseboard showing distinct burn patterns, should be wrapped in plastic and secured with string. Plastic bags secured with tape are not used since volatile substances may dissolve the glue off the tape or diffuse through the plastic, resulting in loss of volatile substances or in introduction of contaminants. Generally, if evidence collected is very dry and the odor of accelerants is not detected, a laboratory analysis will most probably be futile. This is especially true the longer the time between evidence collection and laboratory analysis. The detective packages evidence to assure it will reach the laboratory intact. Different exhibits collected at the fire scene need separate containers to prevent cross-contamination.

The detective should always make a chain-of-custody property receipt or use tags that allow a chain of custody to be clearly maintained. The items of evidence should be handled by as few persons as necessary and maintained in the department evidence room promptly after collection and laboratory examination.

Examination of Ash

Particularly in small fires such as in a fireplace, furnace, incinerator or bonfire, the perpetrator of an arson often seeks to destroy evidence by burning it before setting fire to the structure. The ash often shows the specific type of material burned. This is important when arson also involves a cadaver found in the debris.

Ash fragments are collected carefully, placed in a container large enough to exert no strain or pressure, and taken to a laboratory with as little disturbance as possible. If the ash appears to be a document or cloth with a pattern and is very fragile, spraying it with a thin lacquer should strengthen it enough for handling. Detectives use this method when there is a possibility of decipherable burned documents.

Chemical or spectrographic analysis of ash from burned cloth helps to identify the type of cloth burned. Moreover, visual observation of the ash will sometimes lead to useful information, since different types of cloth vary in mineral composition. Ash from a fire is never to be ignored.

The police detective must make an attentive search of a fire scene for signs of arson and develop a solid case when evidence shows the fire is a crime. He will remain especially alert for suspicious articles and devices, such as fuses, clocks, cans, bottles, wires and dry-cell batteries used to ignite or accelerate the burning. Since a detective might determine the fire has several points of origin, he examines debris, floors, closets, cupboards, attic spaces and other places where an arsonist may have hidden igniters.

Kindling Materials

The most common expedients used by arsonists to assure rapid and intense fires are gasoline, kerosene or other volatile flammable liquids. Other kindling materials are old papers, cloth and packing materials, some of which may be soaked in solvent.

When poured over large masses of papers or trash, gasoline, naphtha and benzene (highly flammable liquid chemicals that accelerate fire) may flow through holes or cracks in the floor and drop to a lower level. If the fire is extinguished quickly, some liquid may remain. Recovery of such solvents must happen immediately after the fire is extinguished.

Paper, trash or other kindling material that is soaked with a volatile and flammable solvent will act as a wick and insulate the underlying solvent from the heat of the fire. Such solvents are recoverable if they are sought immediately after extinguishing a fire that has not grown to major proportions.

Another consideration detectives have in mind at the fire scene involves collection and analysis of old papers, cloth, packing materials or other trash probably brought in by the arsonist. The materials may serve as a source of fibers, glass, hair, soil, metal or other types of evidence that can be connected with the arsonist. They may show his or her identity, environment, occupation and other pertinent information.

Igniters

The most common igniter is the match. Normally, the match is completely consumed and impossible to trace. From force of habit, however, some people will blow the match out and toss it aside. This match can be important as proof if it can be traced to the arsonist. For example, the perpetrator blows out a match and tosses it aside, enabling investigators to recover it from the postfire scene. The police detective may also find a matchbook with an advertisement or with telephone numbers written inside. The laboratory determines the match came from the book, and the numbers and business place, coupled with other investigative effort and evidence, lead the detective to the arsonist.

There are many types of devices an arsonist can build to start the fire in her absence. The most common is the burning candle. Other devices might be a burning cigarette, firearms, ammunition, yellow phosphorus, mechanical match strikers and electric sparking devices. Complex mechanical devices often survive the fire for later discovery and may be traceable to the person who built them.

Searching a Building for Fire Origin

To find fire origins within the interior of a building, police detectives start moving from areas of least or no fire damage to areas of heaviest burning. The place where the charring is deepest and lowest is usually the place where a given fire started, because charring normally is deepest where the fire burned longest, and because fire normally burns upward in a *V*. An inverted *V* pattern might result where accelerants like gasoline have been splashed against a wall before ignition of the fire.

There may be more than one area of fire origin, or multiple points of fire origin within one general area. Because of the long mathematical odds against two or more accidental fires breaking out near each other at about the same time, arson is almost surely shown if true multiple points of fire origin are found. However, before reaching that conclusion, the detective must be sure that what appear to be multiple points of origin are representations of two or more separate fire starts.

Often, the ceilings of a structure may be porous in spots, allowing intense heat from flames to pass through roof areas remote from one point of origin. The damaged ceiling areas may appear to be multiple points of fire origin when in fact they all stem from a single point. Falling curtains or drapes may leave a distinct char pattern on wood flooring after dropping there in flames. Just so, burning beams may fall to a lower floor level, leaving a separate pattern where they land.

Examining Utilities and Appliances

During the investigative search of the fire scene, the condition of all gas and electric appliances is examined. Detectives look to see whether control valves are in the off or on position and look for ruptured gas lines or appliance connectors. Because natural gas is lighter than air, a natural gas fire will normally leave its lowest charring mark above the floor near the source of ignition, often a pilot light. If a stove appears to be heavily involved in a fire originating in a kitchen, gas connectors or electric wiring would, of course, be closely examined, but the detective must remain alert for other possible reasons for the fire. Far too often stove fires begin when a distracted cook leaves hot grease to ignite in an unattended frying pan, and then the burning grease is unintentionally spilled or spread by water foolishly poured on in panic at the fire's discovery. It is also common for such persons to deny that anything happened.

All wiring and circuitry of electrical appliances near apparent points of fire origin must be carefully inspected. A thorough inspection of this sort may include opening junction boxes and inspecting wiring within the space behind electrical wall outlets in the general area of fire's origin.

Fire Origin and Cause Indicators—Arson or Accident?

As I mentioned earlier, arsonists often leave several reliable indicators, like calling cards. A skilled police detective learns to read these telltale signs of incendiaries, much like a pathfinder stalking game through a forest.

Some arsonists make no effort to conceal their tracks. However, the skilled detective never reaches conclusions about fire origin and causes without first thoroughly investigating a fire scene. Spilled gas cans left inside a burned living room, plus flammable liquid-drenched "trailers" or "streamers" of twisted newspapers leading to the remains of a mechanical time-delay device situated at the trailers' intersecting points are sure signs of a planned and deliberately set fire. Similarly, foul play is readily apparent if an investigator finds aluminum foil inserted in the sockets of S-type fuses to thwart overcurrent protection, or nails are driven through cartridge fuses to totally bypass overcurrent protection. If suspicious signs are found, the detective won't be surprised to find doctored wires near the point of fire origin that were calculated to simulate an accidental electrically oriented blaze.

Most of the time, several clues will have to be tallied before a detective can intelligently pinpoint a fire's cause. The degree that glass is cracked by heat, called "crazing," can show whether heat built up near that location rapidly or only gradually. Small crazing commonly signifies that the glass was exposed to intense heat and that heat increased rapidly. This might indicate an accelerant was used. Large crazing shows a smoldering fire and is consistent with the slow buildup of heat. This might indicate the fire started without the use of accelerants, but a clever arsonist who does not have a tight time frame might create circumstances where heat is built slowly before flames erupt. Doing that can supply an alibi for the arsonist who ensures credible witnesses see him far too far from the fire to become a suspect. Melted glass is associated with exposure to intense heat. Depending on the contents of the burned building, the intensity coupled with other clues might lead the investigator to believe arson was involved in the fire.

Smoke, too, carries meaning when attached to glass. Heavy, dark smoke on glass usually signifies slow heat buildup remote from the fire's point of origin, while light smoke stains on glass can be made by intense heat close to the point of origin, or they may happen when the fire produces only minor property damage. Glass that is melted and unstained by smoke has usually been exposed to intense heat, probably quite close to the fire's origin.

Multiple points of fire origin, separate and unconnected, are the hallmark of arson. So are flammable liquid burn patterns etched into flooring or carpeting. When tiles are blistered, it is probable that a flammable liquid flowed and burned over their surface. "Ghost marks" occur when asphalt-tile squares are attacked by a burning flammable liquid seeping below them and dissolving the adhesive affixing them to concrete below. "Spalling," the sudden pitting and cracking of concrete, quite often occurs from flammable liquid burning intensely on the surface of the concrete, followed by a cold stream of water from a fire hose.

The detection of flammable vapors and flammable liquids by a mechanical "sniffer" and portable gas chromatograph usually indicates arson. Ultraviolet light can also detect flammable vapors, but the human nose remains the most sensitive of all detectors. The detective investigating arson must remember that, if the case goes to court with a suspect, more evidence than just one person's sense of smell will be needed to convince a judge or jury. For example, the investigator might explain that he smelled a flammable liquid at the fire scene and then verified that suspicion with a mechanical "sniffer." The mechanical equipment will also have a graph maker that supplies more evidence of the test's validity.

A fire originating in upholstered furniture is likely to lead to annealed springs if the burning continues long enough and the springs are subjected to rapid heat buildup. When this type of annealing occurs, the furniture springs lose their elasticity. The blistering of wood from charring commonly suggests whether a fire was accelerated by a flammable liquid, based on the pattern left on the wood. Generally, large, shiny char blisters (known as "alligatoring") reflect fast-burning fires while small, dull blisters signal a smoldering blaze. Irregular blister patterns are associated with the splashing of an accelerant on the wood. However, recent tests have shown that the reliability of alligatoring as an indicator of fire type is not always absolute.

Finding the unusual at a fire scene can telegraph an arson fire. For example, candle wax in the center of an area of fire origin could very well be the remains of a time-delay device. A brass flex connector to a natural gas line cut with a hacksaw is a sure sign of a set fire, if the fire involved natural gas. The absence of normal furnishings or other contents normally found in a house should tip the detective about the cause of a fire, because arsonists commonly remove valuable contents before torching their home or place of business.

Establishing an Arsonist's Motives

Willful and malicious intent is normally an essential element in arson and it is important, if possible, to establish a motive for the suspected crime, especially in cases that depend on circumstantial evidence. The identification of a positive motive for the suspect may add to the weight of the evidence obtained at the crime scene and lead to successful prosecution of the perpetrator of the crime. The following list contains the most common motives.

Defrauding an Insurer. Destruction by fire and explosion may be used to defraud an insurance company. Examples of an attempt to defraud an insurer might be:

1. An owner of a financed motor vehicle who cannot make payments is threatened with repossession and damaged credit rating. She normally strips the vehicle of valuable items such as radios and tape or disc players and speakers, drives the car to an isolated location and after soaking its interior with gasoline or other flammable liquid, sets it afire. The following day, the owner reports the car stolen to a police agency and then to her insurance company. When the vehicle is found by the police, a report shows the vehicle was stolen, presumably to steal the stereo system and other items, and then burned. Unless the police or insurance company can prove the owner staged the event, the insurance company must pay the claim, settling the debt and maybe giving more money to the owner. This is a common crime that has been prevalent for at least the past thirty years.

2. A business owner faced with bankruptcy is being harassed by creditors, and not wanting to suffer the embarrassment of a failed business, litigation and damaged credit for years to come, he slips in late at night and sets the fire to the business building. The following day, he files an insurance claim and, when payment is made, pays off creditors and is free from the ordeal. This is another common event, too often poorly investigated and never solved if the arsonist is intelligent and careful to make it appear accidental.

3. A home owner facing repossession of a home is seriously in debt and wants to avoid disgrace. She sends her family on a trip, then using any number of schemes, sets the house afire and collects the insurance. Normally, in a dwelling fire, a detective always looks for items of value, clothing, trophies, photo albums and the like or for their absence. If they are not in the postfire debris, the fire was probably started by an owner-arsonist.

In all three cases, it's possible the owner hired another person to do the task, offering the owner an ironclad alibi for the time of the fire. This may leave the insurance company without the choice of denying the claim on suspicion of arson. Although arson is suspected, when the owner has a solid alibi and no connection between the owner and arsonist can be readily established, the insurance company must pay.

Revenge. Because fires may inflict physical, mental and/or financial injury, a person who wants to revenge a wrong, either real or imagined, may seek this means to cause injury or hardship to the person by whom he has been wronged.

Civil Disturbances. Arsons or attempted arsons have become common occurrences in civil disturbances. Agitators may resort to arson as a means of making or furthering a civil disturbance. Such acts attract crowds, destroy property, cause confusion and panic and divert police attention.

Concealing Other Crimes. A criminal may try to hide or destroy evidence of another crime such as murder, burglary, embezzlement or theft by use of an apparently accidental fire. For example, an accountant or bookkeeper who has embezzled large sums of money learns that an independent auditor is coming to review the company books. At night or on a weekend, the bookkeeper finds a way to create a fire that will damage and destroy the company books and records. Or, in another scenario, a person who has committed a murder sets a house or building on fire. Depending on the way the murder happened, the burning can make it appear a person died because of the fire. Remember that a charred cadaver does not always show bullet or knife wounds. However, X rays of a cadaver will probably show the true cause of death in such cases. An analysis of carbon monoxide in blood or tissue from the charred cadaver will show whether the person died from poisoning instead of the fire.

Suicide. A person may use fire to commit suicide or to fulfill a suicide-homicide plot.

Pyromania. Whenever a series of burnings of unknown origin happens under like circumstances in a given geographical area, especially in isolated parts of buildings such as cellars and storage areas, it may be that fires were set by a pyromaniac. The pyromaniac commits the crime of arson to satisfy some sort of impulse. She usually does not seek any insurance indemnity or other material gain. In explaining her act, the person may state it was done simply for a thrill or excitement.

Since the pyromaniac may be among the first observers present at the fire, law enforcement officers and fire fighters arriving at the scene should be alert for suspicious-looking persons. Normally, pyromaniacs have sexual motives for their arson. Because of that, they often wear garments that can conceal fondling or masturbation, such as raincoats or overcoats even when the weather is not inclement. Others might have a look of fascination and may have no apparent reason for being in the area. Photographs of spectators are excellent information sources for this crime, especially if taken routinely at fires. Later comparison may show the same person present at several fires, even at those started by someone else.

Accidental Fires. A police detective never overlooks the possibility that a fire might have resulted from an accidental cause instead of arson. Accidental fires may be produced by many causes, including faulty wiring, overheated electric motors, spontaneous combustion of oil or chemically saturated materials, improperly cleaned and regulated heating systems, or careless cigarette or pipe smokers.

Police Liaison and Coordination During Fire Investigations

The owner of the damaged property is asked about his or her activities at the time of the fire. The detective also checks for prior arrests, previous fires, financial standing, business and domestic conditions, and hobbies or amusements that could have caused reverses in an owner's financial situation.

All witnesses should be questioned. The detective asks the last person leaving the premises about the time of his or her leaving, the condition of the premises then, how he or she secured the premises, location of the keys, and identity of other persons who had keys or access to the building. Suspects questioned by police detectives should be cautioned according to their constitutional rights, even when not in custody.

Close liaison and coordination with proper fire fighting, legal and other investigative authorities are essential to successful arson investigation.

While the detective is examining the crime scene and questioning witnesses, other steps important in the investigation may be underway or completed. Autopsy and medical laboratory results may be obtained and examined; other important documents, such as inventories; financial statements; bills of sale; personnel rosters of employees and those recently discharged; fire department records of previous fires; insurance records; blueprints; law enforcement records of known arsonists in the local and surrounding areas; and records of recent repairs and alterations may also shed some light on the case.

The detective also reviews reports from fire insurance experts. These reports cover the point of origin, damage suffered, classification of the property, and other pertinent facts. The opinions of these experts may be an important aid to a police investigation.

Arson-Related Explosions and the Police Investigation

An explosion is the rapid and violent combustion of a material— solid, liquid or gas—with resultant pressure and heat. Explosions are generally classified as low- or high-order, according to the speed (in feet per second) of the expansion made by combustion. The difference between the two types is important to an investigation because the first type is usually accidental, while the second is usually deliberate or planned.

Low-Order Explosions (Diffused)

An explosion in this category involves a slow expansion over a wide area into a combustion known as deflagration. Most explosives causing this type of explosion have a pushing instead of a shattering effect, and a twisting and tearing type of deformation results.

In a building, walls force outward, making the roof fall into the interior. Objects are scattered in erratic directions in no particular pattern. Other normal characteristics are absence of local shattering and craters combined with a clearly found area of special damage or discoloration. Such explosions result from gas, liquid fuel, solvents, dust and chemicals.

High-Order Explosions (Concentrated)

An explosion in this category is characterized by a rapid combustion, known as detonation reaction, caused by explosives such as dynamite, TNT, nitroglycerin, pentaeythritoltetranitrate (PETN), and various "plastic" explosives.

No atmospheric oxygen is needed since the explosion carries its own oxygen supply in compounds with high oxygen content. An explosion of this nature produces a large volume of gas, expanded by the heat of the reaction. Its origin point forces radiate equally in all directions. Near the center, there will usually be shattered or fragmented materials, including small, high-velocity fragments. Movable objects and debris blow out in a radiating pattern from the center of the explosion. Suction effect or deflection of forces by objects may change this pattern, but identification of the pattern remains possible. X ray films of cadavers burned by the explosion may show foreign objects helpful in police identification of the explosive device used.

Explosive Accessories

Safety Fuses normally have a train of black powder in waterproof casing. The fuse is the medium for carrying a flame to the explosive charge.

Detonating Cord is PETN explosives wrapped in a protective casing that makes them insensitive to shock. Detonating cord and detonating fuses are used to detonate main charge explosives.

Blasting Caps and Detonators are copper or aluminum cases filled with a starting charge and detonating charge. They may be nonelectric or electric. Blasting caps and detonators ignite in one of two ways:

- Ignition by safety fuse. Crimpers used to clamp the detonator to the fuse leave toolmarks on detonator case fragments found at the scene of the explosion.

- Electrical ignition. Detonators are wired to an electrical source. Closing the circuit leads to instantaneous or timed (interval) explosions. Connecting wires usually stay intact after explosion and may leave valuable trace evidence.

Boosters is a term for an explosive charge sometimes used to amplify or boost the shock supplied by detonators or blasting caps to detonate main charge explosives.

Timing Devices are electrical, mechanical or chemical devices used to trigger an explosive charge at a predetermined time.

A Detective's Search for Explosives

Point of origin is based on the patterns resulting from the explosion. In a diffused explosion, the random pattern of energy movement should be apparent. A detective investigating the source of the explosion will look for volatile solvents and like items stored there and for a presence of dust.

When the detective finds no obvious source, he looks for volatile solvents deliberately or accidentally placed. Vapors from such solvents lead to diffused explosions. The detective makes a thorough search for containers and detonating mechanisms in such circumstances.

When evidence shows a concentrated explosion, the detective searches the entire area with care to recover any trace of a detonating mechanism or any other item foreign to the explosion site. His search may reveal the type of explosive as well as yield valuable evidence leading to the perpetrator. All kinds of detonating mechanisms contain metallic materials, and if such a mechanism was used, some traces must remain.

Signs of forcible entry such as toolmarks, broken glass or fibers may be found that will have a significant effect on a solution.

Evidence of Explosive Devices

Homemade bombs and internal devices may leave behind pieces of pipe, parts of tin cans, cloth fragments, tape, wire, fuse sections, batteries, clock mechanisms, parts of detonators, glass particles, parts of boxes or similar fragments. These items might be traced to the person who built the bomb or to the place where it was built. The detective keeps the following points in mind:

- Amounts of explosives may be found undetonated. Sometimes entire blocks of explosives do not explode, and the detective may find them intact at considerable distances from the origin of the explosion.
- Liquid explosives may leave splashes and stains on drapes, curtains, wallpaper, floors or clothing of victims. Traces of wax or paraffin used in bombs improvised from liquids and acids may be found.
- The walls, floors and ceilings of the buildings and the outside walls of nearby buildings may contain some embedded bomb fragments.

Condition of Utilities

Electrical and telephone equipment may serve as a power source for detonating a prepared explosive or may cause an accidental explosion when in contact with an explosive gas or chemical. A police detective examines all fuse boxes and fuses. Any wires added to bypass the fuses, any metal plates, such as coins, placed under fuses or substituted for fuses, and the presence of fuses of rated capacity or type other than that prescribed for the fuse box may show tampering.

Telephones, electric clocks, clock radios and any other type of timed electrical outlet or device that can be preset or whose operation can be predicted (including stoves and coffeepots with timing devices), or any outlet or device that can be set in operation or manipulated from outside the premises or from a safe place within the premises should be examined carefully by an appliance mechanic or a skilled electrician.

The detective gives particular attention to any suspicious device or substance substituted for parts of electrical appliances. For example, a vial of incendiary or explosive material or a fuse or detonator could substitute for the ringing mechanism in a telephone.

Electrical systems of various types of combustion engines may be used as power sources for attached explosive devices or materials. Detectives examine the wiring systems of vehicles and similar equipment near the explosion.

An explosion may result from a faulty gas line or fixture, or from a gas valve carelessly or intentionally left open. Fingerprints or toolmarks may be found on the valve handles or at ruptured places in pipes or fitting.

Stored Fuels, Gases and Chemicals

Since many chemicals and gases can explode, a list should be made of all chemicals and fuels stored on the premises and samples taken of each. Also, fire extinguishers and control systems should be examined to see if they were tampered with or removed to prevent their use in fighting the fire or in neutralizing the explosive.

Crime Laboratory Examination of Explosive Devices and Residue

By analyzing evidence a police detective obtained from the crime scene, laboratory examiners may be able to identify the cause of the explosion and possibly link a suspect with the crime. Laboratory examiners can partly or completely reconstruct a bomb, depending on the evidence police collect and preserve. From the evidence submitted to the laboratory, examiners may be able to determine:

- Type of explosive, detonator, fuse and timing device used and skill needed to prepare the device.
- Kind and characteristics of binding, wrapping and camouflage materials used.
- Postal information contained on a burned or mutilated mailed bomb package.
- Types of materials used in a bomb and the probable manufacturers of the material.

After a police detective identifies suspects, a search of their personal and real property, vehicles, and places of employment may yield items that will lend themselves to comparison with evidence found at the crime scene. Through these comparisons, the laboratory may be able to determine whether:

- Explosives taken from suspects are similar to those used in the crime.
- Tools taken from the suspect made the marks found at the crime scene.
- Wood and metal fragments, nails or screws recovered from the scene are identical with similar materials seized from the suspect.
- Wire, tape or twine found at the crime scene was cut from a roll or piece of like material seized from the suspect. If the instrument that was used in cutting is found, the identification may be more positive.

The detective looks for traces of explosives, acids or chemicals from the bomb; dust, mud or grime from the crime scene; wood splinters or metal dust from the bomb; and blood, skin or hairs from the victim in the following places:

- Fingernail scraping or earwax of the suspect.
- Clothing of the suspect.
- Trash and dust from the suspect's vehicle.
- Dust taken from work benches or tools that belong to the suspect.

The detective also tries to find:

- Handwriting or typewriter exemplars from the suspect that match writing on the covering of a bomb package.

- The perforated tear lines on stamps from a mailed bomb package that match those on stamps in the possession of the suspect.
- Shoes of the suspect that match casts of footprints taken from the crime scene.
- Tires on the suspect's vehicle that match casts of tire tracks found at the crime scene.

HOMICIDE AND VICE

Police detectives spend a lot of their time in two more areas of crime: homicide and vice. Likewise, crime writers spend a lot of time writing about these areas. Both areas are complex, involving a variety of investigative factors, but the focus in this chapter will be on how detectives investigate and solve these crimes. I have intentionally avoided discussion of specific drugs and guns since these are covered extensively in two other books in the Howdunit series: *Deadly Doses* by Serita Stevens and Anne Klarner and *Armed and Dangerous* by Michael Newton. The Howdunit series also offers two books that explore homicide investigation: *Cause of Death* by Keith Wilson and *Scene of the Crime* by Anne Wingate. To avoid extensive overlap with these books, I have kept discussion of those topics to a minimum.

The Vice Detective

During their careers, many police detectives are assigned to enforce drug and narcotic laws. This assignment requires a creative detective and often calls for convincing role playing. An effort to identify, arrest and convict the major supplier of drugs is the police detective's primary goal. The connection from the separate street abusers to the head of a drug supply ring smuggling drugs into the country, manufacturing synthetic drugs, selling prescription drugs and other illicit trafficking is long and disguised. To make effective arrests, detectives must act temporarily as drug suppliers and buyers.

Having worked a few years in the drug investigation and enforcement areas, I will supply the writer with an authentic checklist that we used regularly, both to train our task force members and also during operations or on the street to ensure that procedures and arrests remained uniform and would lead to convictions. Keep in mind that drug abusers are very low on the enforcement priority list. However, the information abusers provide a detective may lead to drug suppliers. Detectives who work in the area of vice assignments know that:

- One means of tracing illicit drug sources involves determining supply outlets. Many techniques are available to the police detective, such as a thorough review of completed reports of past drug investigations, undercover investigations, information informants, surveillance and direct effort to buy drugs.

- In direct buy methods, it's desirable to make more than one buy from a peddler if possible. That procedure gives law enforcement officers and investigators an opportunity to find the peddler's cache of drugs, including his source of supply. It also serves to identify other customers and helps establish that a peddler is a regular participant in the illegal drug/narcotics traffic and not a one-time or opportune offender. As sources of supply and customers of a peddler become known, the possibility of formulating a conspiracy involving other persons increases.

Direct Purchase Guidelines

- It's desirable to make more than one purchase of drugs from a supplier.
- If an arrest will happen immediately after a buy, it may be desirable to dust the currency used with fluorescent powder.
- The series and serial numbers of currency used to purchase drugs should always be recorded for later comparison with any

money recovered from the defendants. (It is important to include the series number, since each series repeats the numbers. A clever defense lawyer can use the lack of a series number coupled with a serial number to create doubt about the validity of currency alleged to have been used during a buy. Even when a jury convicts, the appeal may reverse a lower court decision on a minor, but important deficiency.)

- The currency may reveal an unsuspected link between known and unknown narcotics traffickers and show a conspiracy.
- Recovered money that has been used for the purchase of drugs becomes evidence.

Informant Purchase Guidelines

- If a peddler will sell only to an informant and not to an undercover law enforcement officer or agent, the informant must be strip-searched before the controlled buy to ensure he has no other money or drugs in his possession. Soon after the purchase of drugs, a second search assures his integrity.
- The detective must be able to testify in court that the informant had only the money supplied by his department in his possession and that he had no drugs.
- It's prudent to list all the personal items allowed to stay in an informant's possession; for example, brown wallet containing (list contents), a bone-handled pocket knife, purse containing (list contents), etc. Keep the possessions at a minimum, only enough to make him appear to be a normal person who would have various personal items.
- Any money in the informant's possession when the detective conducts a search as well as excessive personal items should be placed in a box, sealed, and kept safely at the department or place where the informant is released to make the buy.
- Between the two searches (before and after the buy), the detective must keep the informant under constant surveillance so his testimony can be corroborated.
- Police detectives should always maintain the tightest possible surveillance of the informant during the buying process. If possible, when the buy happens in a bar or other place of business, place undercover officers inside as customers to observe and

sometimes provide protective cover should the trafficker discover an informant works for the police.

- If inside observation isn't possible, maintain surveillance outside at entrances and exits. Detectives can testify that throughout the controlled buy, the informant was in their visual contact except for the period he was inside a specific place and again under police surveillance upon leaving.
- When a buy is in progress, detectives use opportunities to photograph the illegal sale.
- Evidence obtained through informant buys, when handled carefully as noted above, is admissible in court but normally calls for the testimony of the informant.

Arresting Drug Violators Guidelines

- The arrest of a drug violator is best done as unobtrusively as possible to prevent the knowledge of her arrest from reaching her collaborators.
- Often, a detective's investigation may benefit from the discreet arrest of the violator.
- The detective must apprise the suspect of her rights (Miranda) promptly after the arrest.

Approaching a Drug Suspect to Make an Arrest.

- When approaching a drug suspect, a detective has to observe the suspect's hands.
- The user may try to get rid of drugs in his or her possession by dropping, throwing, flushing, eating or otherwise destroying the contraband.
- When a police detective finds drugs on the ground at some distance from the suspect, it may be difficult if not impossible to connect the drug with the suspect.
- Addicts can be dangerous, unpredictable and uncooperative. Detectives must be alert to the suspect's being armed. Quickly after arrest, the detective makes the suspect place his hands in the air or behind his head to prevent further disposal of evidence.
- A detective always needs to ensure that drugs taken from a person suspected of being in illegal possession aren't pre-

scribed for the suspect's health and well-being.

- If the suspect claims seized drugs are for health and welfare, the detective must obtain a physician's opinion and verification promptly.

- The mere possession of a prescription for a drug shouldn't be justification for stopping a police investigation, because it could be forged by the suspect or purchased from a backstreet forger.

Searching a Suspect.

- After arrest, the police make thorough strip-search of the suspect and examine her clothing and the area within her immediate control immediately after arrest.

- The detective records names, addresses, telephone numbers, and other pertinent information from notes or lists the suspect has in her possession (that information may be of value in identifying dealers or persons who buy from dealers).

- Small packages of illegal drugs normally dispensed are often concealed in very small spaces.

- Possession of even the minutest of particles may be enough for a conviction, especially coupled with other evidence.

- Detectives must remain alert to the presence of all tablets, capsules, small pieces of paper and liquids as well as the more conspicuous types of equipment such as syringes, needles, medicine droppers, and bent and discolored spoons.

- When police find it necessary to arrest a drug violator in a building, they try to position themselves between the suspect and the bathroom or any sink.

- Toilets, drains, sinks, basins, bathtubs and showers are favorite hiding places for drugs and narcotics since they offer a quick and easy destruction capability.

- Another favorite method of operation is to hang drugs out a window by a string held in place by the closed window. Merely opening the window releases the cache and permits it to fall to the ground. Unless a police officer observes the drugs falling from a window, the possibility of connecting the suspect to the cache is remote.

- Detectives also check religious artifacts thoroughly during a search for hidden drugs. Religious artifacts often provide hiding places for drugs in a hope that searching officers will overlook them.

- The variety of hiding places for drugs and narcotics is limited only by the ingenuity of the offender.

Quick Guide for Police Officers Arresting Drug Offenders

1. Be unobtrusive.
2. Watch the suspect's hands as you approach.
3. Watch for a weapon.
4. Search suspect immediately.
5. Check justification for drugs.

Quick Reference for Police Officers on Hiding Places for Drugs and Narcotics

- Hatband
- Coat lining
- Sleeves
- Pens
- Lighters
- Boots
- Seams
- Shoes
- Cigarettes
- Cuffs
- Waistband
- Chewing gum
- False heels
- Tobacco
- Pants
- Pipes
- Pencils
- Hair
- Body
- Neckties
- Belts

Processing Drug Evidence.

- A detective processes drug evidence in the same way as other evidentiary material.
- Detectives remain attentive to ensure that none of the substance is in contact with a skin opening or inhaled.
- Detectives must meticulously maintain the legal chain of custody, which is important for introducing drugs as evidence in court.

- Good police procedure includes limiting the number of police authorities taking possession of drug evidence.

- Often, detectives find drug evidence in minute quantities and in small containers.

- Detectives place drug evidence items in suitable protective containers quickly, then mark containers with their initials, date and time they obtained the evidence.

- Marijuana cigarettes can be marked on the cigarette paper.

- Without chemical analysis by a competent chemist, pills, capsules, powders and vegetable matter can't be legally identified.

- Whenever a detective writes in his reports about substances suspected of being illegal drugs or narcotics, he uses physical descriptions of their appearance, such as "a white crystalline powder suspected of being codeine" or "a vegetable matter suspected of being marijuana."

- The detective writing a report avoids exact weight statements and instead describes the amount as "about one cup of vegetable matter," "about one quarter teaspoon of powder," or "twenty-four tablets (or capsules)." This keeps a defense attorney from getting the court or the jury mired in how the detective could be so precise, the detective's qualifications, and equipment available to make precision measurements. Surprisingly, a clever attorney can seize on opportunities like this to confuse a jury and often make them doubt the arresting officer's accuracy. However, avoiding that precision leaves the defense without an issue to attack.

- Drugs and drug evidence should be stored in a safe or security container inside the evidence room for proper security.

- Detectives must ensure that seized drugs are always secured and not taken from the evidence room except for controlled transfer to a laboratory for analysis and as called for in legal proceedings.

A Writer's Police Procedural Guide

- Field tests are preliminary and only indicate that a drug may be present.

- Crime laboratory examinations are precise, expert and usually positive proof of drug existence.

- When suspected drugs are shipped to a crime laboratory for analysis, police exercise care that the packaging container is completely sealed and packed to avoid spillage or breaking in transit.

- Police detectives pack tablets and capsules in sterile cotton and place in a suitable container.

- Detectives always send shipments of any kind to a crime laboratory by registered mail, return receipt requested, and include a chain-of-custody copy for the laboratory receipt and for when it's returned to the submitting detective or the police department.

The Police Guide to Making Drug Field Tests

When detectives have a suspect, a field test often will be conducted while the person is detained at the scene instead of making an arrest. The officer needs probable cause to detain a suspect and conduct a field test and that requires seeing something that, based on training and experience, makes her believe the suspect has possession of illegal drugs. If the field test is positive, the officer then has probable cause to arrest the person. The field test, however, will not in itself stand as evidence in court; only a crime laboratory analysis can do that. Instead, the field test is used primarily to serve the probable cause rule of law. Detectives using the field test techniques must always remember that the tests are not infallible and generally follow the guidelines shown below.

- The field test kit is extremely reliable on negative tests showing no drug present.

- The reliability of positive tests varies between the different tests, and this changes occasionally due to added cutting agents that interfere with the tests.

- The detective should also refer to the *Physician's Desk Reference* in the police department library. (*Physician's Desk Reference* is published by Medical Economics Company, Inc., Oradell, New Jersey, and is updated yearly.)

- Any drug used as evidence must be identified by a qualified chemist. He must use approved procedures in an adequately equipped laboratory to make the identification.

- When the quantity of a suspected material is minute, detectives must forgo field tests, making the arrest based on training and experience. The small quantity of material excuses the failure to conduct a field test and its use as probable cause for the arrest.
- Often, the color reactions produced by field tests only indicate that the suspected sample is a drug product.
- Many noncontrolled substances give color reactions similar to those given by controlled substances.
- Many controlled drugs yield no color reactions or yield color reactions other than those that are usually described by field test kits.
- Testing of a suspected material through sampling should never be permitted because the material may be a poison. (Leave the taste test to TV actors pretending to be law enforcement officers.)

A Writer's Quick Reference Checklist

Police Obtaining Information.

- Have police exploited available information to obtain leads (through researching reports, and by using informants and surveillance)?
- Have police coordinated with other law enforcement agencies and departments to obtain and disseminate drug information?

Arrest.

- Did police arrest a drug abuser or peddler because of a direct buy, or have a person under police control make more than one buy?
- Did police record the series and serial numbers of the money used for the buy?
- Did police use fluorescent powder on the "buy" money?
- When police used an informant, did they search him or her before and after the drug buy?
- Did the informant under police control use only money supplied by the police department for the drug buy?
- Did police maintain constant surveillance?

- Did police photograph the informant buying the illegal drugs from a drug peddler?
- Did police make the drug arrest as unobtrusively as possible?
- Did police inform the suspect about his or her legal rights?

Search.

- Did police always observe the suspect closely?
- Did the suspect dispose of any drugs before police arrested him or her?
- Did police make a thorough search of the suspect's person, clothing and immediate area of control?
- Did police check the suspect's fingernails for possible trace evidence?

Search of a Room or Building.

- Did police take photographs?
- Did police do floor sweepings?
- Did police check paraphernalia for fingerprints?

After a Raid.

- Did police designate one officer or investigator to assume responsibility for all evidence collection procedures and accountability?

Processing Evidence.

- Have police maintained an exact chain of custody?
- Did police make field tests on suspected illicit drugs?
- Did police send suspected drugs to the crime laboratory for analysis?
- Did police package the evidence properly to avoid breakage, spilling or contamination?
- Did police confirm the seized drugs are secured properly?

The Homicide Detective

A good mystery is seldom complete without at least one murder. Since all murders must involve the police, I have provided an overview of police techniques and procedures for investigating deaths. I've included those that I have used to investigate dozens of homicides and other deaths and also used as a framework for teaching hundreds of police officers and detectives across the country.

Responsibilities of the Coroner in a Death Investigation

The coroner's office is responsible for determining the cause of death. A medicolegal autopsy is authorized or ordered by the coroner's office in cases of accidental, suicidal, homicidal, unattended or unexpected death, not only to determine the cause and manner of death, but also to protect society and ensure administration of justice. Sometimes the autopsy may not reveal the cause of death, and microscopic, toxicologic, and other special laboratory studies are called for. In a small percentage of cases, the cause of death is undetermined.

Responsibilities of the Police Detective in a Death Investigation

The police detective always maintains a liaison with the coroner's office or pathologist who performs the autopsy. The investigator needs to inform the pathologist of the circumstances of death and preliminary investigative findings before the autopsy. Knowledge of the circumstances of death enables the pathologist not only to choose proper procedures for determining the cause of death but also to offer an opinion about the manner of death.

How the Police Detective Proceeds With a Death Investigation

This investigative checklist addresses the investigation of deaths under other than natural circumstances. The determination of whether a death is homicide (murder), suicide or accidental may be a difficult problem a police detective will face only occasionally in her law enforcement career. This type of investigation calls for seasoned skill, training and experience, plus supporting technical knowledge from crime laboratories, as well as the cooperation of medical doctors and forensic pathologists. This checklist is lengthy and invaluable to all levels of the investigation from discovery to conclusion, from the patrol officer responding to a death scene to detectives and prosecutors alike.

As we proceed into this complex subject, remember that a good detective follows two important rules. First: Despite how the death of a person appears, always treat it as murder. When following that rule, the detective's investigation will always be complete. The second rule: Do not make assumptions or let appearances draw the conclusion. Instead, information must decide. A successful death investigation always begins with a detective having a clear understanding of the types of deaths, including the legal definitions and landmark court decisions (case law) associated with the subject. The following checklist supplies the writer with a quick guide to that authenticity.

Homicide

Homicide is the unlawful killing of one human being by another. The killing of a human being is unlawful when done without justification or legal excuse. Homicide is not necessarily a crime. It is a necessary ingredient of the crime of murder or manslaughter, but in other cases homicide may happen without criminal intent and without criminal consequences, such as in the lawful execution of a judicial sentence, in self-defense, or as the only possible means of arresting an escaping felon. The term "homicide" is neutral; while it describes the act, it pronounces no judgment on its morality or legality. (People v. Connors, 13 Miss. 582, 35 N.Y.S. 472)

Homicide is ordinarily classified as "justifiable," "excusable," and "felonious." Examples are:

Murder. The unlawful killing of a human being by another with malice aforethought, either express or implied. (State v. Hutter, 145 Neb. 798, 18 N.W. 2d 203, 206). Murder is the unlawful killing of a human being or fetus, with malice aforethought. (Cal. Penal Code, §187). The crime is defined by statute in most states. The Model Penal Code definition is as follows:

Criminal Homicide is murder when: (1) it is committed purposely or knowingly; or (2) it is committed recklessly under circumstances manifesting extreme indifference to the value of human life. Such recklessness and indifference are presumed when the actor engages or is an accomplice in the commission of, or an attempt to commit, or flight after committing or attempting to commit robbery, rape or deviate sexual intercourse by force or threat of force, arson, burglary, kidnapping or felonious escape. (Model Penal Code §210.2)

Degrees of Murder. In most states murder is divided into two degrees, for awarding a more severe penalty for some murders than for others. All murders perpetrated through poison, or by lying in wait, or by any other type of willful, deliberate and premeditated killing, or which are committed in the perpetration of, or attempt to perpetrate any arson, rape, robbery or burglary, are commonly deemed murder of the first degree, and other kinds of murder are deemed murder of the second degree. This general pattern applies to the crime in most states, although some have slight variations. Some state statutes, for example, have omitted any reference to "poison" while a few have added "torture" to "poison." To the felony murder clause of the statute several have added "mayhem" and included other felonies, such as kidnapping, sodomy or larceny. In certain states there is also the crime of murder in the third degree.

Felony Murder Doctrine. In common law, one whose conduct effected an unintended death in the commission or attempted commission of a felony was guilty of murder. While some states still follow the common law rule, today the law of felony murder varies largely throughout the country, largely because of efforts to limit the scope of the rule. Jurisdictions have limited the rule in any of the following ways: (1) by permitting its use only regarding certain types of felonies; (2) by stricter interpretation of the requirement of proximate or legal cause; (3) by a narrow construction of the time period when the felony is in commission; (4) by requiring that the underlying felony be independent of the homicide.

Culpable Homicide. Described as a crime varying from the lowest culpability to the very verge of murder.

Excusable Homicide. The killing of a human being, either by misadventure or in self-defense. "Excusable homicide" describes a perpetrator's manner of action the law does not prohibit, such as self-defense or accidental homicide. (Law v. State, 21 Md. App. 13, 318 A. 2d 859, 869). The name itself (homicide) imports some fault, error or omission, however being excusable, the law removes it from guilt of felony. This homicide occurs in two general ways—either per infortunium, by misadventure, or se defendendo, upon a sudden affray. Homicide per infortunium is where a person doing a lawful act, without any intention of hurt, unfortunately kills another; but if death follows from an unlawful act, the offense is manslaughter and not misadventure. Homicide se defendendo is where a person kills another upon a sudden affray, merely in his own defense, or in defense of his wife, child, parent or servant and not from vindictive feeling (that is, in self-defense).

Felonious Homicide. The wrongful killing of a human being of any age or either sex, without justification or excuse in law, of which offense there are two degrees, manslaughter and murder.

Homicide by Misadventure. The accidental killing of another person, where the slayer is doing a lawful act, unaccompanied by any criminally careless or reckless conduct. This is the same as homicide per infortunium.

Homicide by Necessity. A species of justifiable homicide, because it arises from some unavoidable necessity, without any will, intention or desire and without any inadvertence or negligence in the party killing, and therefore, without any shadow of blame (self-defense).

Homicide per Infortunium. Homicide by misfortune or accidental homicide, as where a person doing a lawful act without any intention of hurt accidentally kills another; a species of excusable homicide.

Homicide se Defendendo. Homicide in self-defense; the killing of a person in self-defense upon a sudden affray, where the slayer had no other possible (or at least, probable) means of escaping from his assailant; a species of excusable homicide.

Justifiable Homicide. Homicide committed intentionally but without any evil design, and under such circumstances of necessity or duty as to make the act proper and relieve the party from shadow of blame; as where a sheriff lawfully executes a sentence of death upon a malefactor, or where the killing happens in the endeavor to prevent the commission of felony which could not be otherwise avoided, or as a matter of right, such as in self-defense or other causes provided for by statute.

Negligent Homicide. Criminal homicide results from a death happening because of actions clearly negligent when conditions and circumstances show no prudent reason for the commission or omission creating the negligent act. (Model Penal Code §210.4)

Reckless Homicide. A species of statutory homicide in some states characterized by a willful and wanton disregard of consequences and resulting in death. In some states, it may amount to manslaughter.

Vehicular Homicide. Vehicular homicide is the killing of a human being by the operation of an automobile, airplane, motorboat or other motor vehicle in a way that creates an unreasonable risk of injury to the person or property of another and is a material deviation from the standard of care which a reasonable person would observe under the same circumstances.

Suicide. The taking of one's own life, ironically illegal. When a person dies who is subject to or within a specific area of jurisdiction, an investigation is normally conducted to determine if a criminal act was associated with the cause of death. An exception to that action happens when a person dies from natural causes with a doctor in attendance or in a hospital.

Accidental Deaths. This category often happens under circumstances that appear suspicious. The police detective may be called to investigate the way these deaths happened. They deserve as much diligent investigation as would an obvious homicide or suicide.

Manslaughter. The unlawful killing of another without malice, either express or implied. Such may be either voluntarily, upon a sudden heat, or involuntarily, but in the commission of some unlawful act. The unlawful killing of a human without any deliberation, which may be involuntary, in the commission of a lawful act without due caution and circumspection. (Wallace v. U.S. 466, 16 S.Ct. 859, 40 L.Ed. 1039)

- The unlawful killing of a human without malice and without premeditation and deliberation. (State v. Wingler, 238 N.C. 485, 78 S.E. 2d 303, 307)

- It is of two kinds: *voluntary* — upon a sudden quarrel or heat of passion — and *involuntary* — in the commission of a lawful act in an unlawful manner, or without due caution and circumspection, which might produce death. (18 U.S.C.A. §1112)

- Criminal homicide is manslaughter when (a) it is committed recklessly, or (b) a homicide that would otherwise be murder is committed under the influence of extreme mental or emotional disturbance for which there is reasonable explanation or excuse. The reasonableness of explanation or excuse stems from the viewpoint of a person in the actor's situation in the circumstances as he believes them to be. (Model Penal Code, §210.3)

- The heat of passion, which will reduce a murder to manslaughter, must be such passion as would be aroused naturally in the mind of the ordinary reasonable person under the same or like circumstances, shown by the evidence of the case. Various degrees of manslaughter are recognized by different states. For example:

Involuntary Manslaughter. Such exists where a person in committing an unlawful act not felonious or tending to great bodily harm, or in committing a lawful act without proper caution or needed skill, unguardedly or undesignedly kills another. (Model Penal Code §210.3[1][a])

Voluntary Manslaughter. Manslaughter committed voluntarily upon a sudden heat of the passions; as it would if, upon a sudden quarrel, two persons fight, and one of them kills the other. (Model Penal Code §210.3[1][b]). It is the unlawful taking of human life under circumstances falling less than willful or deliberate intent to kill and approaching too near thereto to be justifiable homicide.

The absence of intention to kill or to commit any unlawful act that might produce death or great bodily harm is the distinguishing feature between voluntary and involuntary homicide.

Death Involving Firearms

Most writers have their victims fall from gunshot or more exotic means, such as poison. In this first summary, I will discuss death by firearms to supply you with the most common type of murder in stories and real life. Also you should refer to *Deadly Doses* (on poisons) and *Armed and Dangerous* (on a spectrum of guns), two excellent books in the Writer's Digest Books Howdunit Series, for specifics in those areas.

Gunshot wounds account for the majority of successful homicides, and guns are also the most prevalent weapons used for suicide. These deaths, like other forms of homicide and suicide, are often not witnessed. Additionally, death due to accidental discharge of a weapon is common. Unlike some other forms of violent or unnatural death, firearm fatalities frequently are attended by important trace evidence of the weapon left in or on the victim's body. This trace evidence lends itself to scientific comparison with suspect weapons and frequently demonstrates many of the circumstances surrounding the death.

- In the medical-legal investigation of fatal injury by firearms, scientific evidence is particularly important, and solution of the crime or differentiation between homicide, suicide or accident often hinges on the gathering and evaluating of the scientific evidence. This evidence is collected and evaluated by a detective's investigation, coupled with investigations conducted by the pathologist and laboratory technicians.

- Some more important investigative objectives that may be deduced or confirmed by attentive evaluation of the scientific evidence are: identification of the weapon and ammunition and their characteristics; relative position of the weapon and victim; and the cause and manner of death.
- Evidence in firearm deaths may include wounds, empty cartridge cases, spent bullets, and powder residues on the clothing and body of the victim. The basic items of evidence or information revealed from the above sources include: make, model and characteristics of the weapon and ammunition; direction, angle and range of fire; number of shots; and possibly even the time the shooting happened.

Firearm Investigative Terms. The detective should use terminology in describing gunshot wounds that has meaning for both investigators and pathologists.

- **Contusing.** Causing a bruise
- **Glancing.** Striking the body without making any visible injury.
- **Penetrating.** Entering the body or an organ with no exit wound.
- **Perforating.** A shot passing completely through with both an entrance and exit wound.
- **Superficial perforating.** A lacerating type of wound. This type of wound is often mistaken for a cutting wound made with a knife or similar instrument.
- **Pseudo perforating.** A wound when the bullet stays in the body with an exit wound caused by a bone fragment.
- **Secondary missiles.** Environmental or body components struck by a bullet and becoming missiles themselves. Equipment, wood from bunkers or trees, stones and bone fragments may become secondary missiles. X ray equipment often shows the location of a bullet in a body when no exit wound is discernible. Stab wounds have been mistaken for bullet wounds.

Recognition of powder marks and residues is an important factor in early differentiation of entrance and exit wounds.

- The pattern and composition are useful in deducing the range of fire and the type of ammunition used.
- Accurate range of fire tests can be conducted by laboratory test-firing the same weapon and ammunition at test targets.

- Types of powder residues can also be differentiated by chemical, photographic, radiographic and spectrographic lab tests.

Characteristics of Shootings. As in medical-legal death investigations, a police detective's basic objective is determining if the wounds happened because of homicide, suicide or accident.

Location and Character of the Wound(s).

- A detective should, in cooperation with a pathologist, determine whether the victim could, considering the location and character of entrance wounds and bullet tracks, conceivably have inflicted the wounds on him or herself.

    Unless there's a special contrivance arrangement, self-inflicted gunshot wounds require that the gun have been held within twenty-four inches of the body.

- Suicide wounds are characteristically single, close-range or contact wounds involving a part of the body easily reached.

- Often, the suicide uncovers the part of the body being attacked, such as drawing a shirt aside before placing the muzzle of a gun against the chest.

- The temple, mouth and chest over the heart are the most commonly selected sites for suicidal attacks with a firearm.

- Most suicides with a firearm happen with a gun placed to the head slightly in front of and above the ear.

- Occasionally, a suicide will shoot himself or herself more than once before being incapacitated or killed.

- When using a rifle or shotgun for suicide, the person usually chooses the chest and abdomen as the target.

- Rifles and shotguns are normally discharged by using a stick or string hooked around the trigger guard or by pushing the trigger with a toe or other contrivances.

Origin of the Weapon.

- Circumstances, such as the victim being on a hunting trip or cleaning, loading, or otherwise working on the weapon may show a logical reason for the weapon's presence and the potential for accident.

- Evidence the victim was handling the weapon unsafely, demonstrating how another person committed suicide, or playing "quick-draw" may show the accidental nature of the shooting.

- Evidence may indicate the person acquired the weapon for no other apparent reason than suicide.

- The absence of a weapon suggests that the shooting was homicidal. However, a suicide victim may live long enough to dispose of the weapon or may arrange contrivances to cause the weapon to disappear after being discharged.

- One way of making a weapon disappear after suicide is to rig a strong elastic band to pull the weapon into a concealed place.

- Other persons with an interest in life insurance claims or fearful of disgrace may tamper with evidence to conceal the suicidal intent and circumstances.

- A murderer may try to conceal homicide by manufacturing circumstances suggestive of suicide or accident.

Condition of the Weapon.

- Evidence that a weapon is defective, that it had no safety or a defective safety device, or that it could be discharged by dropping it, suggests accidental circumstances.

- Evidence may show that the trigger caught into something, discharging it accidentally.

- A weapon in excellent operating condition, needing normal force to pull the trigger, with effective safety devices, etc., may disfavor accidental shooting.

- Presence of contrivances designed to pull the trigger, such as strings or removal of a shoe, are strong indications of suicide.

Multiple Gunshot Fatalities.

These happen less often than homicides and suicides, and are often witnessed or reported by the person who discharged the weapon.

- Accidental gunshot victims usually become shot because of careless handling of a weapon or because of ignorance about the operation of the weapon.

- Sometimes accidental gunshot deaths occur when persons are "quick-drawing" with supposedly empty weapons or pointing weapons at others as a prank.

- Accidents also happen while hunting, or while cleaning or loading and unloading weapons.

- In some instances, particularly with old or defective weapons, the gun may discharge accidentally when dropped on the floor.

- Children and young people often become involved in gunshot accidents while playing with firearms.

- Accidental gunshot fatalities when not witnessed may closely resemble suicide. Usually, however, the known attitude and life-style of the victim plus the lack of apparent motive for suicide present strong indications of the accidental nature of the incident.

Techniques for Death Investigations

At the Scene

- Detectives should make every reasonable effort to arrive at the scene of a reported homicide, fatal accident or suicide before the scene has been disturbed.

- Upon notification of a death and arrival at the scene, the detective should record: (a) time of police arrival, (b) the exact address, (c) temperature, and (d) weather conditions. This information will be of value throughout the investigation and in any future legal proceedings. When detectives lack positive information, their future testimony may be vague and reduce the true value of the remainder of their testimony.

At a scene at which the victim remains, a detective should follow these procedures:

- Immediately upon arrival, examine the victim for indications of life, in cases where no medical doctor is present.

- If victim is dying or in critical condition, try to obtain a statement and make notes of any circumstances that might permit the statement to qualify for admissibility in evidence as a dying declaration.

- Determine the identity of the person who discovered the incident or scene and the identity of the person who made the first official report.

- Photograph the victim and entire scene.

Author's Note: It is usual to investigate an alleged homicide or other death scene after the body has been removed and the scene has returned to its normal use or activity. Sometimes, the body might have been interred. In an investigation of this type, aside from reconstructing the scene, closely examine records of any previous investigations of the death to create and explore investigative leads. It may be necessary to have the body exhumed for an examination by pathologists.

Many problems emerge from curious onlookers at the scene. They may destroy evidence, such as latent fingerprints, or may deposit materials that are mistaken for evidence. It is a police responsibility to ensure the crime scene is not contaminated. To ensure this, persons not directly involved should be evicted from the scene, but detectives need to learn the names of these persons and when they arrived before their departure.

Police never release the scene of a death until certain it's no longer needed to develop leads. Premature release of the scene will destroy evidence and prevent any follow-up investigation that may be necessary. The same guidelines dictate when to release the body.

Identification of the Deceased

Detectives do not place complete reliance on a visual identification of the victim nor on written identification and personal articles found on the deceased.

The following methods assist in positive identification of the victim (listed in the order of reliability):

- Fingerprints are the most positive means of identification if the deceased has known fingerprints on file.
- Dental charts.
- Medical records that show injuries or operations, such as broken bones, surgical repairs or removal of parts of the body.
- Records of tattoos and scars.
- Clothing. Articles may call for laboratory examination and extensive tracing of chronological possession. Of particular importance are the (a) size, type and condition of the clothing; (b) laundry and dry cleaning marks; and (c) foreign substances sticking to the clothing.
- Identifying tags and documents. Metal tags or bracelets, identification cards and other documents may help the police identification effort. If a document appears to have been tampered with or if it has been mutilated or burned, it should go to a crime laboratory for examination or restoration.

- Metal articles. Although metal articles such as pocket knives, watches, rings, cigarette lighters and belt buckles may be separated from the victim or mixed with like objects from other victims, they are seldom consumed by fire or destroyed by an explosion. Unless detectives record the exact locations of these articles, their value for identification purposes is reduced.

Motive and Opportunity

If the perpetrator of a homicide remains unknown or a suspect denies involvement in the incident, it's of prime importance to:

- Establish a motive (although not a legal necessity).
- Identify any persons who had an opportunity to commit the offense.

Author's Note: These two factors are of equal value. The choice of which one to consider first depends on the circumstances of each incident the police are investigating.

- If detectives find a person had an apparent motive, it should be determined if he had the opportunity to commit the offense.
- Conversely, if a person appears to have had an opportunity to commit the offense, it should be determined if he had a motive.

The facts surrounding motive and opportunity usually develop through questioning. Here are some suggestions. Detectives should:

- Question witnesses about what they observed, giving particular attention to unusual incidents that may indicate a motive.
- Question acquaintances and relatives of the victim to develop the identity of each person who may have had a motive or opportunity.

Author's Note: Homicide is often a crime of passion committed by a person who is well known by or related to the victim. Detectives should:

- Question associates of the suspect to determine their knowledge of her relationship with the victim.
- Question the suspect about her relationship with the victim and her whereabouts and activities before, during and after the incident.
- Conduct surveillance, undercover or an intensive investigation to develop leads that may establish motive.

- Investigate excuses having a bearing on opportunity for corroborative support.

Estimating Time of Death

- Depending on the circumstances, a pathologist can often provide an opinion about the time of death. It is desirable for the pathologist to take part in the investigation at the scene to note: (a) condition of the body, (b) postmortem changes, (c) environmental conditions, and (d) circumstances of death.

- When certain control factors, such as climatic conditions and time of exposure to the elements are known, the pathologist may give a broad estimate of the time elapsed since death based on: (a) rigor mortis, (b) livor mortis, (c) loss of body temperature, and (d) state of putrefaction of the remains.

- Changes in brain, rectal and liver temperature help to estimate the time of death, but none of these methods are reliable in every case.

- An examination of the stomach contents may also be of value. Remember, however, that the estimation must remain broad; the benefit to the detective's investigation will most likely be negligible.

Autopsy

A pathologist determines the cause of death. A detective should always develop a rapport with the pathologist and usually arrange to attend the autopsy. A police detective's presence at the autopsy as a close observer provides her the opportunity to:

- Discuss all known facts and any special considerations or information needed.

- Ask and answer questions.

- Receive evidence or specimens recovered from the victim.

- Discuss with the pathologist any findings that might seem inconsistent with the known facts before the body is released from medical control.

Questions to which an investigator should obtain answers, if possible, when investigating deaths resulting from violence include:

- Time of death?

- Cause of death and which wound was fatal?

- Type of weapon or substance used and manner of use?
- Interval between wounds received and death? (Was the victim capable of movement?)
- Drug or alcoholic content in the blood?
- Evidence of sexual assault, pregnancy, venereal disease?
- Opinions about manner of death?

Suicide

The techniques of investigating suicide and homicide are the same. As noted earlier, a suicide should always be investigated as a homicide despite appearances. In both instances, it is important that motive be established. Opportunity should be considered where any indication exists that an apparent or alleged suicide may actually be a homicide.

Police detectives must consider the following factors when they are investigating a death that appears or is alleged to be a suicide:

- A person seldom commits suicide in the nude.
- A suicide victim usually opens his clothing when attacking parts of the body.
- In a suicide, a person seldom if ever shoots himself in the eye.
- Males are more prone to use weapons or violent means. Females are more prone to use poisons.
- Persons who commit suicide by cutting and stabbing usually leave hesitation marks. These are slight cuts or scratches the person makes with the suicide instrument before he gains the resolve to make the fatal cut or stab.
- Whether the suicide victim is right- or left-handed (of importance in shooting and stabbing, but remember that a right-handed person can shoot himself with his left hand and vice versa).
- A person usually jumps feet first to his death.
- Seldom will more than one deep wound be inflicted when an instrument such as a cleaver, machete, hatchet, axe, knife or ice pick is used to commit suicide, although it is possible for there to be more than one.

Does the police investigation reveal:

- Previous suicidal attempts or tendencies?

- Financial difficulties?
- Psychiatric problems?
- Unwise or indiscreet emotional involvement with a member of the opposite sex?
- Domestic troubles?
- Homosexual activity?
- General depression caused by family problems? Ill health? Psychiatric problems? Domestic troubles? Pain? Revenge? Other serious problem? Divorce?
- Escape from an intolerable situation?
- Loss of love, self-esteem, purpose, position and usefulness?
- Alcoholism or narcotics addiction?
- Fear of compromise and punishment?

Death by vehicle should not be overlooked in relation to suicide. Some considerations are:

- Are the wounds incurred compatible with the position? With damage? With interior protrusions of the vehicle?
- Do wounds indicate death before the time of the collision?
- Were the lights on at the time of the collision?
- What is the personal history of the victim?
- Are there letters to next of kin?
- Were there social problems? Marital Problems?
- Is there another motive for suicide?

The following points may help ensure a police investigation has considered all necessary aspects in any type of death:

Initial (Notes).

- Time notified and by whom?
- Time of arrival at the scene?
- Time first law enforcement officers at the scene? Who?
- Temperature, humidity and weather conditions at the scene?
- Who found the victim and the exact time and place?

Scene.

Indoors ☐ Outdoors ☐ Both ☐
- Properly protected

- Diagram — interior/exterior
- Black-and-white photographs
- Street plan (if applicable)
- Color photographs
- Latent fingerprints
- Other latent marks
- Aerial photographs
- Measurements taken
- Artifacts noted
- Casts and molds taken
- Evidence Collected:
    Weapons
    Fibers
    Blood
    Soil samples
    Hairs
    Toolmarks
    Scene vacuumed
    Stain samples

Victim's Body.
- Note position
- Cloudy cornea and/or pupil
- Presence or absence of rigor mortis in following muscles:
    Jaws
    Neck and fingers
    Wrists
    Elbows
    Shoulders and knees
    Hips
    Abdomen
- Mucous membrane dryness
- Blisters of the skin

- Livor mortis — does skin blanch (turn white) when finger pressure is applied?
- Venereal discoloration (genitals)
- Factors indicative of time of death (such as snow on top of but not beneath body, run-down timepieces, spoiled food, or insect invasion of the body)
- Area underneath the body when moved
- Condition of blood at scene:

  Liquid

  Clotted

  Dry

Victim's Clothing.

- Disheveled
- Penetrated or opened
- Stained (blood, semen)
- Lab tests _____
- Torn, cut, punctured
- Fastened
- Secured from _____
- Is clothing proper for circumstances?

Hair (Head, Body and Pubic).

- Samples
- Foreign hairs

Blood.

- Location _____

Victim's Hands.

- Bagged at scene
- Nail scrapings taken
- Evidence found in hand of victim collected
- Elimination prints taken from body
- Wounds photographed, measurement reference

History of Victim.

- Identity of person who saw victim last (time, date, place)

- Association with known or suspected criminals
- Known enemies
- Police record
- Recent change in marital status
- Trouble in relationship with family or loved one
- Recent change in victim's behavior
- Did victim do anything differently on the day of her death than she usually did on that day or at that hour?
- Motives indicated:
    Large insurance policies
    Substantial estate
    Known threats

Medical History of Victim.

- Recent complaints regarding health (time, date and place of complaint, also name of physician and treatment)
- History of nervous disorder or previous mental illness or nervous breakdown
- History or suspicion of alcohol dependency, drug abuse or addiction
- Victim's recent mental state (unhappy, upset or depressed)
- Access to or possession of poisons, drugs or medication
- History of any condition or illness that would suggest a fatal outcome

Autopsy.

Investigator's Duties

- Presence at autopsy
- Photographs
- Copies of all reports
- Notes and sketches
- Tell pathologist of connected circumstances

Gunshot Wounds

- Was wound treated before death? How?
- Shape of wound (star-shaped, round, etc.)

- Description of wound
- Photographed
- Presence of abraded area around wound
- Intermediate targets documented (doors, walls, windows, clothing, etc.)
- Muzzle impression
- Sooty material
- Powder embedded
- Autopsy procedures:

   Were X rays taken to find the projectile(s)?

   Was the angle of the path of the projectile detected?

   Was a full autopsy conducted?

   Was a toxicology study conducted?

Cutting and Stabbing

- Body position
- Wound type and location:

   Stab

   Cut

   Laceration
- Wound characteristics:

   Hesitation marks

   Defense wounds

   Scrimmage wounds

   Fatal wound
- Artifacts noted:

   Post mortem injuries

   Embalmer's wounds

   Prosector's incisions

Drug overdose

   Scene Investigation

- Signs of poisoning (vomit, chills and fever, intense thirst, diarrhea, etc.)
- Paraphernalia (tourniquets, syringe, cooker)

- Capsules, decks, pill bottles
- Prescription items, Milk of Magnesia, antacid, Maalox
  Body
- Position
- Rigor
- Lividity
- Froth at nose or mouth
- Needle mark
  Autopsy Points
- Tissues for microscopic examination:
    Skin (subcutaneous tissues and vessels, injection sites)
    Lung (granulomata, edema, congestion, pneumonia, fibrosis)
    Lymph nodes (axillary, portal)
    Liver
    Heart
    Spinal cord
    Toxicological investigation
    Bile (presence of opiates)
    Subcutaneous tissue and vessels (fresh injection site — source of narcotics)
    Urine (opiates)
    Blood
    Gastric contents (examine for capsules or tablets, last food digested)
    Liver, kidney, lung and brain tissue

Suspect.
  - Photographed when arrested:
    Wounds/cuts/scratches noted
    Photographed clothed
    Photographed nude (sex offense cases)
  - Searched
  - Suspect's clothes and shoes obtained

- Fingernails scraped
- Body hairs obtained
- Head hairs obtained
- Blood type determined
- Hands swabbed (neutron activation analysis)

S E V E N

ARREST AND PROCEDURE

Among the many critical discretionary decisions a police officer or detective makes regularly during his career, the decision to arrest is one of the most significant for him and the person arrested. Although laws may seem cut and dried, and officers may seem to have little choice in deciding whether to arrest, the officer remains the only person who can, and should, make that ultimate decision. The moment a police officer announces to a person that he is making an arrest, he is in great peril. At that point, he may meet violent resistance or an attempt to escape. In this chapter, I will cover the confrontation of a suspect, some general laws of arrest, plus procedures and guidelines police must follow in arresting and searching a suspect.

Confrontation of a Suspect

The first, and often critical, stage of a criminal prosecution is the point at which the police officer or detective comes face to face with a suspect. A mistake by the police officer during this first confrontation can often make otherwise good evidence unusable and make a conviction impossible.

The general guidance that governs police conduct during a confrontation, wherever it happens, depends largely on the officer's knowledge of the suspect and the crime, plus the extent the officer is depriving the suspect of his freedom and the suspect's perception about his detention.

The police officer must know what constitutional rules she must follow and how her actions depend on whether she simply questions a person without depriving him of his freedom or whether she detains the suspect for any time, however brief, or takes the person into custody through a formal arrest.

For example, when the police officer has reason to believe a certain person merely knows something about a criminal act but has no reason to believe the person is involved in it, the officer's general questioning of that person is not governed by the self-incrimination and right-to-counsel rules (that is, the Miranda Rules).

Even when a police officer does suspect the person of criminal involvement, these rules do not apply to the questioning when the suspect understands he has no obligation to answer the officer's questions and is free to stop talking and leave any time he wishes. (The non-custodial rights caution was discussed in earlier chapters.) However, if the officer gives the suspect reason to believe he is not free to go, then the rules of conduct based on the Fifth Amendment and Miranda Rule come into play.

Once the police officer formally detains a person, search and seizure rules also take effect. When the officer arrests a suspect, further personal search and seizure rules apply (shown below).

Ordinarily, a person is not detained when the officer simply asks him for his name and identification. However, when an officer takes additional steps that suggest the person is not free to go, then a detaining situation has occurred.

Temporary Detention

When a police officer knows specific facts that lead him to suspect criminal involvement of a person, he may briefly detain the person for questioning even without probable cause for an arrest.

- The basis for the police officer to stop and temporarily detain a person cannot be a hunch or an educated guess. The officer must be able to point to specific facts that support his suspicion. His basis for a decision to act stems from an assessment of the whole picture, including the reasonable conclusions his experience enables him to draw from the facts. If a police officer cannot articulate specific facts and conclusions justifying his act, then any evidence resulting from his stopping and detaining a person becomes inadmissible for prosecution.
- The "criminal activity" the detective is investigating can be ongoing at that moment; it can also be crimes that have been committed or crimes he thinks the suspect will commit.
- During a stop, the police officer may question the suspect, have her viewed by witnesses, and detain her while he follows other avenues of investigation. Also, the Supreme Court has indicated that an in-the-field stop may include taking fingerprints from a suspect.
- A detaining on less-than-probable cause should remain brief, and although there's no absolute time limit, the duration of the stop is a factor the court will examine to determine whether the officer's "stop" was really an "arrest." The police officer cannot detain a person longer than is reasonably necessary to accomplish the legitimate purposes of the stop.
- The police right to transport a suspect away from the place where she was first stopped is uncertain. Some courts have allowed transporting suspects short distances so that witnesses could identify them; other courts have disagreed. Taking a suspect to the police station will probably turn the stop into an arrest and require probable cause.
- Some states have statutes allowing the police to obtain a warrant based on reasonable suspicion and to detain a suspect at a police station to obtain his fingerprints. The constitutionality of such statutes remains untested and uncertain.
- When nothing occurs during the stop to give the officer probable cause for arrest, he must allow the suspect to continue.

A Stop

Pursuing a person amounts to a "stop" requiring "reasonable suspicion," if police actions would lead the person to the reasonable belief that he is not free to leave.

No "stop" happens when police merely drive alongside a suspect with no signal from the police officer that the person must stop his vehicle. However, a show of force, such as sounding the police car siren, coupled with flashing lights, may turn the situation into a "stop." It is still unclear what type of force, or how much, would be necessary to convey to a person not yet under actual police control that he is not free to leave.

When a suspect's car crashes during pursuit, obviously the suspect is in the ordinary sense of the word "stopped." However, deciding whether this situation creates a "stop" by a police officer in the legal sense depends on the particular facts. If the suspect crashes into an obstacle an officer has put in the road to force him to halt, police have "stopped" the person for Fourth Amendment purposes. It would not matter that the police expected the suspect to come to a safe stop. However, if a suspect loses control of his car while police pursue him and crashes into a wall, his crash would not, of itself, establish a police stop.

Use of Police Roadblocks

Police cannot legally make random, arbitrary stops of automobiles on the public roadways. However, brief, systematic stops at highway roadblocks and checkpoints can be constitutional.

According to a variety of court rulings, the rule against arbitrary stops applies whether the police purpose is to investigate a suspected crime or just check the motorist's documents or the condition of her vehicle. Although police can stop a vehicle on a public roadway, ordinarily they must observe specific facts that supply them with a reasonable suspicion that the vehicle, its operator or other occupants are in violation of some law.

The Supreme Court has ruled that police may establish highway checkpoints that stop vehicles without individualized suspicion to check motorists for signs of drunken driving. Such stops must be brief, and they may not be truly random; that is, the police officer may not exercise any discretion in deciding whom to stop but instead must use some neutral selection system.

Courts generally require such stops to be conducted according to a detailed plan devised by supervisory officers, that care be taken not to make motorists fearful or surprised, and that motorists' safety be protected. Each state and jurisdiction may have other requirements as well, or it may forbid sobriety roadblocks on state constitutional grounds.

Requiring a Driver to Get Out of His Vehicle

Once a police officer has made a legal stop of a traffic offender's vehicle, she automatically has the right to order the offender to get out of his vehicle.

This action has been recognized as a reasonable safety precaution for an officer. If the officer has ordered the offender out of his car, and his appearance or actions lead the officer to reasonably fear he has a weapon or is otherwise involved in criminal activity, the rules of stop and frisk come into play.

Stop and Frisk

Police officers have the authority to stop and frisk a suspect even though they do not have sufficient cause to arrest him, *if*:

- The officer has knowledge of facts that reasonably lead her to believe the suspect is involved in criminal activity and may be armed and dangerous.

- The officer clearly identifies herself as a police officer (when in street clothes) and makes reasonable inquiries about the suspect's conduct.

- The suspect's response to the officer stopping and questioning him does not relieve the officer's suspicions and fears of danger to herself or others.

- For example, a police officer or detective observes two men loitering outside a bank, conferring several times with each other, and walking in front of the bank several times, looking through the bank's windows. Each man wears a topcoat although it is a warm day. One of the suspects, just before the noon hour, goes to a car parked directly across from the bank and sits behind the wheel. As a bank guard leaves the bank, the second suspect starts to walk into the bank. The officer can then stop the suspect, ask for an explanation of his conduct and frisk him if he does not give answers that relieve the officer's suspicions. The officer has reasonable suspicion to believe that criminal activity is afoot, that the person is a bank robber and likely armed, and that he poses a threat to public safety and the officer.

- Court cases generally imply that the rules establishing guidelines and control for police officers "stopping and frisking" a person usually require them to have a "reasonable suspicion" of ongoing criminal conduct. However, police can also stop and, if appropriate, frisk someone they suspect of being involved in an earlier crime.

Note: To justify a stop, the officer's "reasonable suspicion" must be based on specific objective facts and the logical conclusions her training and experience enable her to draw from those facts. However, such general considerations as the high crime rates of the area are no substitute for specific facts about the suspect or his conduct. For example, a police officer who works in a neighborhood that is a hangout for junkies and pushers sees two men in an alley, a few feet apart from each other and starting to walk in opposite directions. The officer has not seen enough to justify a stop of the men even though, because of the area, she suspects a drug buy has just taken place.

Facts that are innocent in themselves, when considered together in light of an officer's experience, may provide grounds for a stop. Such facts may be part of a "profile" or list of characteristics sometimes used to identify persons likely to commit certain crimes, especially the transporting of drugs. However, it is not a good idea for the police officer to rely mechanically on a profile. The question must always remain whether the "whole picture" would lead a reasonable, experienced police officer to believe a crime has happened or is about to happen.

Making an Arrest and Following Legal Procedure

The police officer and detective must evaluate the fruits of their observation and investigation and make determinations about the arrests of persons investigated. Two crime categories are the first element in decisions to arrest: misdemeanors and felonies. Misdemeanor crimes can receive a maximum of up to one year's confinement; felony offenses carry more than one year confinement to life in prison or execution, depending on the crime committed and the state or federal laws applied.

Three General Rules of Arrest

Although the laws and procedures of police arrest have lengthy conditions, three general rules apply. The police officer or detective may arrest legally when:

1. The officer has reasonable cause to believe the person to be arrested has committed a public offense while in the officer's presence.
2. The person arrested has committed a felony, although not in the officer's presence.
3. An officer has reasonable cause to believe a person he arrests has committed a felony, whether the officer has officially received notification of the felony or not; for example, when the police officer observes a man wearing a ski mask leaving a convenience store with a gun in one hand and a bag in the other.

Misdemeanor Arrest

The first factor of a misdemeanor arrest stems from the "reasonable cause" consideration that requires intimate knowledge of statutes the officer is enforcing. Each statute discusses succinctly the "elements of proof" for each crime that lead the officer to make a judgment about reasonable cause, reasonable belief and probable cause, each concept being generally synonymous.

From the first step of establishing reasonable cause, the officer moves to the next step of determining whether he can deduce from his observations that an act, or failure to act, by a specific person to be arrested is a violation of that law. Several court decisions over the years have played a key role in shaping the procedure of arrest for misdemeanor crimes. For example:

A federal court in 1924 noted that "presence" continues to be a requirement for the police officer to make a warrantless arrest "only if he had reasonable cause to believe it had been committed in his presence." "In presence" means that which is directly perceived by any of the senses. Of the senses by which law violations can be perceived, eyesight is the most common, including use of binoculars or a telescope. Eyesight aided by flashlight is acceptable. Courts have ruled the validity of a police officer hearing without artificial aids in People v. Goldberg. During a key court decision in 1922, the sense of smell also received a permissible ruling for police officers in these circumstances.

The sense of touch has importance during shakedown or pat down searches when the officer detects an object through the suspect's clothing that feels like a pistol or knife. Perception might also be accomplished through a team effort to qualify for the "presence" requirement, such as the 1968 case (Robinson v. State, 4 Md. App. 515, 243 A.2d 879) in which one officer observed a burglary and described the fleeing suspects in a radio broadcast. Another officer heard the broadcast and stopped the suspects on the basis of the description.

Felony Arrest

The second rule of arrest law, which specifies "when a person arrested has committed a felony, although not in the officer's presence," also presupposes the police officer has sound knowledge of state statutes and elements of proof necessary to establish a felony crime. This element would depend on the officer's perceptual abilities; although her presence was not required, she must be able to explain to the court how she knew the person arrested had committed a felony. That information might have come from detectives working burglary cases, or from a radio broadcast, or from reading a bulletin listing wanted felons.

The third rule of arrest is more complex and deals with the officer's suspicion of questionable activities. The officer charged with protection of life and property in her jurisdictions must remain diligent and exercise an inquiring mind. An officer's interpretation of her observations, plus reasonable cause to believe certain things as true when related to other facts, creates the basis for her to legally arrest a person. In this chapter, I will break down the elements police officers must consider before making a decision to arrest a person.

When an Arrest Takes Place

The police officer or detective makes an arrest as soon as he indicates by word or action his intent to take a person to the police station or before a judicial officer, or otherwise to take a suspect into custody. The following important points delineate the complexities of arrest:

- Picking up a suspect for questioning is an "arrest" even though the officer does not tell the person formally he is under arrest, does not tell him he must go with the officer, and even though he intends to let the suspect leave if the interrogation proves fruitless.

- However, when the officer merely invites a suspect by telephone to come in and talk, and does not bolster his invitation with any show of authority, it is not an arrest.
- The mere questioning of a witness who is not in custody is not an arrest of that witness. A motorist stopped for a driver's license or car registration check or for a traffic violation is not, at that point, under arrest.
- The officer has not made an arrest when he briefly detains a person suspected of criminal involvement simply to question him for a moment.
- When a police officer arrests a suspect, he may keep the suspect under constant and close surveillance, as his judgment dictates, until safely transported to the police station or other holding facility.

Probable Cause

The process of arrest stems from the Fourth Amendment of the constitution that says: *"The right of the people to be secure in their persons . . . against unreasonable searches and seizures, shall not be violated, and no warrants shall issue, but upon probable cause. . . ."* However, many states have more stringent requirements, particularly when an informer has provided the information allegedly establishing probable cause. The following important points control the legal actions of police officers and detectives across the country. When violated intentionally by an officer, that officer becomes personally liable in a civil action and often criminally liable in a prosecution. It is a matter of importance within the criminal justice system and is strictly enforced by the courts.

All arrests by police officers, with or without a warrant, must be based on probable cause. Probable cause requires the police officer to have reasonable belief, based on reliable evidence, that a suspect has committed a crime. It must go beyond mere suspicion or an officer's educated hunch. However, it is less than absolute certainty. The evidence a police officer or detective needs to make a valid arrest doesn't have to amount to proof of guilt. It must show that the suspect has "probably" committed a crime.

Arrest Without Personal Observation

A police officer (including detectives) can, without personally observing the commission of a crime, establish probable cause and make a warrantless arrest.

For example, an officer hears a burglar alarm sounding and as she rounds a corner to investigate, she notes the alarm seems to come from an appliance store. A moment later, she observes a man running toward a parked car with several appliances in his hands. When the man sees the officer, he throws the appliances to the ground, gets in the car and tries to start it. The officer arrives and orders him from the car and he complies. In this situation, the officer has probable cause to make a warrantless arrest.

However, more than the observation of suspicious behavior, it is necessary to establish probable cause to arrest. For example, during the midafternoon, a police officer is patrolling an area where several residential burglaries have recently happened. The officer observes a person who residents have said is a "suspicious character" walking along a street carrying a portable television set. The person arrives at a parked car with another person at the wheel, and puts the TV set in the rear seat of the car. The officer has not received any reports of burglary or theft but approaches the person and asks where he got the television set. He tells the officer the television set was purchased from a friend. The officer has no probable cause to arrest him, or any authority to detain him any longer.

Given the same set of facts as above, except with the officer receiving information by radio or personally receiving a complaint of burglary in the area, he would have good reason to at least detain the person until determining whether the television set was stolen.

Evidence From Other Persons

Probable cause to arrest might come in many ways besides the police officer's personal observation of a suspect's activities. For example:

- Probable cause might come from police radio bulletins, tips from "good citizen" informers who chanced to see criminal activity, reports from victims, anonymous tips, and tips from "habitual" informers who mingle with people in the underworld and who themselves may be criminals. Probable cause for arrest might have a valid basis from various combinations of these sources.

- When an officer or detective receives information from a sufficiently reliable source or sufficiently detailed information, she may have probable cause to arrest without having to conduct any personal surveillance of the suspect's activities. The detective may need no more corroborating evidence than the observation that the suspect matches the description of the alleged criminal.

Official Reports

A police radio bulletin announcing a crime and describing the alleged criminal justifies an officer's arrest of a person meeting the alleged criminal's description, provided the person could have been at the scene of the crime at the time it happened. For example, if a radio bulletin broadcast about an armed robbery five minutes earlier supplies a good description of the assailant, and a patrol officer sees a person meeting the description on the other side of town a minimum of twenty minutes from the robbery by the fastest means, there is no probable cause. However, if the robbery happened twenty or thirty minutes earlier, probable cause might exist, depending on closer investigation of the suspected person. Other factors about a police radio bulletin include:

- A radio bulletin must specify that a crime happened.
- The bulletin that describes a person wanted only for investigation purposes does not justify an arrest.
- The bulletin should authorize arrest on reasonable belief, however when it does not, the officer should always clarify his authority before making an arrest that relies on the bulletin alone.

Crime Victims or Witnesses

A crime victim's report and description of an assailant could justify a warrantless arrest within a reasonable time. However, a prudent police officer or detective will understand the victim or witness may often have a "relative" perception that can lead to false arrest. For example, a victim may have observed a person earlier who seemed to act suspicious; later, after being robbed by a person in a darkened street, the victim supplies a description of the person she noticed earlier in a well-lighted area. Unless the officer has good reason to rely upon the victim's or witness's perception, he does not have "reasonable" belief although based on the description he might have "probable cause." However, without reasonable belief, the probable cause element will not protect the officer from false arrest charges.

"Good Citizen" Informers

Generally police officers can assume the reliability of informers who are just good citizens doing their duty. If the information received does establish that the suspect described has probably committed or is probably committing a crime, the arrest could happen without either personal surveillance of the suspect's activities or checking into the informer's reliability. However, that concept has several cautions attached for the prudent police officer.

For example, a waitress tells a police officer she has personally seen a person selling narcotics in the restaurant where she works. She gives the officer a detailed description of the person and describes the manner of the sale. Technically, the officer has probable cause to arrest, if the person remains in the restaurant and the waitress points him out, or the person receiving the narcotics remains in the restaurant and the waitress points him out.

The officer or detective must determine the motives of the waitress. A veteran officer knows well-meaning people have a tendency to exaggerate or perceive they have observed something they have not. For example: I was once involved in a situation similar to this. I had the seasoning to remain attentive but diplomatic. I told the waitress we would make the arrest outside the restaurant and that later she would have to come to the station, make a statement, identify the persons in a lineup, and testify in court. The waitress immediately began to waver on her report, and after I pressed her to tell us exactly what she observed, she admitted that she had watched the two people exchange envelopes. Having heard that one of the men sold drugs, she "assumed" the transaction involved drugs. Had we arrested the two men, no drugs would have been found. We knew that because the case involved a public official (the man receiving the alleged drugs) and an undercover law enforcement officer who had established a successful cover as a drug dealer. We persuaded the waitress that an arrest based on her testimony would create problems, but tried to make her feel appreciated, for coming forward took great courage. Doing this salvaged the undercover officer's position, and based on the deal in the restaurant and others, the grand jury handed down an indictment on the public official, who later went to jail for corruption. Had the officers responding to the call from the waitress been rookies instead of two seasoned detectives, the situation might have turned out differently, with the officers bearing the brunt of liability that the public official would surely have pressed to clear himself. It's important to add that if the situation had been a legitimate drug deal or suspected as one, the waitress could not have provided the credibility for probable cause to make a valid arrest. Witnessing two men swap envelopes, even when she believed the men were engaged in a drug deal, would not legally enable an officer to make an arrest. Had the waitress seen one man hand the other man a small clear plastic bag with a white substance in it, and the other man hand over a twenty dollar bill or some other currency, and had she been willing to testify to that, an arrest could have been made with reasonable belief and probable cause.

Anonymous, Paid or Habitual Government Informers

A tip from either an anonymous informer or a habitual one, such as an informer who mingles with the "criminal element" and who works for pay or for some other motive, must be addressed with caution. Such an informant's information might have credibility or lack credibility. An officer should never act on such testimony alone. The determination of whether the information received has credibility depends largely on several circumstances, such as:

- Has the informer been shown to be consistently credible?

- Has the informer been shown to be reliable?

- Has the informer personally observed the suspects commit crimes or prepare for crimes?

- When the informer reports hearsay from another person, can the officer check on that source carefully before giving any credence to the information?

- Has the detective receiving the information been able to verify some or all details of the tip?

- Have other information sources corroborated the informant's information?

Obviously, if the informer remains anonymous, the detective will have a difficult task demonstrating just from the tip itself that the information is credible or reliable. Equal difficulties stem from the paid informant who might just have need for fast money and create information that sounds good. This difficulty increases when the informant's identity must remain secret for his safety and continued use as an information source.

While what an informer of proven reliability has personally observed may furnish probable cause for arrest, it is far safer to corroborate what she has told the officer by keeping the suspect under surveillance. The prudent officer or detective treats the informant's information as a lead instead of "reasonable belief" or "probable cause" for an arrest.

Suspect's Reputation or Past Record

Among the factors a police officer or detective must consider when determining whether he or she has valid probable cause for arrest is the suspect's reputation. For example, when a person has been arrested, indicted or convicted regularly for some type of crime, and an informant tells a detective the person has committed a similar crime or plans to soon, the credibility of the information is greater than if the suspect has a clean record. However, a detective should not make an arrest based solely on that element, and the best test includes having probable cause without considering the suspect's past record as a factor in establishing "reasonable belief."

Misdemeanor Arrests

The probable-cause requirements above govern arrests for felonies with or without a warrant, but an arrest for a misdemeanor committed outside the presence of an arresting officer generally may not happen without a warrant even if the officer has probable cause. An arrest for a misdemeanor may happen without a warrant if the offense is committed in the officer's presence. These are not constitutional rules, and they differ somewhat from state to state.

Use of Force to Make an Arrest

Police officers can use whatever "reasonable nondeadly" force they believe necessary to make an arrest and to protect themselves and the public from bodily harm while making the arrest.

Deadly force however, has far-reaching restrictions. Before using deadly force a police officer must weigh several factors. First, he must consider the seriousness of the crime. Although the statute allows deadly force use for felonies, including an escaping felon, it's normally that type of action that destroys an officer's career, creates civil lawsuits against him and his department, and might land the officer in criminal court and prison. An example from real life: A police officer or detective responding to a burglary complaint saw a person in dark clothing exit a window of a house and run, although the police officer repeatedly yelled, "Police — stop where you are!" Reaching a nearby backyard fence, the suspect began climbing over it. Once clear of the fence, the officer believed the suspect would escape. The police officer perceived that the person had committed burglary, a felony in that jurisdiction (and most others). As the person reached the top of the fence the officer fired his handgun twice (to arrest a fleeing felon with deadly force); the person collapsed to the ground and died. In this real situation, the "suspect" was found to be the sixteen-year-old son of the owner of the house; he lived there. His parents had restricted him for getting into trouble at school that day, and he probably ran from the police because in his pocket were five marijuana cigarettes. The youth had trouble with the police earlier for drinking alcohol in a public place and was later caught buying and possessing marijuana. Another factor in this case emerged when the tape of the dispatch revealed the officer went to the wrong address. A resident of the neighborhood had called in to report a suspicious activity in the yard of a house where the occupants were known to be away. That house was across the street from where the shooting occurred. Investigation later revealed that the mysterious person with a flashlight was another neighbor looking for a lost cat. The officer was technically within the law since he "perceived" the person fleeing from him was a burglar; however, because of his poor judgment (seriousness of the crime, and no apparent threat to officer or public safety), public outrage and work history, the officer resigned from the police department. The parents of the child sued and won a multimillion dollar judgment against the police department and officer jointly.

Had the officer used prudence — and his radio — the entire situation would have been avoided. This story serves as an example of how easily the use of deadly force can get out of hand. The rule of thumb a seasoned, well-trained police officer or detective uses before employing deadly force is based on the seriousness of the crime and immediate situation. First, is the suspect a danger to the public if he or she escapes? For example, a suspected burglar poses less of a threat to the public than a suspect known to be a rapist, murderer or kidnapper. Second, use of deadly force is clearly justified when the officer must protect himself or other persons against deadly force. A person with a large knife coming at an officer or another person in rage with the perceived intent of attacking the officer or other person and failing to respond to the officer's orders to stop creates a clear situation where the officer must act quickly to stop the attacker. Sudden attacks such as a person firing a gun at an officer also clearly justify use of deadly force.

Breaking Into a Building to Make an Arrest

This authority falls in two categories: (1) When a police officer looks through a window or other opening and sees a crime committed or in progress, such as a life-threatening assault on a person by another person in the building, or sees a body on the floor and a person standing nearby with a gun in hand; (2) When an officer believes a wanted or suspicious person is within a building. A prudent officer will not break into the building without an arrest or search warrant in hand and then only after knocking at the door and trying to gain entry without forcing the entry.

A clear example of how breaking into a building can do much harm stems from a real case. After several days' investigation by detectives of the No Name Police Department, the officers established probable cause to believe that "Ralph" had murdered a gas station attendant during an armed robbery a week earlier. Without bothering to obtain a warrant, the detectives and several uniformed police officers approached Ralph's known residence about midnight. They could see lights in the house and could hear sounds coming from a television set or radio. A detective knocked on the door but received no response. After a few minutes, the officer broke into the apartment, but no one was there. However, on a table in plain view were several items of physical evidence that linked "Ralph" to the murder. The court did not convict Ralph of murder because the evidence obtained after breaking in was inadmissible, and Ralph moved on, probably to commit other crimes, possibly murder. The police in this case needed a search warrant, and if sufficient probable cause existed, an arrest warrant. Then breaking in would have been legal and all evidence seized would have also been admissible.

Resistance to Arrest

If police officers clearly identify themselves to a suspect, removing any question of their authority at the time of arrest, the person resisting the arrest commits a crime. Detectives in street clothes have to ensure that the person recognizes them as police officers. If the suspect just physically resists, the added crime would normally involve a misdemeanor, while pulling a knife or gun, or running from the officer after arrest usually evolves to a felony.

Warrant Arrests

One of the most important aspects of a warrant to arrest concerns the validity of the warrant. A warrant must state the specific charge for which a person is to be arrested and provide a description of the person to be arrested. Generally, a person's name is considered his or her identification, but there is room for error when arresting by name only. A police officer must be sure that she arrests the person for whom the warrant is intended. There are several principal identifiers useful for a warrant, including name, address, driver's license number, date of birth, place of birth, sex, color of hair and eyes, height and weight, race, ethnic orgin and visible scars and marks.

The warrant must also bear the signature of the issuing judge or magistrate. If the warrant is for a felony, the arrest can happen at any time. In the case of misdemeanors, the warrant must specifically state that it is for nighttime service or be served for arrest only during daytime.

The warrant requires that the person named be taken to the judge who issued the warrant or to the court of issue. In most jurisdictions, it may be a standard procedure to take the arrestee directly to jail to go through the "booking" process. The suspect then posts bail and receives a specific time to report to the court. In these cases, the arrestees do not generally go directly to the judge unless they demand it. Once the person named on the warrant has been arrested and processed according to its instructions, the officer signs that part of the document known as the "notification of service," and the document is returned to the court.

Arrest Without a Warrant

Except when obvious that the officer is arresting the person for the crime that he is committing at the time of arrest, or arrests him immediately following a pursuit, it's mandatory that an officer identify herself and announce her intention to arrest the person for the crime on which the arrest is based. Before arresting without a warrant, a seasoned police officer will review the facts she has to ensure a justifiable arrest.

Experienced officers prepare for an arrest by arranging for adequate support if time permits. They use common sense and distinguish between bravery and foolhardiness. A single-handed arrest accomplished by a brave police officer looks good in his personnel file, but he also risks losing the suspect or causing injury to himself, to the suspect or to someone else. Charisma, or commanding presence, is essential in this type of arrest. The officer must demonstrate command in his actions and appearance. He must give clear and concise orders and use only what force is necessary.

Diplomatic Immunity

Diplomatic officers, their families, official staff and servants, who are not citizens of or permanent residents of the United States are totally immune from arrest, detention or prosecution for a civil or criminal offense when they fall within the specifications of federal law (22 U.S. Code 252). They have credentials issued by the U.S. State Department.

Consular officials are accorded some limited immunities, but their families and other members of their household or entourage are not covered by the immunity. A foreign career officer may not be arrested or held pending a trial for any criminal charge except a grave crime, defined by the State Department as a felony offense that would endanger the public safety and pursuant to a decision by the competent judicial authority.

A consular office building and the official papers and documents it contains are protected by diplomatic immunity. Entry of such official premises may be made only with the permission of the head of that post or the head of that diplomatic mission. Officers may enter without permission if there is some urgent need, such as to put out a fire or provide some other protective service.

Entrapment

Often, an entrapment issue will be raised when an officer makes an arrest, particularly when the arrest involves some type of undercover or decoy operation. Because the officer is not standing before the suspect in full uniform, she is suspected of entrapment, especially when so accused in court of that action by clever defense attorneys. The issue of entrapment was first publicized during the court case of Sorrels v. United States in 1932, when the Supreme Court stated: "Society is at war with the criminal classes and courts have uniformly held that in waging this warfare, the forces of prevention and detection may use traps, decoys, and deception to obtain evidence of the commission of crime." Although some rules involving interrogation and lineups have eroded over time, that statement still carries considerable weight. Undercover activities may include placing an informer among criminal ranks to build a case and collect evidence; having police officers pose as "hit men" to gather evidence against people who are looking for someone to kill a friend or relative for insurance purposes; having an officer pose as a prostitute or a "john" on the streets to arrest solicitors; or having a team of officers go out on the streets posing as derelicts and drunks so they may attract muggers.

Undercover operations, plants, informants and decoys have all been used at one time or another in this "war with the criminal classes." It's legal; however, the tests about whether entrapment occurred is "with whom did the idea to commit crime originate?" The narcotics dealer, the mugger or the prostitute are all plying their trades on the streets, and the officers working such clandestine assignments are not putting the ideas to commit crime in the offenders' minds. They are merely increasing the odds for protecting other people and in catching the offenders at their illicit occupations. Whenever an officer works on such an assignment, she must make herself available for the criminal to act in her presence, doing nothing to induce the suspect to commit the crime.

Investigative Detention

There are many occasions when a police officer will temporarily detain a person in the field or transport that person to the station for a time to investigate the person and circumstances that seem to warrant further inquiry. The field interview situation and the field identification of people who happen to be near a crime are just two examples of such temporary detention. In the court cases United States v. West (1972) and United States v. Allen (1973), the courts stated, "The local policeman . . . is also in a very real sense a guardian of the public peace, and has a duty in the course of his work to be alert for suspicious circumstances and, provided that he acts within constitutional limits, to investigate whenever such circumstances indicate to him that he should do so."

A temporary detention for additional investigation beyond the frisk may be necessary, according to the courts. The Fourth Amendment is not so restrictive that a police officer should allow a crime to occur or a criminal to escape arrest just because the officer lacks the precise amount of information necessary to show probable cause for an arrest. For example, an officer may have probable cause to search a person, but at that moment not have enough cause for an arrest. Then, during the search, the officer finds a weapon or contraband and now has the probable cause for an arrest. With the continued validity of court decisions reinforcing age-old police procedures of stopping persons for investigation and searching for weapons and the constitutionality of temporary detention upon reasonable cause, officers may perform these jobs when they can show probable cause for their actions at each step along the way.

Searches Incident to Arrest

The police officer may, incident to a valid arrest, make a warrantless search of the arrested person at the time and place of the arrest. The officer may also search the area into which the arrested person might reach for a weapon or to destroy evidence and adjacent spaces from which a person in hiding could attack the officer.

The area a police officer may search for weapons or evidence incident to an arrest is strictly limited. It does not extend beyond the area into which the suspect could reach to obtain a weapon or destroy evidence. This means that if an officer arrests a person in one room of his house, she may not search other rooms, or even places in the same room if the suspect could not get to them quickly and easily. Once the officer has taken the person into custody, she must obtain a search warrant if she wishes to search the premises where she arrested the suspect.

The police authority to make a warrantless search incident to an arrest remains very narrow. If the officer exceeds her authority, she may spoil evidence that could have been obtained and admissible with a search warrant.

The search must be "contemporaneous in time and place with the arrest." This means the limited search must happen immediately after the arrest and at the place of arrest. This is particularly true if the officer intends to search any of the area surrounding the person arrested.

Exceptions

Under certain circumstances, an officer may make a search incidental to arrest immediately before the arrest. For example, the officer encounters a robbery suspect whom he has probable cause to arrest. The suspect is carrying a briefcase. The officer stops the person and searches the briefcase before arresting him. The search is reasonable because even without the search, the officer has probable cause to arrest and could then search it after. An officer might conduct a search before the arrest to prevent a mistake. For example, an officer or detective receives a radio broadcast informing him that an armed robbery happened one block from his position at the time of the broadcast, and that the suspect left the store two or three minutes earlier. The broadcast supplies a detailed description of the suspect; however, there's nothing especially distinctive about the person compared to other people on the street at the time. The broadcast also describes the person as carrying a briefcase in which the store manager said the suspect put the money. The officer notes other people on the streets also carrying briefcases. However, when he sees the suspect coming toward him, the person looks scared, looks behind him often and walks hurriedly. Although the suspect attempts to blend with the other people on the street, his actions plus description tells the seasoned officer that he is the person who committed the robbery. The officer also wants to ensure that no mistakes happen. The person might, for example, only be avoiding being served with civil process, or believe someone is following him to collect a debt. But, he may also have just stolen the petty cash from an office or robbed a bank. The officer pats down the suspect for weapons first, and finding none opens the briefcase, where he finds the cash and a revolver. When making this arrest, the officer knows he has the right person in custody.

When a police officer arrests a person in an automobile, he may at the time of the arrest and incidental to the arrest search the passenger compartment of the automobile and any containers within that limited area. The word "container" as used in this rule includes any object capable of holding another object, including closed or open glove compartments, consoles or other receptacles located anywhere in the passenger compartment including luggage, boxes, bags, clothing and the like. Once the arrest is completed, however, and the officer has taken the suspect away from the scene, he must obtain a search warrant if he wants to continue searching the automobile.

When necessary, a police officer can delay a search of the arrestee's person for a time after taking him or her into custody. For example, when an officer wants to seize the clothes of a jailed burglary suspect for evidence analysis but cannot obtain replacement garments for several hours, he may delay the seizure for a few hours without having to obtain a warrant.

Police officers are authorized to make a warrantless search incidental to a valid arrest whether or not the officer has an "arrest" warrant. Once the officer removes the suspect from the arrest area, he cannot search that area without a search warrant. He also may not make a delayed warrantless search of an arrested person's luggage or other personal containers seized at the time of arrest. Instead, the officer places the items in custody without search and obtains a search warrant. For example, police arrest a suspected drug courier at a train station because they have probable cause to believe marijuana is concealed in the suspect's footlocker. The police arrest the suspect and take the footlocker into custody at the police station property room unopened until they obtain a search warrant to legally open and search the footlocker. An exception would include a valid reason of emergency and that depends on the case the arrest involves. There is no distinction between containers such as luggage, commonly used to transport personal effects, and flimsier containers such as cardboard boxes and plastic or paper bags. If a container is sealed or closed in such a way that it indicates the suspect wants to keep its contents private, the police officer who wants to search it must first obtain a warrant. If, however, the container allows the contents to be immediately apparent, and the officer recognizes it as evidence or contraband, he may search it.

A search of the person may be made incident to an arrest for an offense that does not involve weapons or other tangible evidence only if the officer has good reason to take the suspect into custody.

Note: A traffic violation is not a crime in itself. Added offenses, such as attempting to escape from the officer in pursuit or driving under the influence of alcohol or drugs, can elevate a traffic violation to a misdemeanor.

Recognition of a dangerous suspect during a traffic violation stop might prompt a frisk search, but an officer can take no further action unless he finds a weapon or contraband. Another exception could arise if the officer saw weapons or contraband within the automobile in plain view.

Evidence obtained by a search incident to arrest cannot be used if the arrest itself is unlawful. A police officer cannot make an arrest as an excuse to justify a warrantless search. The validity of the search depends on the validity of the arrest, and the officer must have probable cause to arrest if he is to obtain usable evidence in a search incident to an arrest.

The Rule of Plain View During an Arrest

Officers making a valid arrest may, without a search warrant, seize items found in plain view at the time of an arrest when they have probable cause to believe the items establish contraband or evidence of a crime. For example, when an officer legally enters an apartment to make an arrest and sees white powder and narcotics paraphernalia on a kitchen table, she may legally seize this evidence, and it becomes admissible in court under this rule. The officer need not be absolutely certain the items seized are contraband or evidence; she only needs reasonable belief.

The Hot Pursuit Arrest

When a police officer pursues a person with probable cause to believe the suspect is armed and has just committed a serious crime (for example, armed robbery, murder or arson), the officer may — for her own safety, the safety of the public, and the prevention of escape — search the building where the suspect was pursued.

This is a warrantless search that happens before arrest. The officer's authority is limited, and once the suspect is arrested and in custody, the search must stop immediately. For example, an officer receives an armed robbery report and shortly thereafter learns that a person matching the robber's description has just entered a two-story dwelling. The detective, accompanied by several police officers, may enter the dwelling without a warrant and search for the suspect or for wherever he may have hidden a weapon, such as in closets, under beds or in drawers. However, once police find the suspect, their search must stop immediately, and they must obtain a warrant to continue a search of the premises.

Sweep of Premises Where an Arrest Has Been Made

Officers might be allowed to make a limited "sweep" of a home or other premises where a lawful arrest has been made to find other persons. This happens when the circumstances give the arresting officers a basis for reasonably believing other persons hiding on the premises will pose some type of danger to those at the arrest scene or to public safety.

For example, within a few hours of an armed robbery, police obtain warrants to arrest two suspects and to stake out the home of one of them. After two days, during which the detectives do not see the suspect enter or leave, they have a call placed to the home and verify the suspect is there. The detectives, backed with uniformed officers, enter the home to execute the arrest warrant. After looking unsuccessfully for the suspect on the first and second floors, the detectives call down into the basement that anyone there should come upstairs. After repeated calls, the suspect emerges and officers place him under arrest. He is not carrying the gun used in the robbery, nor have the officers observed it on the first or second floor. They then go down into the basement to see if his accomplice, who may be carrying the weapon, is there. The detective's check of the basement is reasonable, and evidence they find there is admissible. The facts suggested that the suspect went to his home soon after the robbery and hid in the basement. Under the circumstances, it was reasonable to think that the second suspect might be there too, armed with the gun and prepared to ambush police officers.

This rule is similar to, but distinct from, the rule on searching the area into which an arrestee might reach for weapons or evidence. A protective sweep incident to arrest may extend to the entire premises, not just within the arrestee's reach. On the other hand, it's limited to areas in which a person could be found; in other words, the officer in this example could search a closet in the basement but not a drawer. The sweep may not continue after the suspicion of danger has been dispelled, and it may last no longer than is necessary to complete the arrest and leave the premises.

Obtaining Physical Evidence From the Body of a Suspect Under Arrest

Police officers are not required to warn or to obtain the consent of a suspect under arrest before taking physical evidence from his or her person.

For example, police can compel a person under arrest to submit to photographing for identification purposes, fingerprinting, the cutting of hair samples, the testing of his breath, the collection of urine, the extraction of blood, and the removal of objects hidden in body cavities, so long as the force exerted or procedure used is not so outrageous as to be considered "shocking."

- The pumping of an arrested person's stomach to obtain a capsule of swallowed drugs has been deemed "impermissible and shocking" by the courts.
- The routine extraction of blood by a person competent to do so has been allowed.
- Police can force a person to disgorge from his mouth evidence he is attempting to swallow.

Other things police can do to retain admissibility of evidence obtained include:

- Making an arrested person remove his clothing either to permit a search for concealed evidence or to allow an inspection of his body for tattoos, scratches, birthmarks, or other identifying peculiarities. However, strip searches in some circumstances have not been permitted.
- Compelling a suspect to appear in a lineup for identification.
- Making an arrested person try on articles of clothing associated with the crime.
- Compelling an arrested person to speak so her voice may be identified by a witness or victim. However, police cannot compel the suspect to say anything that might incriminate her.

Obtaining Physical Evidence From the Body of a Suspect Not Under Arrest

Police officers may, without warning or consent, briefly detain a suspect whom they have probable cause to arrest for the limited purpose of taking highly destructible physical evidence from his body, even though they do not intend to arrest him then.

For example, a police officer interviews a suspect she has probable cause to think has strangled his wife. The officer does not wish to arrest the person until further investigation takes place. However, because the victim's neck was lacerated, the officer thinks that bits of skin and blood cells may be under the suspect's fingernails. The police may take fingernail scrapings from him, against his will, to obtain and preserve evidence that he could otherwise easily destroy.

Note: The police authority to make this kind of detention and "search" without arrest is extremely limited. The police must have a definite kind of evidence in mind, and can intrude on the suspect's right of privacy only to the extent necessary to seize it; they cannot make the kind of "full" search that is permitted incident to arrest. There must be the probability that the evidence will be lost if the officer doesn't seize it at once.

E I G H T

INTERVIEWS AND INTERROGATIONS

The best sources of information about people are the people them-selves. Probably the best way of getting information from people is to ask them for the information. Effective police officers and detec-tives have learned to become proficient in the art of interviewing people. There are two basic methods for getting information:

Interviewing. The questioning of a person who has or is believed to have information of interest to the police officer or detective. The person interviewed is usually a victim or witness but may be an informant or someone esle who can provide information, even if not always directly related to the crime under investigation. During an interview, the police detective will encourage the interviewee to give his or her account of an incident or crime. "Probing" is a good way to describe the technique of interviewing. A skilled interviewer will "probe" a person's memory to draw out key information, even infor-mation the interviewee doesn't realize he has.

Interrogation. An interrogation involves questioning a person suspected of having committed a crime, having complicity in the crime, or having direct knowledge about the crime but who is reluctant to supply the information to police. "Prying" is the best word to describe an interrogation. The person being interrogated is normally unwilling to part with the information the police want or need, including confessions, location of a murder weapon or victim, names of others involved in the crime, who hired the suspect to commit a crime, and other incriminating information.

The Decision to Interview or Interrogate

The distinction between interviewing or interrogating is not as clear-cut as it might seem. An interview may become an interrogation or vice versa, and the police detective has to remain alert to which will be appropriate at the time. Interrogation conjures up images from the past of hot lights, the rubber hose, and a horde of detectives — ties loosened, sleeves rolled up, and shoulder holsters in clear view — hovering over a sweating suspect. That's where the term "sweat it out of him" originated. However, in this age of computers, fax machines and sophisticated crime-solving techniques, as well as strict court rules and aggressive defense lawyers, the traditional methods are now mainly of historical interest.

Note: A common myth suports the idea that a confession resulting from an interrogation closes a case. However, a confession without corroborating testimony, physical and circumstantial evidence does little to solve a case. I learned early in my career that interrogations can often create more trouble than good. For example, a tainted interrogation that discloses information leading to collection of solid evidence can destroy a case in court if a good defense lawyer can persuade the court not to admit the suspect's confession or any of the evidence gained from his confession. I always wait until the last investigative step to interview or interrogate the suspect. Then I do it only to let the suspect "tell his side" of the story should he choose to do so.

Legal Considerations of Interviews and Interrogations

The police question a wide variety of people, most of whom are not criminal suspects. They interview victims, witnesses, informants, complainants, interested participants, disinterested parties, women, men, children of both sexes, professional people, blue-collar workers, white-collar workers, no-collar workers, people who arouse their curiosity, people who behave in a lawful manner, and people who do not. In each category, the police officer and detective must have an intricate knowledge of the law, the crime and what information they need.

When interviewing children, for example, parents or guardians normally must remain in the room. Depending on the situation, another person — normally a nonpolice female — can suffice. Some children don't want to talk in front of their parents because of potential repercussions; some parents coach or answer for their children. Whenever police interview a child, especially on sensitive topics, the prosecutor should advise them legally on the procedure before the interview begins.

Male officers interviewing females must also consider legal aspects, especially when the interview involves references to sexual matters. A male officer or detective interviewing a female victim or witness should always have a female officer present; often, but not always, a female officer can conduct a more productive interview.

Every citizen is protected by the Fifth Amendment of the constitution. The Supreme Court's 1966 ruling regarding the Miranda v. Arizona case clarified the protection and set forth certain guidelines of police conduct that have become famous as the Miranda Warning. However, the Miranda Warning applies legally only upon the arrest of a person, or for those already in custody for another crime. The Fifth Amendment does not specify that a person only gets this protection after he's been placed under arrest or taken otherwise in custody. It leaves a gap that most police fall into unless they apply the noncustodial rights warning to any person the officer suspects or any person who "might" become a suspect. Noncustodial rights follow the language of the traditional Miranda Warning with this difference: The suspect does not have the option of having a lawyer appointed for him, and is advised he can leave anytime he desires. Suspects must know and understand that they are not under arrest. If the police suspect a person of a crime but only later gather enough evidence to arrest him, the noncustodial rights may subsequently establish that the police gave the suspect every opportunity to exercise his constitutional rights.

Other legal aspects the police officer and detective must cope with involve the witness. A cooperative witness may consent to giving a detailed description of what she knows but refuses to testify in court or changes her story in court. Many cases never reach the courtroom because of these problems. Detectives should always obtain a written statement of the interview and have the interviewee sign it with a witness. Doing that will not ensure the witness won't recant or refuse to testify, and since the statement cannot be admissible in court as evidence, why bother? When the police detective depends heavily on the interviews to create other evidence and later establish probable cause for arrest and search warrants, the witness may back out with an excuse that she never told the detective the information he says she did; the detective can quickly lose credibility and get into legal trouble as well. He can be sued for false arrest, illegal seizure, and a variety of other charges brought against him and the department. In rare situations, the officer might face criminal allegations, suspension or dismissal. Taking the time to obtain a written statement from this type of witness protects and supports the detective's actions.

Importance of Human Factors

Human factors affect a police detective's success in stimulating an interviewee to talk and influence the accuracy or truthfulness of the information she receives from the interviewee. The detective evaluates each interviewee and the information furnished, attempting to understand the person's motivations, fears and mental makeup, then uses her understanding of the interviewee to gain useful information.

When selecting an interview or interrogation technique, a police detective must consider perception or memory, prejudice, reluctance to talk and personality conflicts.

Perception and Memory

The validity of the information disclosed during an interview or interrogation depends on the interviewee's ability to correctly perceive what happened in his or her presence, to recollect that information, and to communicate the information correctly to the detective. A mistake made in recalling a particular incident is often due to one or more of the following:

- Location of the interviewee relative to the incident at the time it occurred. Rarely do two people give the same account of an incident they both have witnessed.

- Weakness in the interviewee's ability to see, hear, smell, taste or touch.

- Lapse of time since the incident occurred, or lack of reason for the interviewee to attach much importance to the incident when it occurred. The account given of an incident later is often colored, consciously or unconsciously, by what the interviewee has since heard or seen regarding the incident. Further, an interviewee may bridge gaps in his knowledge of a particular incident by rationalizing what he did see or hear; he may repeat the entire mixture of fabrication and fact to the investigator as the truth.

- A police detective should interview witnesses and victims as soon as is practical after an incident occurs. Even then, all the detective's skill is required to discover what the interviewee observed and can recall accurately. A suspect who is interviewed immediately has less time to formulate alibis with potential conspirators or to establish an otherwise viable sequence of events that could minimize his responsibility in the incident.

Reluctance to Talk

The detective may encounter a person who is reluctant to divulge information and must overcome this reluctance — in a legal manner — to secure the information she needs.

The most common reasons for reluctance to talk are:

Fear of Self-involvement. Many persons are not familiar with police methods and are afraid to aid the police. They may have committed a minor offense they believe will be brought to light upon the least involvement with the police. They may think the incidents that occurred are not their business, or that guilt lies jointly on the victims and the accused. They may fear publicity. They may fear reprisal by the suspect or the suspect's associates against them, their family or property.

Inconvenience. Many persons disclaim knowledge of incidents because they do not wish to be inconvenienced by being subjected to questioning or required to appear in court.

Resentment Toward Police and Police Methods. This resentment may be particularly prevalent among persons who have no loyalty to the organized community. Sometimes the resentment manifests itself as sympathy for the accused person, who is regarded as the underdog pitted against the impersonal, organized forces of society and their chief representatives—the police.

Detective-Interviewee Personality Conflicts. Lack of success in an interview or interrogation may be due to a personality conflict between the detective and the interviewee. For example, racial and gender factors will often create personality clashes. When that is the case, the detective should voluntarily withdraw in favor of another investigator before all chances of success are lost. An interviewee may feel compelled to talk to a new detective after his experience with the first detective whom, for one reason or another, he found objectionable.

Witnesses to Interviews and Interrogations

There is usually no requirement to have a witness attend a nonsuspect interview; however, it is advisable to have witnesses to an interrogation. The written statement serves as the best witness to an interview, especially when its signing is witnessed by another officer or other credible person. With suspects, however, someone should be present to witness the rights warning, oath-taking and signing of any written statements obtained from the suspect.

Nothing prohibits a police detective from excusing a witness to the interrogation after obtaining the waiver of rights when the detective prefers certain psychological advantages that come from a "person-to-person" encounter with the suspect. The witness should return to hear a suspect confess to the crime and witness the signing of any statements.

Normally, no more than two detectives should be present in the interview room, since interrogating a suspect in the presence of many law enforcement officers has been held by the courts to suggest duress and coercion. Guns and handcuffs should not be visible to the witness, victim or suspect during an interview or interrogation because this also suggests coercion.

The officer who witnesses the rights warning should be the same person who witnesses the signing of statements; this prevents having more than two detectives or officers appear in court to testify.

Female Interviewees

The police detective should be sensitive to the fact that a woman may be reluctant to talk in other persons' presence about intimate topics. However, when it is necessary to question a female, the male detective should, for his own protection, have a female witness within hearing. The use of a two-way mirror and concealed microphone is also appropriate in such a case. The fact that the interviewee believes she is alone with the detective may assist in overcoming her reluctance to talk. Whenever possible, a female detective should interview or interrogate female suspects, witnesses and victims.

Types of Persons Interviewed and Interrogated

During criminal investigations, police detectives may question a variety of people as noted earlier in this chapter. In the following sections, I'll discuss what the police detective must consider about each category of persons before tailoring his or her technique to gain the most from the effort.

Victims

A victim is normally interviewed to develop the facts of an incident. This interview may take place in a hospital, at the victim's home, or at another location not of the detective's choosing.

A victim is not always a reliable or cooperative witness, sometimes due to fear of retaliation from the perpetrator or his associates; a state of mental or physical shock; poor memory; possible involvement of relatives or friends; or fear of publicity.

Also, a victim may be too eager to please and, in an attempt to cooperate, may exaggerate and distort facts. It may be necessary to interview a victim several times before all facts are correctly and accurately disclosed.

Occasionally, it is necessary to interrogate a victim. Victims commonly inflate the value of property to obtain large insurance claims or to win sympathy from bill collectors. Victims may also attempt to hide their involvement in an offense, a common ploy of victims in rape and drug-related investigations.

Witnesses

A witness is a person, other than a suspect, who has information concerning an incident or crime. A witness may also be the victim, complainant or accuser who first notified the police of the incident or crime. Although some witnesses are eager to tell the police what they know or think they know, others remain elusive or uncooperative.

The police detective often has to search out witnesses who do not voluntarily come forward to present their knowledge of a crime. A witness to a crime may be:

- A person who observed the crime being committed.

- A person who can testify as to the actions and whereabouts of the accused at the time the crime was committed.

- A person who knows facts or heard the accused say certain things that would tend to establish a motive for the commission of the crime.

- A scientific specialist who has examined the physical evidence and can give impartial testimony in court concerning the collected evidence.

- A person who by his or her knowledge of certain facts or occurrences can contribute to the overall knowledge of the case.

A witness is usually interviewed, but may be interrogated when suspected of lying or withholding pertinent information. It is not necessary to warn a witness of her rights under the Miranda decision unless she has said something to the detective that makes him believe her status as witness has changed to that of suspect. Under these conditions, all questioning should cease, and the suspect must be informed of her constitutional rights.

Informers

The success and efficiency of investigations often depend to some extent on persons who, for pay or for other reasons, furnish information about criminals and their activities. This source of information is protected by the police detective, who often interviews the informer under conditions of the informer's choosing.

Complainants and Accusers

During an investigation, one person may report on or accuse another. The complainant or accuser is usually interviewed. In some cases, however, the detective may have to interrogate accusers or complainants suspected of lying, of distortion, of concealing the fact that they provoked the accused, or of attempting to divert suspicion from themselves.

Others

To understand the motives and actions of persons involved in a crime or incident, the police detective interviews persons acquainted with the victim, suspect, witness or informer. These interviews are regularly conducted in the office, home or place of business. Rarely do these interviews result in an interrogation.

Distracting Persons

The police detective may encounter persons who have no real connection with a crime or possess no knowledge of it, but who nevertheless present "information" to the police. They may claim to be witnesses or victims—or even perpetrators. Despite the lack of any real basis for their statements, the prudent detective will listen to their stories, evaluate what they say in relation to the known facts, and take the necessary action.

Sensation or Publicity Seekers

Persons in this category are not often encountered during investigations. Emotionally disturbed persons, however, occasionally present themselves as witnesses, as additional victims of known suspects, or as accomplices to suspects who have received considerable publicity. The investigator must make every effort to handle publicity seekers in such a way that neither the investigation nor the reputation of the police department suffers. Detectives must be aware of "attention-seeking" behavior. Police regularly encounter people who confess to crimes after reading about them in newspaper accounts. The best way to protect against these persons and to judge the legitimacy of other persons who do come forward is to withhold some key details that only a person who was actually involved would know about.

Grudge-bearing and Lying Witnesses

Because of previous conflict with an accused or suspected person, or to settle an old score, a person with no real knowledge of a crime or incident may volunteer information about or profess to be a witness to an event. A thorough familiarity with the known facts and details of the event will often enable the detective to detect inconsistencies in the story of such a person.

The testimony of the grudge-bearing or lying witness may closely parallel the accounts of the incident released to the media or allowed to circulate through other channels. What the real motives of these persons are remain obscure to the detective. However, he or she will check their background information to disclose the untruths and the motivation for their statements.

False Accusers

A false accuser may make a charge that later investigation will disclose to be groundless. Sometimes, such a charge will persist until a trial is conducted. False charges are, at times, exaggerated versions of actual crimes of lesser nature, but sometimes they are made when no offense has been committed. False charges are particularly prevalent in sex cases and are not uncommon in other crimes.

A false charge may represent the sincere though erroneous thinking of the victim or may rest on the victim's reaction to previous ill-will, suspicion or jealousy. All the detective's skill is required in the first interview with an accuser to separate truthful from unfounded accusations. This must be done in a diplomatic manner. Anything the detective does to slight a person who volunteers such information or to make him feel that his reporting of the matter was foolish may cut off a possible future source of reliable information.

Conducting Interviews

There are four basic objectives of an interview and interrogation:
1. Secure complete and accurate information.
2. Distinguish fact from fantasy.
3. Proceed according to a well-thought-out plan.
4. Have truth as the objective.

Information

It's important that a police investigation reveal the real truth. The police detective may be able to verify the statements of one person by interviewing several other people who witnessed the same event. Not everyone sees the same things through the same set of eyes or experience. Any number of factors may influence the perception, memory and articulation of those observations in a later interview with a police officer. When two eyewitness accounts differ, it does not necessarily mean that one person is lying, nor is it impossible for two witnesses to tell stories that sound quite similar. The police detective should also test the information that a witness shares by personally visiting the crime scene and location of the witness's reported observation. The detective places himself at the exact spot described by the witness and observes (or hears, or smells) for himself if it is possible for the witness to have perceived what was reported.

Fact Versus Fantasy

The skilled police detective checks the witnesses for honesty and reliability. She checks records and finds out what other people who know them have to say about the witnesses' sobriety, emotional state, and reputation for truthfulness. She compares statements of several witnesses and walks through the event as it was described to determine what could have happened and what could not have happened. People who remember events have "landmarks" in time because they actually happened. The detective will remember the sequence, the people present and attendant items that tend to verify a witness's statements. For example, the witness describes an event, names other people who were present, and may even be able to tell the detective what show was on television at the time. The witness will remember these things even if asked to recount what happened in reverse, or to skip around and go back and forth among his various observations. A fabricated story will sound different every time and will probably fall apart when the witness is asked to recount certain observations out of sequence.

Plan

When the police detective has examined the crime scene and learned all she can about the crime and the person she is to interview, she will have a good idea about questions to ask the witness. Detectives often make an outline of their questions and keep police reports, sketches and pictures of the crime scene handy to help prepare them for the interview.

Truth

This is the ultimate focus of every investigation the police detective conducts. Although the detective may have certain information that leads her to believe she knows what the suspect, witness or other interviewee is going to tell her, she has to keep an open and nonjudgmental mind. A preconceived notion that certain people are innate liars or that others speak nothing but the truth will get an officer into trouble.

Interviewing Techniques

Preparing for an Interview

The police detective prepares himself adequately to maximize the effectiveness of his interview. Often it's hasty, maybe no more than a mental review of his knowledge of the case or a quick briefing by the patrol officer who first arrived at the crime scene. When time permits, however, a more formal preparation takes place. The police detective's six key elements of preparation include:

Familiarity With the Case. The detective must fix in his mind what he currently knows about the crime following the "who, what, when, where, why and how" guide. He needs to give special attention to the specific details, especially those that have not become public knowledge.

Familiarity With the Background of the Interviewee. The police detective must acquire some background knowledge about the interviewee before the interview. Normally, he obtains that information during a preinterview session. The detective also attempts to develop a rapport with the person interviewed. One of the best "warm-up" techniques includes having a person talk about himself. The detective should ask the interviewee for the following personal information:

- Name and address.
- Age, place of birth, nationality and race.
- Educational background.
- Present and past occupation, skills, places of employment.
- Habits, hobbies and associates—how and where leisure time is spent.
- Information about past problems with police or other legal troubles.

The detective should ask these questions and others that come to mind in a casual manner, taking an interest and trying to find some common topic he can talk with the person about. For example, maybe the interviewee was born in Wyoming and the detective is from Northern Colorado, or they might have attended the same college or have similar hobbies, such as boating. These important techniques can create an environment that enables the interviewee to remain at ease. Often they will reveal far more information than they would have in a cold, traditional police setting. This "warm-up" precedes advising them of their rights, since none of the identifying information is incriminating.

Estimate of Information Sought. The police detective must have an objective for the interview, yet remain attentive to added information. All known information, plus information obtained from each interviewee, has a cumulative effect and the skilled detective uses this to his advantage. Each interview he conducts should be reassessed in light of any additional information that can be gained from each person.

Establishing Physical Environments. Whenever possible, the police detective arranges to have a private area for the interview, free from outside interference such as telephone calls or other interruptions. The best location is a specially furnished interview room at the police station.

The traditional interview room at a police station will be austere and sterile; these "police" environments rarely produce the desired interview or interrogation results. Much of the reason these facilities remain stark stems from traditional thinking, especially among the older police officers who normally have control of how the station house operates. As time, education, training and new thinking spread throughout police ranks, many of the old ideas, customs and traditions will be replaced.

A skilled, successful interrogator will choose or create an environment that has a moderate "official" feel but will also try to put the interviewee into a setting he doesn't expect, a setting that's more like a business office instead of a police station.

Note: I've created several interview rooms over the years at police stations. My technique transforms the standard austere and "official" interview room into a pleasant environment with fish tanks, pictures on the wall, lamps and other furnishings so that it resembles a business office. When an interviewee enters this pleasing, businesslike environment, she has temporarily left or "escaped" from the "police environment." I found that interviewees coming into police stations were tense and uncomfortable, and wanted to provide just enough information to satisfy the detective and then get out. Other interviewees would become hostile and refuse to talk or would say they didn't know or see anything, even when the detective knew those persons might hold the key to investigative success. Hostile witnesses often make more trouble for the detective than no witnesses, especially in court, where a person testifying might say the opposite of what she said to a detective or become evasive and make the court doubt her testimony.

Establishing the Right Seating Arrangement. Depending on the effect the detective wants to create for the interview, the seating arrangement in an interview often plays a key role. For example, the detective may choose to have a table or other barrier between him and the interviewee, and sit in a bigger chair for psychological advantage. Size and design differences in furniture indicate relative importance or superiority. The same concept plays an important but unspoken role in offices of government officials, business executives and others. The skilled detective plays off that unspoken sense of superiority when necessary to impress or ensure that interviewees clearly understand their role.

However, the detective doesn't want to take advantage of his superior position, so he moves away from the desk and big chair to one of the same size as the one occupied by the interviewee, demonstrating an air of openness and trust between them.

Often, a detective will arrange the seating so the two sit face to face, knee to knee, and assume the attitude of a "concerned uncle." After first creating an impression of authority and distance, the detective uses this casual seating to give the interviewee a sense of closeness to the detective, somewhat like an old friend, someone to whom he can tell all he knows without fear.

Ensuring Comfort and Social Necessities. The police detective has a responsibility for the safety, health and comfort of the person she interviews if it takes place where she controls the environment, such as in the police station.

The detective must ensure availability of restroom facilities, water or other refreshments when the interview is prolonged. The detective must also ensure that the interviewee experiences no psychological abuse or duress beyond normal nervousness. Statements made under stressful conditions will probably be recanted. Witnesses or suspects may claim they said what the detective wanted to hear just to get out of there as soon as possible (which could also be true).

Interview and Interrogation Strategies

A successful interviewer or interrogator must learn to do some acting that satisfies the situation and the personality of the interviewee. The type of image the detective wants to project to the interviewee depends largely on the background information available plus the preinterview discussion noted earlier. The following "roles" will normally cover any interview or interrogation situation the police detective might encounter and includes those used by seasoned investigators.

Personality

To become truly proficient at interviewing or interrogation, a police detective learns the importance of portraying a variety of personality traits. She must adjust character to harmonize with, or dominate, the many moods and traits of the interviewee, becoming so involved in the part that she begins to feel the emotions and attitudes she's pretending to display. The detective must be able to feign anger, fear, joy and other emotions without allowing that to affect her judgment or reveal any personal emotion about the interviewee.

Sympathy

A police detective soon learns that people like to complain and gossip. He can use that knowledge to considerable advantage in most interviews. Depending on the interviewee, the detective finds the right opportunity to begin his act of sympathy for the interviewee who has to endure the situation, such as a victim of a crime, or for a witness having to endure the responsibility of possessing valuable knowledge. During interrogation of a suspect, the detective might project sympathy and a seemingly genuine understanding of why the person committed the crime.

Note: Over twenty years ago, in an advanced criminal investigation school, I received some good advice from a salty old instructor. He said: "What you want to do is develop a strong preinterview rapport, then advise the person of his rights, and when you do it right, the person will say, 'Why do I need a lawyer? I have you.' " The sympathy approach has rarely failed me over the years, and there are many criminals still in jail because of it. Many "hardened" criminals — including rapists, murderers, professional arsonists, burglars and armed robbers — confessed when I used this approach, proving that even they wanted to tell *someone* and, when taken from the "police" environment and traditional attitudes, told all they knew despite understanding they would go to jail for it. I've even had criminals come out of the courtroom on the way to prison for ten, twenty, thirty years or life, and shake my hands as they passed, thanking me for my fair treatment and understanding. Although it has happened many times, I'm still amazed, especially in those cases where the suspects provided me with evidence I probably would not have found without their confession. I've also never had one of the suspects I've interviewed or interrogated challenge or recant their statements or confessions.

Sincerity

Sincerity plays a large role when detectives interview children and the elderly. The detective must convey a sincere sympathy, and normally that's easy to do. Children and elderly people can sense when a detective lies to them, even when it doesn't involve words. They see through an act that's insincere. Once the image shatters, all the techniques known to a veteran detective won't salvage the situation, and rarely will another detective or officer fare better, because the suspicion will remain. Even when it's difficult to feel sincerity toward the interviewee, the police detective must project sincerity effectively.

Impartiality

A skilled police detective conducting interviews or interrogations must appear totally impartial, neutral and openminded about the situation and the person. Police detectives are traditionally portrayed as becoming "involved," but in real life involvement is the fastest route to failure during interviews. It often leads to interviewees saying whatever they perceive the detective "wants to hear." Whenever the detective cannot project the neutrality he needs, he should not participate in the case investigation, especially in the interviews of suspects, victims or witnesses.

Empathy

Empathy differs somewhat from sympathy. The successful detective knows she must project the understanding needed to draw out important information. The skilled detective approaches these techniques by placing herself in the interviewee's position and asking how she would react in that situation. When the detective can do that, she will know how to obtain the total cooperation of the interviewee.

Firmness

There are times when the police detective must be firm with the interviewee, and often that technique serves to emphasize the importance of the information sought. Most people like to feel needed and important; they want the detective to tell them firmly just how important they are to the successful outcome of an investigation. Certain people the detective encounters during interviews will be indecisive and may signal that they would like the detective to be firm. The projection of firmness often supplies the "excuse" that interviewees are looking for to tell what they know or confess to a crime.

Note: The traditional portrayal of police detectives hovering over a suspect or witness or using "macho" treatment went out with the rubber hose and the hot lights. Certainly, instilling fear in the heart and mind of an interviewee or suspect will bring desired results eventually. The "tough" approach of earlier years led to the Miranda Rule decision and others regarding treatment of people by the police. Today only the unskilled, untrained or plain stupid law enforcement personnel force testimony or confessions from people with these techniques. They are easy to spot—they're the ones who lose all the cases in court. Courts across the country have taken a strong stand on interview and interrogation techniques used by the police. The purpose of investigating a crime and bringing the perpetrator to prosecution in court is to win a conviction. The greatest percentage of cases lost in court result from shoddy investigation including inept interviews and interrogations.

Techniques of Taking Written Statements

Earlier I mentioned that the smart police detective or officer always obtains a written statement from the interviewee and suggested how important that document could be to the credibility of the officer and outcome of the investigation. However, understanding the techniques of "taking a statement" is important. The idea of "getting the facts" and putting them in a report can backfire; putting them in the report and supporting them with the person's written and signed statement can make all the difference.

Who Writes the Interviewee's Statement?

The detective should always write the interviewee's statement based on information revealed during the interview. The detective must define the focus of the statement and cover elements of proof. The written statement should contain the "relevant" information an interviewee is prepared to testify about in court. Most interviewees will ramble on about all types of things related and unrelated to the crime. During the interview, the detective listens, takes notes and shapes a written statement from what he hears that has importance to the case. For example, a typical interviewee will digress into all sorts of suppositions, guesstimates and anecdotes. The detective, the prosecutor and the court are only interested in the narrow parameters of the crime under investigation. The written statement must emphasize information that establishes "elements of proof," identifies other relevant aspects, and focuses on the credible knowledge of the interviewee. Only a rookie would have an interviewee write his own statement. However, after three hours of talking, the interviewee might expect a long multipage statement and be confused or disappointed when the detective hands him a one- or two-page written statement to read and sign. The detective must explain the reasons to the interviewee. This will have the additional benefit of helping the interviewee understand what might be expected of him later when testifying in court.

Recorded and Verbatim Statements

Police detectives often record the interview on tape or have a stenographer in the room taking down everything said. Both have advantages and disadvantages for the detective.

Tape Recording the Interview

Tape recording an interview will supply an absolute record of what went on and what was said by whom during an interview or interrogation. However, many interviewees don't consent to being recorded, and often the interviewee becomes very uncomfortable in the presence of a microphone or tape recorder. It affects what they say and when they talk; they may appear to measure each word. Normally, the interviewee must be told the interview is being taped. Most detectives use their judgment about using a tape recorder on a case-by-case, interviewee-by-interviewee basis.

Verbatim Statements

Few police departments have the budget necessary to provide stenographic personnel for each interview; however, high-priority cases such as murder will normally require a stenographer in the interview room. Verbatim statements place great demands on the skill and experience of the stenographer. For example, when the interviewee begins to ramble about how she doesn't like chocolate cake or ice cream, the stenographer must stop until the detective gets the interviewee back to the relevant information.

Note: One common problem of verbatim or recorded statements results from the ramblings of interviewees, often going into guesstimates, supposition, hearsay and other matters that have nothing to do with the case at hand. Interviewees also tend to name a variety of people, some perhaps relevant but most not so. A defense attorney has the right through "discovery" to obtain the tapes or transcripts and might win approval to have the tape played for the court. If the interviewee expressed a variety of opinions and mentioned names that the detective discarded as irrelevant to the case, a skilled defense lawyer could make it sound as if the police had run a shoddy investigation, picking and choosing evidence to frame the defendant. Although untrue, the jury might begin wondering, and that could lead to "reasonable doubt" and acquittal.

Closed Circuit Television (CCTV)

CCTV has come into widespread use in police departments and serves a valuable purpose, both in patrol functions and for the detective. Many departments now have a mobile version of CCTV mounted in police vehicles to record stops and activities of patrol officers or detectives and the occupants of stopped vehicles. Most departments now have CCTV in the booking area of the police station to record the activities and conduct of officers and arrested persons from the point of entry until booking processes end. This prevents accusations of brutality or improper behavior by police officers and records belligerence or intoxication of persons brought in. Jails and prisons also use CCTV extensively to monitor and control inmates.

The CCTV is also of value to detectives for recording their interviews and interrogations. But just as recorders and stenographers pose problems, there are a variety of pros and cons associated with CCTV use. Often the CCTV will not be used by the detective until after the preinterview session and perhaps the interview itself is completed. When the information has critical importance, or the suspect wants to confess, the CCTV is turned on to record that part. Each situation has its own requirements, but with discretion and skill, the officer or detective interviewing or interrogating can take advantage of a CCTV system.

Use of Lie Detectors

One of the largest myths in law enforcement concerns polygraph systems, often called "lie detectors." The reality of the polygraph is that they're unreliable. Polygraph and voice stress evaluators both operate on the same principles; neither "detects lies," but both might or might not detect stress, and that's much different from a conclusion that a suspect or witness has lied about some information. This weakness of the system also works in another way as well. If a person takes a polygraph test and, although guilty of a crime, does not perceive or believe his or her acts created a crime, the polygraph or voice stress test will not indicate any deception characteristics.

Note: During my thirty years as a law enforcement officer, the last twenty as a criminal investigator, I've caused suspects, witnesses and victims — about twenty-five in all — to take a polygraph test. Despite using highly trained and skilled polygraph operators in various places throughout the United States and in a few foreign countries, I've received the wrong information from the tests every time. I stopped asking for polygraph tests, as many detectives who gain experience over the years believe they waste time and rarely show guilt or innocence accurately.

The Interrogation

Interrogation techniques come into play primarily with a suspect of a crime when the objective is a confession. Normally, a suspect will ask for a lawyer when the Miranda Warning is given them at the time of arrest and that prevents questioning until a lawyer talks with them or is present at the interrogation. A smart lawyer will tell the suspect not to answer any questions, especially if she knows or suspects the person is guilty of the crime. However, the exception that leads to an interrogation is the suspect who says he's innocent and doesn't need a lawyer and agrees to questioning. When that situation happens, the following key elements guide the police detective.

When to Interrogate

A person should be interrogated only if she definitely and with good reason is believed to be guilty of a crime, to be an accomplice to a crime, or to be withholding information directly pertaining to a crime. A person who can be successfully interviewed is never interrogated.

Planning the Interrogation

The police detective bases her plan for interrogation on the facts of the case and on the background information she's able to develop on the person interrogated. Statements of the victim and witnesses, added to information derived from the physical evidence of the case, enable the detective to reconstruct the crime mentally and to anticipate some of the facts she may obtain from the suspect during the interrogation.

Time of Interrogation

The time of interrogation depends largely on the crime, when the suspect is identified, and who the suspect is. I personally leave talking to the suspect to the last step in my investigation when I have all the facts. I try to be in a position where I don't need the suspect's cooperation. Instead I give her an opportunity to tell her side of the story or express her denial of involvement.

It's important to note that a suspect, even when waiving her rights and consenting to an interrogation (or interview), has no obligation under the Fifth Amendment to tell the truth if it incriminates her. A witness, for example, might be guilty of a crime for lying or giving false information; however, a suspect can legally lie, give deceptive information, or sign false confessions or proclamations of innocence and she cannot be charged with a crime for doing those things.

Place of Interrogation

Normally, an interview room or detective's office in the police station provides the best environment for an interrogation. There's little basic difference between the interview and interrogation in this respect.

Categorizing Suspects

Suspects are categorized according to the approach most likely to induce a successful interrogation. The categories are:

- Known offenders whose guilt is reasonably certain because of evidence available. This category may be further divided into suspects more readily influenced by sympathy or understanding and suspects more readily influenced by logic.

- Suspects whose guilt is doubtful or uncertain because of the lack of essential facts or because of weaknesses in the available evidence. Persons in this category are interrogated to determine truth, falsehoods and distortions of facts.

Note: Some suspects cannot be placed precisely in any of the above categories. The accuracy of the detective's efforts to classify a suspect depends upon his own ability and experience and upon the availability and accuracy of information developed about the suspect or the case. An incorrect classification may lead to an unsuccessful interrogation if the approach based on the original classification is not skillfully and quickly changed before the suspect becomes aware of the detective's error.

Introduction and Warning in the Interrogation

Even though the suspect was advised of his rights at the time of arrest, a prudent detective will readvise him before starting an interrogation. In the stress of arrest, a person might not understand or even remember if the officer told him his rights. If the suspect confesses and supplies much information about the crime—for example, where money or weapons or bodies are hidden—and his attorney can later have the confession ruled inadmissible, probably none of the evidence collected from the confession will be admissible (fruits of the poison tree). Detectives always need to ask suspects if they can read and write English; sometimes they cannot, and that can negate the Miranda Warning and any confession or admission in a written statement they sign. The prudent detective having any doubt about a suspect's ability to read and write English must have him read something (not the Miranda Warning) he could not possibly have memorized and make that remark in the notes. Once the suspect agrees to continue, the detective can begin to interrogate.

Police Detective's Approach to Interrogations

Several approaches are available to the police detective when questioning a suspect including direct, indirect, psychological or other means. Each of these techniques is explained below.

Direct Approach

The direct approach is normally used to interrogate a suspect whose guilt is reasonably certain. The detective assumes an air of confidence concerning the suspect's guilt and stresses the evidence or testimony indicative of that guilt. Two modifications of the direct approach are:

Sympathetic and Understanding Attitude. A person who is a first offender or who has committed an offense in the heat of passion, anger or jealousy is normally responsive to a sympathetic and understanding attitude. The detective should treat the suspect as a normal human being who, under the stress of circumstance or extreme provocation, has committed an act that is alien to his or her true nature. The detective should strive in every way to gain the confidence of the suspect and to minimize the moral implications without giving any intimation about the penalties of the crime.

When dealing with such a person, the detective should, in a confident manner, emphasize the evidence against the person. Signs of nervous tension should also be pointed out to the suspect as evidence of his guilt. The suspect is repeatedly urged to tell the truth; the use of words with sinister meanings or connotations must be avoided. The question design enables development of a complete and detailed account of the crime from the moment it was first conceived by the suspect until it happened.

Logic and Reasoning. The habitual criminal who feels no sense of wrongdoing in having committed a crime must normally be convinced by the detective that his guilt can be easily established or is already established by testimony or other evidence. The detective points out to the suspect the futility of denying his guilt. The suspect should be confronted at every turn with testimony and evidence to refute his alibis. When the suspect admits to commission or complicity in another crime or to any act or motive connected with the crime under investigation, the admission can be used as a wedge to help secure a complete confession.

Indirect Approach

The indirect approach is exploratory and used normally when interrogating a suspect whose guilt is uncertain or doubtful. Detectives check the suspect's alibis to determine their truthfulness. Facts definitely known to the detective that suggest the suspect's guilt will formulate questions to test the person's reactions and determine whether he or she is inclined to lie.

When evidence is lacking or weak, the detective must proceed cautiously to place the suspect in a position where he or she will be forced to distort or alter facts definitely known to the detective. The suspect should then be requested to explain satisfactorily any discrepancy or distortion of information. The detective may at times imply that much more is known by making statements or by asking questions that lead the suspect to believe that the answers are already known.

After this situation has developed, the detective may revert to direct questioning to obtain an admission or confession. In the indirect approach, the question design develops a detailed account of the suspect's activities before, during and after the time an offense was committed.

Psychological Approach

This approach is designed to focus the thoughts and emotions of the suspect on the moral aspects of the crime and bring about in the person a realization that a wrong has been committed. Great care is taken in employing this approach to ensure that the suspect does not become so emotional as to render any statement made as inadmissible.

The detective may begin this type of interrogation by discussing the moral seriousness of the offense, by appealing to the suspect's civic-mindedness or to responsibilities of citizenship, or by emphasizing the effects of their acts on their spouse, children or close relatives. From this beginning, the detective may proceed to such matters as the sorrows and suffering of the victim and the victim's relatives and friends.

The suspect may tend to become emotional when discussing his mother or father, his childhood and childhood associations, his early moral and religious training, and persons he holds in high esteem, such as school teachers, religious instructors, athletic coaches, neighbors or friends. This tendency is particularly true when a suspect is guilty of a crime that he feels violates the moral values he associates with these people. Often, the emotional appeal of some person or personal relationship increases in intensity with the passage of time and with the distance separating the suspect from his former environment. By emphasizing the contrast between the suspect's present and former ways of life, the detective may intensify the suspect's emotional response, especially when he has deserted his family, has become orphaned or otherwise separated from his family, or when he has forsaken the way of life prescribed in his early moral and religious training.

The psychological approach is often successful with a young person and with a first offender who has not had time to develop a thinking pattern typical of a hardened criminal.

Skill is required in utilizing this approach. The basic emotions and motivations most commonly associated with criminal acts are hate, fear, love and desire for gain. By careful inquiry into the suspect's thinking, feeling and experience, the detective is likely to touch upon some basic weakness and thereby induce in the suspect a genuine desire to talk. The detective should make every effort to establish a common ground of understanding. She should help the suspect to construct a face-saving rationalization for his motives for committing the criminal act, and thereby make talking about the crime easier for him.

Other Approaches

After all other interrogative methods and approaches have failed to produce an admission of guilt or confession, techniques of a more subtle nature may be employed. Detailed planning and realism are prerequisites to the successful use of these techniques. The detective should plan the use of these techniques carefully so that the approach will not be obvious to the suspect. Furthermore, the detective must be careful not to jeopardize the success of further interrogative effort by disclosing to the suspect just how much or how little information has been obtained by the police.

The Cold Shoulder. The suspect is invited to the detective's office. If the suspect accepts the invitation, he is taken to the crime scene. The detectives accompanying the suspect say nothing to him or to each other; they simply await the suspect's reactions. This technique permits the suspect, if guilty, to surmise that the detectives may have adequate evidence to prove his guilt, and this may induce him to make an admission or confession. If witnesses whose identities are known to the suspect are available, they may be requested to walk past the crime scene without saying or doing anything to indicate to the suspect they are aware of his presence. This procedure serves to intensify the impression that the facts of guilt have already been established.

Playing One Suspect Against Another. This technique may be used if more than one person is suspected of having been involved in the commission of a crime. There are many variations of this method. In all variations, one suspect is played against another by purposely encouraging the belief of one suspect that her companion in the crime is cooperating with the police or has talked about the crime and has laid the blame on her.

Suspects are normally separated and not allowed to communicate with each other. Periodically, they may be allowed to glimpse or to observe each other from a distance, preferably when one is doing something that the other may construe as cooperation with the police and as prejudicial to observer's interests. The detectives may sometimes confront the stronger suspect with known facts that have been allegedly furnished by the weaker suspect. Known details of the crime may be mentioned in the presence of the stronger suspect under conditions that compromise the weaker suspect. One suspect may be cordially treated or even released, while the other may be given the "cold shoulder." This method is most successful when investigators infer rather than assert that one suspect has confessed to the crime.

Evaluating the Information

The police detective has ample opportunity during the interrogation to observe and evaluate the physical mannerisms and the emotional state of the suspect. The detective must remain alert for any signs of emotional disturbance or nervous tension that may indicate deception or guilt. The detective should evaluate the information given by the suspect in light of known facts, the testimony of the victim and witnesses, and the physical evidence available. The detective should verify by other investigative means every pertinent statement made by the suspect.

Telltale Body Language

During interviews and interrogations police detectives must watch for telltale body language. The seven areas considered most important are:

1. **Eyes.** No matter what their mouth says, the interviewees' eyes will tell the detective what they are thinking. If the pupils widen, they have heard the detective say something pleasant to them. The detective made them feel good by what she said. When pupils contract, the opposite is true. If eyes narrow, the detective has said something they don't believe, and a feeling of distrust is setting in.

2. **Eyebrows.** If one eyebrow is lifted, the detective has told them something they don't believe or that they perceive to be impossible. Lifting both eyebrows indicates surprise.

3. **Nose and ears.** If they rub their nose or tug at an ear while saying they understand the detective, it generally means they're puzzled by what she is saying and probably don't know at all what the detective wants them to do.

4. **Forehead.** If the interviewees wrinkle their forehead downward in a frown, it means they're puzzled or don't like what the detective has said. If the forehead is wrinkled upward, it indicates surprise.

5. **Shoulders.** When interviewees shrug their shoulders, it usually means they're completely indifferent. They have no interest in what the detective is telling them.

6. **Fingers.** Drumming or tapping fingers on the arm of a chair or top of a desk indicates either nervousness or impatience.

7. **Arms.** If interviewees clap their arms across their chest, it usually means they're trying to isolate themselves from the detective or they're actually afraid of the detective and are trying unconsciously to protect themselves.

THE JUSTICE PROCESS – COURTS AND THE POLICE

The court system administering the criminal process includes lower criminal courts (misdemeanors), superior courts (felonies), appellate courts (reviewing cases appealed), and supreme courts (deciding cases related to state or federal constitutions). The states and federal government have independent court structures unique to their particular jurisdictions. Prosecution of a crime that is a violation of state law ordinarily happens in the state court, while offenses against federal laws are generally handled by the federal courts.

The Justice Process

The justice process begins with an initial contact with police and ends with the offender's reentry into society. At any point in the process, the accused might no longer remain an offender and can be allowed to return to society without any further penalty for such reasons as:

- The case is considered unimportant or trivial.

- Legally admissible evidence is unavailable.
- The accused is considered not to need further treatment, punishment or attention.
- For personal reasons (discretion), those in power decide not to take further action in the case.

Though each jurisdiction is somewhat different, a comprehensive view of the processing of a felony offender would probably contain the following decision points:

Initial Contact. The initial contact an offender has with the justice system is usually with the police. Police officers may observe a criminal act during their patrol of city streets, parks or highways. They may also find out about a crime through a citizen or victim complaint. Similarly, an informer can alert them about criminal activity in return for financial or other consideration. Sometimes political officials, such as the mayor or city council, will ask police to look into an ongoing criminal activity, such as gambling, and during their subsequent investigations, police officers will encounter an illegal activity.

Investigation. Regardless of whether the police observe, hear of, or receive a complaint about a crime, they may choose to investigate. The purpose of this procedure is to gather sufficient facts, or evidence, to identify the perpetrator, justify an arrest, and bring the offender to trial. An investigation may take a few minutes, as when police officers see a burglary in progress and apprehend the burglar at the scene of the crime. It may take months and involve hundreds of investigators, as was true with the Atlanta murders' investigation, which lasted from 1980 through 1981.

Arrest. An arrest happens when the police take a person into custody and deprive the person of freedom for allegedly committing a criminal act. An arrest is considered legal when all the following conditions exist:

- The police officer believes there is sufficient evidence (probable cause) that a crime is being or has been committed and intends to detain the suspect.
- The police officer deprives the person of freedom.
- The suspect believes he or she is in the custody of the police officer and cannot voluntarily leave.

The police officer is not required to use the word "arrest" or any similar word to initiate an arrest, nor does the officer first need to bring the suspect to the police station. For all practical purposes, a person who has been deprived of liberty is under arrest. Arrests might happen at the scene of a crime or upon a warrant being issued by a magistrate.

Custody. After arrest, the suspect remains in police custody. The person will regularly be taken to the police station for fingerprinting, photographing and recording personal information—a procedure popularly referred to as "booking." Witnesses may view the suspect (in a lineup), and further evidence gathered on the case. Normally, police officers or detectives interview or interrogate suspects to get their side of the story, and ask them to sign a confession of guilt or to identify others involved in the crime. The law allows suspects to have their lawyers present when police conduct in-custody interrogations and lineups.

Complaint. After police turn evidence on a case over to the prosecutors, who are entrusted with representing the state at any criminal proceedings, a decision will be made whether to file a complaint or bill of indictment with the court having jurisdiction over the case. Prosecutors use complaints for misdemeanors, and information and indictments for felonies. Each is a formal charging document asking the court to bring a case forward to trial.

Preliminary Hearing — Grand Jury. Since it is a tremendous personal and financial burden to stand trial for a serious felony crime, the U.S. Constitution provides that the state must first prove to an impartial hearing board that there is probable cause that the accused committed the crime and that there is sufficient reason to try the person as charged. In about half the states and in the federal system, the decision on whether to bring a suspect to trail (indictment) is made by a group of citizens brought together to form a grand jury. The grand jury considers the case in a closed hearing, where only the prosecutor presents evidence. In the remaining states an "information" is filed before an impartial lower-court judge, who decides whether the case should go forward. (This process is known as a preliminary hearing or probable cause hearing in most jurisdictions.) The defendant may appear at a preliminary hearing and dispute the prosecutor's charges. During either procedure, if the prosecution's evidence is accepted as factual and sufficient, the suspect must stand trial for the crime. These procedures are not used for misdemeanors because of their lesser importance and seriousness.

Arraignment. An arraignment brings the accused before the court that will try the case. There, a judge apprises the defendant (the accused offender) of the formal charges, informs her about her constitutional rights (such as the right to legal counsel), considers her bail request, and sets the trial date.

Bail and Detention. If a bail decision wasn't made previously, it's evaluated at arraignment. Bail is a money bond, the amount of which is set by judicial authority to ensure the presence of suspects at their trial while allowing their freedom until that time. Suspects who do not show up for the trial forfeit their bail and the judge ("the bench") issues a bench warrant to any law enforcement officer to arrest the person on sight. Suspects who cannot afford bail or whose cases are so serious that a judge refuses them bail (usually restricted to capital cases or where the offender is considered a danger to the public) must remain in detention until trial. In most instances this means an extended stay in the county jail. In many jurisdictions, programs now allow defendants awaiting trial to be released on their own recognizance, without bail, if they are stable members of the community.

Plea Bargaining. After arraignment, it is common for the prosecutor to meet with the defendant and his attorney to discuss a possible guilty plea arrangement. If a bargain can be struck, the accused will plead guilty as charged, thus ending the criminal trial process. In return for the plea, the prosecutor may reduce charges, request a lenient sentence, or grant the defendant some other consideration.

Adjudication. If a plea bargain cannot be arranged, a criminal trial will take place. This involves a full-scale formal inquiry into the facts of the case before a judge, a jury or both. The outcome of the court includes a defendant found guilty or not guilty, or the jury can fail to reach a decision (hung jury), leaving the case unresolved and open for a possible retrial.

Disposition. After a criminal trial, a defendant found guilty as charged is sentenced by the presiding judge. Disposition usually involves either a fine, a term of community supervision (probation), a period of incarceration in a penal institution, or some combination of these penalties. In the most serious capital cases, it is possible to sentence the offender to death. Dispositions usually happen after a presentencing investigation by the court's probation staff. After disposition, the defendant may appeal his or her conviction to a higher court.

Correctional Treatment. Offenders found guilty and formally sentenced come under the jurisdiction of correctional authorities. They might serve a term of community supervision (probation) under control of the county probation department or serve a term in a community correctional center, or they may be incarcerated in a large penal institution.

Release. At the end of the correctional sentence, the offender returns to the community. Most incarcerated offenders receive parole before the expiration of their maximum term given by the court and finish their prison sentence in the community under supervision of the parole department. Offenders sentenced to community supervision, if successful, finish their terms and resume their lives unsupervised by court authorities.

llustration 9-1 (page 232) shows the normal procedure for a criminal case involving the court system.

The Police Detective in Court

Pretrial preparation by the police detective has two phases. The first begins with the crime itself. When a crime happens, the job of the police detective is to see what happened, who caused it and why. Once that's determined, the emphasis shifts from fact-gathering to preservation of evidence and preparation for trial. Detectives realize the latter has equal importance with the former, and that once the "thrill of the chase" is over, their responsibilities continue. The work of the police detective doesn't end until the case is presented in court. The sufficiency of the evidence and its presentation form the yardstick by which their investigation will ultimately be judged.

Investigation for the Courtroom

The investigation phase of case preparation starts at the scene of the crime or with the happening of the crime investigated. Police detectives should be thorough, bearing in mind that someday they will be called upon to testify to the facts and their observations. They must make proper notations, since memory does not improve with time. The success or failure of their case in court may depend

Typical Flow of Events in the Justice Process

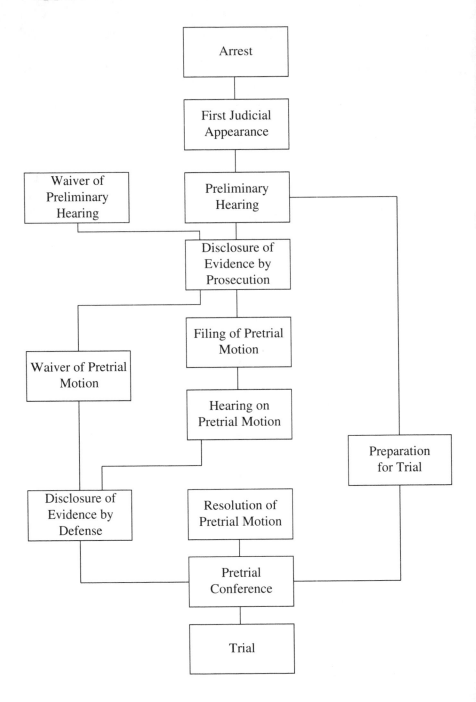

on their ability to explain the facts, the actions taken, and the results or conclusions.

Presentation of the criminal case in the courtroom is the end result of the police detective's investigative process. Both a good investigation and the preparation of the case for the courtroom require action beginning at the crime scene, including locating witnesses and preserving evidence. The duty of the police detective is to gather facts and render conclusions that the crime did happen based on the elements of proof, but not to draw conclusions about offender guilt (they always remain a suspect in police eyes—a court determines guilt or innocence) that later events or a turn of circumstance in the courtroom may prove wrong. For example, if a detective reaches a conclusion of guilt regarding a suspect and decides because of a clouded viewpoint not to take photographs of a crime scene, he runs the risk of having to do so later when crime scene circumstances have changed, or of not being able to do so at all, with disastrous results in the courtroom. Omission of detail, despite how trivial or unnecessary it might seem at the time, can easily cause a person guilty of a serious crime to be acquitted or the trial to be dismissed.

Curiosity is an essential piece of intellectual equipment, but its satisfaction in the detective's own mind without obtaining supporting details is a waste of time. Getting the essential facts without finding witnesses or other sources of proof is of little value. Added effort expended in the initial investigation is worthwhile.

Finding witnesses or assembling corroborating evidence shortly before trial, or even during trail, is far more expensive and time-consuming than doing so while the investigation is in progress. Lack of such material may result in the compromise of the case before trial or inability to go to trial at all. Again added effort during the investigation will more than justify itself in the long run.

The police detective begins with the attitude that the case will someday go to trial. Detectives with experience in the courtroom learn to anticipate trail requirements such as these:

- From case to case, the issues will vary with the evidence available. In one case, the determining issue may be the cause of death. In another, the issue may be the identity of the victim or the assailant.

- When reviewing the detective's report, the prosecutor identifies areas of weakness and then asks the detective to remedy any defects or omissions in their investigation.

- The prosecutor tries to anticipate discovery motions and bills of particulars before trial and to negate possible claims or defenses at trial. An experienced police detective will also act in anticipation of these requirements.

- Processing the scene of the crime is the first duty of the police detective. Physical dimensions and other data are important, not only for the investigation, but also at trial. The detective must be able to reproduce the scene through photographs, floor plans and sketches, including its physical size and dimension, as well as details of weather, visibility, and other climatic conditions at the time. Each detail is made part of the investigative record for future use and court testimony.

- Physical evidence is preserved primarily by photographs. When necessary, the object itself is preserved and maintained in the same condition as when the crime happened. To have the object in better or worse condition than it was at the relevant time is to render it useless at trial.

- Oral evidence, statements of witnesses, cannot be preserved like physical evidence. The detective must first know the applicable rules of law and procedure that apply in the jurisdiction concerning the taking and use of statements of witnesses. The purpose of obtaining such information is twofold. The detective has an interest in obtaining evidence for use in court under the rules of evidence and in obtaining information that, although probably inadmissible in court, will remain fruitful for leading to other avenues of investigation, corroborating the detective's case, or contradicting that of the defense attorney and defendant.

- After the investigation has concluded, the report becomes the principal source of information. Often, it is the basis on which the disposition of a case is decided and the accused is prosecuted.

- An investigation without a report has little or no value. A good report is a communication of information set forth in an accurate, concise, clear and complete manner, serving as a record of a given event. It is a record of what was seen, heard, read, done or considered. Reports are a necessary part of the detective's job. When the report is not complete, the detective has to be contacted, witnesses reinterviewed, and supplemental reports made. Reports from detectives are the material on which prosecutors depend to build their cases as they accept the burden of proof. If the report is inaccurate or incomplete, the results may be disastrous.

Pretrial Preparation

When the police detective knows the case is going to court, she must review the investigation results, including all memorandums, reports and data concerning the crime and entire case folder. Although a detective worked the case from beginning to end, it might have ended several months before she receives notification it's going to trial. However, in many departments a complex investigation might have a responsible investigator with several other detectives contributing fragments of information and evidence.

The pretrial preparation includes a conference between the detective and the prosecutor. Before the conference, the detective prepares to testify based on logical questions that will most likely be asked.

The detective must be familiar with the case, even those aspects handled by other detectives. She must also remember all details of evidence-handling. While a good report requires no oral explanation, such a meeting will enable the trial counsel (prosecutor) to review with the detective the specifics of the case. The prosecutor is then better able to pose meaningful questions to the witnesses in court. The detective must not deny the existence of a pretrial conference because such conferences are an acknowledged and acceptable part of careful pretrial preparation.

As a result of the pretrial conference, the prosecutor may request the detective to conduct experiments or to determine that certain physical facts are accurate. A police detective's testimony validating these facts will be not only admissible but persuasive to the jury.

As trial nears, the prosecutor will become aware of witnesses for the opposing side, either through "discovery" procedures or examination of subpoena lists.

An essential part of pretrial preparation is to determine the identity of opposition witnesses, the probable nature of their testimony, and their strengths and weaknesses, including any criminal record.

When time and resources permit, detectives might assist prosecutors in determining the identity, personal circumstances and other data about prospective jurors. That effort enables the prosecutor to select a jury to fairly evaluate the case. Jury calls to citizens do not include background investigations such as criminal records, pending criminal actions, civil lawsuits and other aspects that might taint their judgment.

Skilled detectives will be thoroughly familiar with the case and prepared to present it in a forceful and convincing manner when testifying, using their experience and knowledge as witnesses to best advantage. By being prepared, detectives can avoid errors and contradictions that may not only leave them flustered, but damage their credibility before judges or juries.

Courtroom Procedures

Under our American system of justice, a trial is the process we use for discovering truth and making decisions. The trial process establishes an adversary proceeding where opposing parties with conflicting interests face each other in the courtroom.

The theory behind the adversary system is that a fair and impartial jury will be best able to arrive at a truthful verdict if each side to the lawsuit is given an opportunity to present evidence and to cross-examine the evidence submitted by the opposing party. In this system, each side has an equal chance to present its proof and persuade the jury of the merits of its position, and each side has the opportunity to attack the opponent's proof and expose its deficiencies. When evidence is presented in this way, the jury will not only be able to hear both sides of the story, but will be able to judge the respective merit of each side as conflicts are developed on cross-examination. By gaining insight in this way, the jury will, theoretically, see the whole picture and make an intelligent decision in reaching a verdict consistent with truth. In the following compendium the key components of the criminal justice court system as it relates and involves the police help to develop a clear picture of how this complex and often perplexing system works.

In a criminal trial, the party with the burden of going forward with proof is the government, referred to as the "United States," "the People," "the State" or a similar reference depending on the practice in that jurisdiction. The accused person in a criminal trial is known as the "defendant."

In a struggle between two sides, prosecution and defense, someone must decide who won. Unlike an athletic event or a card game, where the winner is the one making the most points, the outcome of a trial depends on the evaluation of many intangibles, most of them subtle and subject to difference of opinion. Exercise of this judgment is obviously an important task.

Determining the question of ultimate importance to the prosecution and defense, especially the defendant, comes from a judge or jury.

The role of a jury includes listening to witnesses, considering their testimony, and evaluating other evidence to decide, based on the facts, who is telling the truth plus determine guilt or innocence of a defendant beyond a reasonable doubt.

The job of the judge is to interpret the law applicable to the case and then to advise the jury so they can reach a verdict based on legal principles. Some criminal court defendants choose to have a judge decide their case without requesting a jury trial.

The amount of proof it takes to win, the "number of points" required, varies with the nature of a case. In a criminal case, the defendant is presumed innocent, and the prosecutor (sometimes called a district attorney), must prove the defendant is guilty "beyond a reasonable doubt."

The object of a criminal trial includes proceeding in an orderly fashion to decide the issue in question. The parties are even as the contest begins. However, maintenance of the status quo will not lead to a determination of the rights of the parties. The rules of a trial require the party who initiated the contest (the government) to proceed first. That party is said to have the "burden of proof."

The amount of evidence required to prove a case cannot be explained in precise terms. The statute that brought the defendant to trial has "elements of proof," however, that establish two things: (1) the crime happened as described by law; and (2) the evidence collected by the police established probable cause to reasonably believe the defendant committed the crime. The court must then decide if that's true or false. The court must also determine if all the rules, regulations, procedures, laws and other guidance were followed precisely by the police and later by the prosecutor. When infractions are found, the evidence gained through the infraction may be thrown out and not allowed as points to be decided and that often leads to acquittal on "technicalities" as opposed to proving the person is not guilty.

In a criminal case, the government side must meet the "beyond a reasonable doubt" test. Just a slight tipping of the scales of justice in favor of the prosecution will not be sufficient. On the other hand, the prosecution does not have the burden of proving its case 100 percent or "beyond all doubt." Rather it must establish the case beyond a reasonable doubt—a doubt with reason. Conscience must be satisfied that the correct decision has been made, one that is fair to the accused and to the public interest and safety.

Criminal Trial Procedures

Once the contestants are identified and the required amount of proof known, it is necessary to proceed in an orderly fashion to the final decision of the legal battle. As we have seen, the party that initiated the proceeding has the burden of proof and must go forward with the presentation of evidence.

The procedure in a criminal case follows a systematic course summarized below:

- When the accused pleads "not guilty" to a crime charged by the prosecution, the trial begins. It's important to note that a not guilty plea by the defendant does not establish a denial the crime happened, but rather that he or she did not commit the crime.

- The judge, jury, defendant and lawyer, prosecuting attorney, witnesses and various court officials gather at the appointed time and courtroom. After establishing the parties are ready to proceed, the judge will have the clerk swear witnesses (or they might be sworn separately as they appear), and the judge will normally exclude them from the courtroom so they cannot hear other witnesses testify.

- The prosecutor will make an opening statement. This is the moving party's opportunity to tell the judge or jury what they intend to prove to meet the burden of proof and win the case.

- The "trier of fact," whether judge or jury, is given a preview of the case, an idea of what to expect, without which the case would otherwise be confusing.

- The defendant (through her lawyer) will then have a similar opportunity to explain their case, either before presentation of evidence begins or before they start their part of the case.

- The preliminaries having been accomplished, the State begins to present the evidence to establish its case.

- Evidence is said to be either "direct" or "circumstantial." Testimony of witnesses, documents or such tangible items as photographs or a murder weapon are included in the definition as "direct" evidence. Contrary to popular misconception, circumstantial evidence is not only admissible in court but is sometimes the only evidence available.

- Circumstantial evidence consists of proof of a fact or series of facts that establish by logical inference a matter in issue. For example, it has snowed during the night and you see one set of footprints in the snow leading to your front door. When you open the door, you see your morning newspaper. You "know" the carrier has been there, although you did not see him. The trier of facts will view inferential evidence with caution, but will give it the weight to which it is entitled.

- Witness testimony is the standard method of presenting evidence. To prove the plaintiff's case a logical series of witnesses is called to the stand. Asking questions by the attorney who called the witness is known as "direct examination." Inquiries must be made in a form that do not suggest the answer; otherwise, the opposing party will object to the question as "leading." When the sponsoring attorney completes his or her questioning of the witness, the opposition attorney then has an opportunity to "cross-examine" the witness.

- The purpose of cross-examination is to test the memory, recall and recitation of the facts by the witness. Cross-examination is optional with the attorney, and a skillful trial advocate will use it only if something can be gained. Having decided to cross-examine, the attorney has wide latitude as to the form of the questions. Questions asked in cross-examination would not be allowed on direct examination. Following the defense attorney's cross-examination of the witness, the prosecuting attorney has an opportunity to ask more questions designed to buttress the testimony and repair any damage done.

- It is within the trial judge's discretion to allow each attorney to take turns asking more questions, each series of which is to be limited to the scope of the answers last given. When this procedure has been completed, the witness is excused from the stand and leaves the courtroom unless granted permission by the judge to stay.

- Using a series of witnesses, documents, photographs and other items, the type and order of which will vary with the case, the prosecuting attorney (having the burden of proof) will attempt to prove his or her case. Whether the judge will allow particular testimony or other evidence depends on well-established legal principles known as the "rules of evidence." Upon feeling that the obligation of proof has been met, the prosecutor will "rest" their case. Opposing counsel will then usually ask the judge to dismiss the case for insufficient evidence. This tactic is rarely successful, however, because the prosecutor usually has met at least the minimum requirements of a case.

- After the prosecutor has completed the State's case, the defendant has the opportunity to present evidence. The defendant does not have the burden of proof to present any evidence, but usually does so or otherwise the case would probably be lost. In the presentation of the defendant's case, witnesses are called, tangible evidence is presented, and so on, in a manner similar to that used by the prosecutor.

- The defense attorney conducts the direct examination of defense witnesses and the prosecuting attorney has an opportunity to cross-examine. The defendant proceeds until the opposing evidence appears to have been overcome or surpassed.

- After the defense "rests" the prosecuting attorney may offer evidence in rebuttal. With permission of the court, each side can continue taking turns rebutting the other with additional evidence. In practice, judges are usually reluctant to allow this to continue very long. Each rebuttal is strictly limited to countering the one before it.

- When both sides have completed their cases, the defendant usually will make another motion to dismiss the case, based now on all the evidence, both the prosecution and defense. If it is a jury trial, motions such as this, as well as those to exclude particular evidence, will be made outside the presence of the jury. The attorney making a motion has the obligation to give reasons and to cite supporting law. The opposing attorney will have a similar opportunity before the judge rules on the issue.

- When all motions end, the attorneys have a chance to present final argument. If it is a jury trial, the judge will receive from the attorneys suggested statements of law applicable to the case. These "jury instructions," after review for legal sufficiency, will be read to the jury before or after arguments of counsel, depending on procedure in that court.

- The prosecutor will argue first, pointing out the highlights of the State's case by referring to the evidence presented and the law in support of it, and will attempt to persuade the judge or jury to decide in his or her favor.

- Following arguments of counsel and the judge's recitation of the applicable principles of law, the jury will retire to the jury room to reach its verdict. Once that is done, the bailiff will be so informed and the court will reconvene, at which time the decision will be announced.

- The trial is now complete and the witnesses and jury are excused. The defendant in a criminal trial may make motions to set a verdict aside, based on that side's view of the evidence adduced at the trial and the law applicable to it.

- Finally, there may be a petition of appeal to a higher court.

The Police Detective Witness

Most persons have a natural reluctance to speak to a group. Nervousness as a witness in the courtroom is normal, but there are things that can be done to avoid it. The more familiar the police detective is with the courtroom procedure and the rules of evidence, the better witness for the prosecution he or she will make. Experienced detectives know well that the impression made on the jury is important to the case.

Demeanor on the Stand

The jury's first impression of the police detective happens when he walks into the courtroom and takes the oath. His actions and attire play a large role in convincing the judge and jury that the detective takes his testimony seriously. The following rules generally apply to those practiced by the police officer and detective when testifying in criminal court:

- The detective approaches the witness stand in a deliberate and unhurried manner.
- The detective does not glare at the defendant or act arrogant or overconfident.
- The detective remembers the jury is forming its first opinion of him, and it is difficult to change a negative first impression.
- The detective's appearance as he accepts the oath is critical; all eyes in the courtroom are upon him. He stands erect and gives the impression of taking the oath seriously and giving truthful and conscientious testimony.
- After taking the oath, the detective sits in the witness chair in a comfortable but alert manner. He maintains a full view of the judge, jury and attorneys.
- The detective waits patiently for the proceedings to begin, careful not to make distracting sounds or movements.
- While testifying, the detective exercises care to avoid nervous mannerisms such as rearranging clothing (e.g., necktie), crossing and uncrossing of arms or legs, clearing the throat, putting his hands to his face, or constantly repeating meaningless phrases such as "you know" that distract from his testimony and affect the weight it is given. By avoiding such mannerisms and not appearing to be nervous, the detective lessens the possibility the judge or jury thinks he might have something to hide, or is not telling the truth or the whole truth.

Standard guidance most prosecutors and police departments supply police officers and detectives for testifying in court includes the following:

- Tell the whole truth — an officer is sworn to do so.
- Every relevant fact must be readily admitted, even if it is not to the advantage of the prosecution.
- Do not stop to figure out whether your answer will help or hurt. Just answer the question to the best of your ability.
- Don't try to color or shade testimony to help the prosecutor; it only invites trouble. Doing so makes it appear you are taking sides, and you lose credibility.

- Use normal language; do not attempt to use a vocabulary or jargon that is unfamiliar to you or to the jury. In normal conversation, no one would ever "exit the vehicle" but would simply "get out of the car."

- Do not use obscenities or slang unless they are an indispensable part of your testimony made vital and material by the questions asked.

- No matter how many times you have testified in court, this is the first time this jury has had the opportunity to hear you speak.

- Answer questions politely and courteously, in a conversational tone and loudly enough so that the judge, jury and defendant can hear you.

- When questions are asked of you, listen carefully. If you do not understand a question, ask for it to be repeated.

- Think before answering, and do not allow the questioner, especially the defense cross-examiner to rush you into "shooting from the hip."

- A measured pause before answering has benefits in a variety of ways. It allows you to think about the question and better understand it. It also gives you the appearance of a believable, well-thought-out answer.

- When you respond slowly enough to consider your thoughts before speaking, your testimony is enhanced. Speaking hurriedly can result in the misunderstanding of testimony because your words are improperly phrased. Adopt a deliberate pace, but avoid speaking so slowly as to cause your listeners to doubt your testimony.

- Avoid body gestures with hands or nods of the head.

- If you do not know the answer to a question say so. Never guess at the answer to a question.

- When it's understandable that you would not remember a detail (for example, a license number), it's permissible to refer to your notes to refresh your recollection. Always ask the court if you may be allowed to consult your notes, report, memoranda and other aids. However, remember that once you do that, the defense attorney has the right to examine them and is permitted to ask questions about them.

- When testifying, stick to the facts of the case.
- When you make a mistake while testifying, recognize it and make a logical, accurate correction.
- Avoid becoming trapped into making estimates or approximations on things you should know exactly such as distance, speed and time; have that information before testifying and remain accurate.
- Avoid conclusive statements when there's a possibility of added information surfacing.

Cross-Examination

Cross-examination will often create the worst ordeal a detective must confront because she is placed in a position that she's unaccustomed to—having to take relentless verbal abuse without the authority to do anything about it. Someone once said that cross-examination by a defense attorney in a criminal court takes the place in our society that torture occupied in the medieval society. However, veteran police detectives have developed techniques to deal with the abuse and most adopt the following principles to handle it. The seasoned detective anticipates an attack by the defense attorney on certain categories, including:

- Police notes and memoranda.
- Pretrial preparation with the prosecutor.
- Police interrogations.
- The detective's lack of personal information.
- The defendant's cooperation with the police.
- The defendant's denials to the police.
- Acts of omission by the police.

Attacks on Police Notes

When a defense attorney has access to the detective's notes, memoranda or reports, either before or during the trial, a favorite line of attack on the detective's direct testimony is to highlight any inconsistencies that may exist between the contents of the notes, memoranda or reports and the testimony concerning them. An "inconsistency" can be either a fact that was reported differently in the notes than in testimony or a fact the detective testified about that was not mentioned at all in the notes, memoranda or reports. The detective has to anticipate this problem and prepare to justify these discrepancies. Examples of these problems follow:

- The detective might not be given an opportunity to explain the inconsistency. The defense attorney conducting the cross-examination may be content merely to raise the fact that one exists. When the detective is asked directly whether the version of events in her notes is inconsistent with her present testimony, the detective might want to answer saying that "the inconsistency is only apparent and can be explained" (if this is actually so).

- When the inconsistency consists of the failure to mention something in the reports the detective submitted to superiors during the investigation that is later testified to in court, the fact it was omitted from these reports can sometimes be explained. When the detective's explanation is inadequate, the cross-examiner may continue the attack to create some doubt among the jury about the detective's credibility and ability as a police professional.

- Generally, when the attorney confronts the detective with inconsistencies between what earlier written memoranda reveal compared to present testimony (an inconsistency that is obvious and undeniable), it's better for the detective to concede the discrepancy readily, without apparent embarrassment, and then leave it to the prosecutor to decide whether to pursue the matter further.

The Adequacy of the Detective's Investigation

Defense attorneys will often cross-examine the detective concerning matters that might suggest the investigation was incomplete or inadequate, including:

- The initial failure to uncover certain evidence such as latent fingerprints that a more thorough crime scene search might have uncovered.

- The failure to perform certain tests on physical evidence that, if performed, might have excluded the defendant as a suspect.

- Where tests were performed, the failure to use the most sophisticated methods or equipment.

- Despite thorough testing, the failures to process or preserve the original evidence for independent examination by the defendant's forensic examiners.

Pretrial Preparation With the Prosecutor

The defense may well inquire as to prior discussions between the prosecutor and the detective about the testimony the witness gave at the trial. Their objective with this line of questioning is to suggest to the jury the possibility that the detective has been coached by the prosecutor about what to say and how to say it. If the detective's answers to the prosecutor's questions on direct testimony have been formulistic responses to predictable questions, this line of attack will likely follow.

Lack of Personal Knowledge

Defense lawyers sometimes attempt to capitalize on the fact the detective has no personal, firsthand knowledge of the criminal incident since he did not witness it as it occurred. Most, if not all, of the detective's information is secondhand and circumstantial. There is little the detective can do but concede this fact if it is raised.

Credibility of the Police Witness

As a last resort, the defense attorney may attack the detective's credibility either on the grounds of bias or of untruthfulness. This tactic may have some success since many people believe that police tend to presume the guilt of suspects, having been trained to be suspicious and to conduct investigations to confirm these suspicions.

A more serious charge of bias sometimes surfaces in cases where the defendant is a member of a minority race or ethnic group and the detective and the police force she represents are predominantly of the majority race or ethnicity. The defense may then seek to show that the only reason the defendant was selected as a suspect in the case was the fact of her race or ethnicity.

The police detective will probably face questions not only on the grounds of bias or prior inconsistent statements but also on the basis of her reputation for truthfulness or her habits or character traits. This type of attack occurs with regularity in cases where undercover detectives are called as witnesses for the prosecution. Here the defense attorney will attempt to bring out through admissions made by the detective that undercover work consists of constantly misrepresenting oneself to those with whom she comes into contact. The attorney might contend that deceit was used to extract a confession or a damaging admission. The theme of deceit and duplicity, the betrayal of "friends" who had come to trust the undercover officer, confronts the detective when emphasized by the defense attorney. The undercover detective can do little during such an onslaught except to grin and bear it. There is no denying what is obviously true, that the nature of the work involves deception and untruth.

Common Tactics of Cross-Examination

The police detective becomes a natural prey for the aggressive defense attorney, especially in serious crime trials. The detective needs to remember that the attorney makes his living and charges fees based on successes, not failures. When an attorney accepts a case, his focus remains on winning in court, or on appeal, and the police detective will normally be his greatest problem. The defense attorney knows that his chances of winning probably hinge on discrediting the testimony of the detective, and to accomplish that goal, he creates a general set of tactics. The following list contains the common tactics used by defense attorneys, their procedures and desired results.

There are twelve contrasting types of hostile cross-examination of police officers and detectives by defense attorneys. The first and most common consists of an effort to overwhelm and confuse the detective by rapid-fire questions designed to get her to respond immediately without giving the question or the answer much thought and finally to anger the detective and cause her to make imprudent remarks in the heat of anger. In this type of cross-examination tactic, the detective's answers are frequently cut off in midsentence with another question, even more pointed and hostile than the one that preceded it.

However, the defense attorney might vacillate between the types. A brief discussion of each follows.

Defense Attorney Tactics of Cross-Examination

Tactic — Example — Purpose — Detective's Response

Rapid Fire Questions	One question after another with little time to answer.
Purpose	To confuse the detective; attempt to force inconsistent answers.
Detective's Response	Take time to consider the question; be deliberate in answering; ask to have the question repeated; remain calm.
Condescending Counsel	Benevolent approach, oversympathetic in questions to the point of ridicule.
Purpose	Tries to create impatience, anger or sharp answers.
Detective's Response	Give firm, decisive answers; ask for the question to be repeated if improperly phrased.
Friendly Counsel	Very courteous, polite; questions tend to take detective into counsel's confidence.
Purpose	To lull the detective into a false sense of security so that answers in favor of the defense will be given.
Detective's Response	Stay alert; keep in mind that purpose of defense is to discredit the evidence and detective's testimony.
Badgering, belligerent	Counsel (defense attorney) stares detective right in the face; shouts "That is so, isn't it?"

Purpose	To make detective angry enough to lose sense of logic and calmness. Generally, rapid questions will also be included in this approach.
Detective's Response	Stay calm; speak in a deliberate voice, giving prosecutor time to object.
Mispronouncing detective's name; using wrong rank	Detective's name is Jansen, lawyer calls him Johnson; Detective's rank is Lieutenant, lawyer calls him Sergeant.
Purpose	To draw the detective's attention to the error in pronunciation rather than to the question asked so that the detective will make inadvertent errors in testimony.
Detective's Response	Ignore the mispronunciation and concentrate on the question counsel is asking.
Restrictive Question	"Did you discuss this case with anyone?"
Purpose	A no answer will place the officer in a position of denying having had pretrial conferences. A yes answer would be used to imply the detective has been told how to testify.
Detective's Response	"I have discussed the case with the prosecuting attorney and other police officers working on the case. No one has told me how to testify."
Suggestive Question (leading question allowable on cross-examination)	"Was the color of the car blue?"

Purpose	To suggest an answer to the question in an attempt to confuse or to lead the detective (often used to gain control of a witness, moving to rapid fire, leading questions).
Detective's Response	Concentrate carefully on the facts; disregard the suggestion; answer the question.
Demanding a yes or no answer to a question that needs explanation	"Did you tell my client he couldn't call his lawyer?" (Lawyer knows detective told the defendant he couldn't call his lawyer until finished with "booking.")
Purpose	To prevent all pertinent and mitigating details from being considered by the jury.
Detective's Response	Explain the answer to the question; if the counsel demands a yes or no answer, pause until the court instructs you to answer in your own words.
Reversing the detective's words	Detective says, "The gun was found 22 feet from the victim." Counsel says, "You say the gun was found 72 feet from the victim?"
Purpose	To confuse the detective and demonstrate the detective's lack of confidence.
Detective's Response	Listen intently whenever counsel repeats something you have said and correct any errors.
Repetitious Questions	The same question asked several times slightly rephrased.

Purpose	To obtain inconsistent or conflicting answers from the detective so he can bring that out to the jury.
Detective's Response	Listen carefully to the question and state, "I have just answered that question."

Conflicting Answers	"But, Detective Brown, Officer Smith just said . . ."
Purpose	To show inconsistency in the investigation. This tactic is normally used on measurements, times and other technical information easy to distort.
Detective's Response	Remain calm. Conflicting statements have a tendency to make witnesses nervous. Be guarded in your answers on technical matters. Unless you have exact knowledge, use the term "approximately." Refer to your notes.

Staring	After the detective has answered, counsel just stares as though there was more to come.
Purpose	To have a long pause that one normally feels must be filled to provoke the witness into offering more than the question called for.
Detective's Response	Look at counsel expressionlessly and wait for the next question.

When the detective's testimony has been completed and she has been instructed to leave the witness stand, she does so with an expression of confidence but not a smile. The detective remains businesslike and unhurried, but not acting triumphant or overconfident;

nor should she appear downcast or defeated if things did not go as well as she would have liked. That will be the last chance for the judge and jury to gauge the detective and her testimony; they need to be left with the impression that the detective is knowledgeable, trustworthy, professional and truthful.

Index

Save 15% on these other books in the HOWDUNIT Series!

Get your facts straight with these other books designed to help you commit fictional murder and conduct crime investigations according to the rules.

Police Procedural: A Writer's Guide to the Police and How They Work
Russell Bintliff
Learn how police officers work, when they work, what they wear, who they report to, and generally how they go about the business of controlling and investigating crime. #10374, 272 pages/$16.95, paper

Private Eyes: A Writer's Guide to Private Investigators
Hal Blythe, Charlie Sweet & John Landreth
Covers how investigators really work, and how they differ from their fictional counterparts, allowing you to avoid repeating mistakes many writers have made before. #10373, 208 pages/$15.95, paper

Deadly Doses: A Writer's Guide to Poisons
Serita Deborah Stevens with Anne Klarner
This comprehensive reference book answers all your questions when "poisoning off" a character. #10177, 320 pages/$16.95, paper

Scene of the Crime: A Writer's Guide to Crime-Scene Investigations
Anne Wingate, Ph.D.
A factual, time-saving reference book that gives you facts and details of criminal investigations and police work. #10319, 240 pages/$15.95, paper

Cause of Death: A Writer's Guide to Death, Murder & Forensic Medicine
Keith D. Wilson, M.D.
A comprehensive reference that traces what happens to a body from trauma to burial—and all stops in between. #10318, 240 pages/$15.95, paper

Armed & Dangerous: A Writer's Guide to Weapons
Michael Newton
Never before have firearms been explained in such a completely accessible and easy-to-understand manner—with a literary orientation. #10176, 192 pages/$14.95, paper

To order call toll-free 1-800-289-0963 or send your order to the publisher. Mention #6415 to get 15% off the books in the HOWDUNIT Series. Include $3.00 for postage and handling for one book, and $1.00 for each additional book. Allow 30 days for delivery.

For a complete catalog of Writer's Digest Books call the number above or write to:

Writer's Digest Books
1507 Dana Avenue
Cincinnati, Ohio 45207